Create *Your Own*

Blog

Second Edition

TRIS HUSSEY

SAMS   800 East 96th Street, Indianapolis, Indiana 46240

Create Your Own Blog:
6 Easy Projects to Start Blogging Like a Pro
Second Edition

ISBN-13: 978-0-672-33597-6
ISBN-10: 0-672-33597-2

Library of Congress Cataloging-in-Publication Data is on file.

First Printing May 2012

Trademarks

All terms mentioned in this book that are known to be trademarks or service marks have been appropriately capitalized. Sams Publishing cannot attest to the accuracy of this information. Use of a term in this book should not be regarded as affecting the validity of any trademark or service mark.

Warning and Disclaimer

Every effort has been made to make this book as complete and as accurate as possible, but no warranty or fitness is implied. The information provided is on an "as is" basis. The author and the publisher shall have neither liability nor responsibility to any person or entity with respect to any loss or damages arising from the information contained in this book.

Bulk Sales

Sams Publishing offers excellent discounts on this book when ordered in quantity for bulk purchases or special sales. For more information, please contact

U.S. Corporate and Government Sales

1-800-382-3419

corpsales@pearsontechgroup.com

For sales outside of the U.S., please contact

International Sales

international@pearsoned.com

Editor-in-Chief
Greg Wiegand

Acquisitions Editor
Michelle Newcomb

Development Editor
Todd Brakke

Managing Editor
Sandra Schroeder

Project Editor
Seth Kerney

Copy Editor
Barbara Hacha

Indexer
Larry Sweazy

Proofreader
Sheri Cain

Technical Editor
Catherine Winters

Publishing Coordinator
Cindy Teeters

Designer
Gary Adair

Compositor
Bronkella Publishing

Contents at a Glance

Table of Contents

8 Creating a Visual Artist's Portfolio Blog · · · 177

9 Blogging with Tumblr · · · 191

About the Author

Tris Hussey started blogging on a whim and then found himself as Canada's first professional blogger. Tris has worked for several blogging and media startups and has taught new media at the British Columbia Institute of Technology. Tris teaches blogging, WordPress, and podcasting through the University of British Columbia.

In addition, Tris finds time to speak, guest lecture, and contribute to the social media community in and around Vancouver. When not doing all this, Tris manages the marketing and social media for Simply.ca.

Dedication

For my Dad, who always told me to read the manuals.

Acknowledgments

When I started the first edition of this book, I never in my wildest dreams would have thought that I would have not only written two more books since, but also be writing a second edition to this book! I feel blessed and honored that I'm able to do this. Of course, writing a book—even a second edition—isn't an easy job. So I have tons and tons of people to thank.

This book couldn't have happened without the help, direction, and prodding of many, many people. Thanks to Paul Chaney for believing that I could do this book in the first place and letting the publisher know this. Thank you to my brilliant technical editor, Catherine Winters, for keeping me straight. Thanks to the whole editorial team at Pearson—I couldn't ask for better editors and support. Michelle Newcomb, my acquisitions editor, patiently waits for my tardy email replies. Someday I'll get better, Michelle. Thanks to Rob Cottingham of Social Signals for the cartoon at the beginning of Chapter 5, and to my friends and family for inspiring and supporting me while I've been writing this book. Most importantly, thank you to my beloved wife, Sheila, for supporting me and believing in me through this whole process—again!

We Want to Hear from You!

As the reader of this book, *you* are our most important critic and commentator. We value your opinion and want to know what we're doing right, what we could do better, what areas you'd like to see us publish in, and any other words of wisdom you're willing to pass our way.

You can email or write me directly to let me know what you did or didn't like about this book—as well as what we can do to make our books stronger.

Please note that I cannot help you with technical problems related to the topic of this book, and that due to the high volume of mail I receive, I might not be able to reply to every message.

When you write, please be sure to include this book's title and author as well as your name and phone or email address. I will carefully review your comments and share them with the author and editors who worked on the book.

E-mail: consumer@samspublishing.com

Mail: Greg Wiegand
Editor-in-Chief
Sams Publishing
800 East 96th Street
Indianapolis, IN 46240 USA

Reader Services

Visit our website and register this book at informit.com/register for convenient access to any updates, downloads, or errata that might be available for this book.

INTRODUCTION

About the Second Edition

Wow, a lot has changed in the years since I wrote the first edition of this book, which I started in 2008 and finished in 2009. In the past few years, I've written two more books and, while I was doing that, a lot in the blogging and social media world has changed—and for the better, I think.

This new edition isn't a complete rewrite of the first edition, but it's pretty close to it. Chapters 1–4 have been updated with current examples and the current state of technology. For example, TypePad isn't a major player, but new services like Tumblr and Posterous have made *serious* headway. Chapters 5–10 are, for the most part, entirely rewritten not only to use better examples, but also to reflect how blogging has matured in the past 2–3 years. When I wrote the first edition, using a blogging engine like WordPress to build your "regular website" wasn't commonplace. Now it is, and this new edition has an entire chapter dedicated to doing just that. Also, in the intervening few years, WordPress has truly eclipsed all other blogging engines to become the leading choice for most bloggers. So although the first edition was *extremely* platform agnostic, this second edition uses WordPress and WordPress.com not only for examples, but as the recommended engine of choice for users of all levels and stripes.

I hope you enjoy this new edition, and I would be remiss not to thank all the readers of the first edition for their feedback on what I did right and did wrong.

It's All About Storytelling

Welcome to my book. Pull up a chair, get a drink, and let me tell you some stories. Now, before you put this book down, shaking your head, let me explain what I mean. Blogging is about storytelling. Regardless of the technology, the topic, the style, or business website or personal blog, everything centers around telling a great story. Blogging is about having a platform to express yourself. Your blog is your place to let your expertise and passion show through. I've written this book to help you do just that.

Over the past many years, I've taught hundreds of people how to blog. I've led Blogging 101 classes in person and online. I've guest lectured on the future of blogging and taught continuing education courses on multimedia and creating websites using blogs. If there is one thing that people figure out as soon as I start talking—*I love what I do*. Every day my job is to sit back, think, and read what the news of the day is, and then tell the world what I think. Dream job? Yeah, I'd say so.

So I wrote this book to help everyone I can to use technology to make his or her own soapbox on the Internet. While reading this book, I want you to laugh, cry, smile, and get excited. I write like I blog—I feel so sorry for my editors—and I blog like I talk. I hope you enjoy this book and, if you don't, I hope you leave me a comment on my blog: www.trishussey.com.

Wait, You're a Professional Blogger?

Well, I wasn't a professional at *first*, but I became one eventually. Like many of you reading this book, I started blogging on a whim. I said to myself one afternoon, feeling rather dissatisfied with my job as a market researcher, that if I wanted to revive my Internet consulting practice, I should "learn about this blogging thing." Yep, that's pretty much exactly what I thought—a whim, a "gee, this could be fun" idea that turned into something that I love *and* I got paid to do.

I wasn't always a blogger, of course. After finishing graduate school, I started out in the working world running a lab at Duke University. Yes, I was then and remain today a science geek. I've always been interested in computers (a rather handy skill when pretty much all the instruments—even the microscopes—are computer controlled) and worked in the campus computer lab in college helping people with their computer questions. No, I never managed to get a date helping all those cute girls with their questions. So the progression of my career has *always* been centered around using technology.

After a short while as a lab manager, I left academia to go back to the front lines of tech support. It might not have been glamorous, but I was good at it and had lots of fun doing it. This was also a watershed job because it was at that job where I learned HTML and how to develop websites. That was about 1995.

When I started blogging in 2004, I did it to learn about this new medium and have a place to express myself. As it happens, that's pretty much why and how blogging started in the first place—more on that later. Back in 2004, most people had their blogs on Blogger, so that's where I started out, too.

Because the blogosphere was a smaller place back then, it didn't take too long to get noticed, and by the end of the year I was being paid to write posts on other people's blogs. In 2004, this was a daring thing. There were a lot of people against the idea of people getting paid to blog, much less post on other people's blogs. I was one of the first people in Canada to do this and one of only a handful doing it in *the world*. Between 2004 and 2005 I helped break a lot of new ground in the world of blogging and business blogging. Not to mention I changed blogging engines, platforms, and hosts a couple times during that time as well.

If I thought 2004 was a whirlwind in blogging, 2005 blew it away. That year, professional blogging took off—like a rocket. Businesses started blogging, and conferences focusing *just on* business blogging took off. During this time, I also started to make a name for myself with "live blogging" sessions at conferences. I had some of my first sponsorships and was regularly speaking and teaching about blogging. It was nothing short of mind boggling (or maybe mind "blogging").

Today, we talk more in terms of "social media" than blogging. Social networking sites like Facebook and Twitter have exploded onto the scene, and now we're "tweeting" what we're doing instead of blogging as much. Am I still blogging? You bet. I consider it more "writing" today, but I'm still blogging and helping people and companies blog—or set up websites on blogging engines.

I'm writing this book to share my experiences, tips, tricks, and even spin a yarn or two with you. By the end of this book, I hope that you will be starting off blogging. Yes. Really. By the time you've put this book down, you will know enough to start your own blog and how to structure it to suit your niche.

How to Use This Book

I've written this book so that Chapters 1–5 give you the tools to start blogging, but the rest of the book is tailored to what kind of blog you want to write or the kind of website you want to create. For example, if you want to start a blog or website for your business you might want to skip from Chapter 4, "Building a Community Around Your Blog," to Chapter 6, "Creating a Business Blog," or Chapter 7, "Creating a Website," because those chapters are more tailored to your interests. I've taken the basics from the first four chapters and expanded on them to make them more relevant to a business user. What about the rest of the book? I have a secret for you—it's really hard to draw a line in the sand between the things you need to know and all the different "types" of blogs. They are all very closely related, so although you may want to create only a personal blog, flipping to the chapter on multimedia blogs (Chapter 10) or Tumblr (Chapter 9) will still give you a deeper understanding of how these technologies can be used in *many ways*.

Somewhere along this journey we're taking together, you're going to wonder what my

favorite blogging engine is and whether I have a bias toward it. I'm going to answer simply and openly (like a good blogger should, by the way)—yes and yes. My blog engine of choice is WordPress, and yes because it's my preferred engine, I have a bias toward it. However, I've tried and used many different engines and know one thing for certain: All of them do at least one thing well—create content.

As I take you through the various types of blogs covered in this cookbook, I'll note whether one engine is better than another for one type of blog. Even though I really like WordPress and know the people who developed it, this doesn't mean I don't see its flaws and ignore the strengths of the other engines. In fact, it's because I've used all the engines that I am friends with people at almost all of them—I give them the straight deal and honest feedback.

Throughout the book, I include various informative elements, like sidebars and idea galleries, that elaborate on or complement the current topic. There are also the following types of helpful asides:

TIP

Tips have valuable information that I've gleaned from years of being a pro blogger. Essentially the stuff I wish I knew when I started.

NOTE

Notes that might be a little "Did you know..." or something to watch for when you're working on something. Like, Did you know the creator of WordPress, Matt Mullenweg, wasn't even 20 years old when he released the first version?

CAUTION

This is code for "a mistake I've made in the past, so don't do it!" Things like: When someone says, "Back up your database files like this before proceeding…," it's a good idea to listen.

NEW TERM

Sometimes in the text, you'll see a new piece of jargon that is bolded. When you see that, you'll see an accompanying New Term element like this one that explains what it means.

If I were teaching this book as a class, I'd answer questions as I go along. Unfortunately, this isn't a live class, so the best I'm going to be able to do is direct you to the book's blog where you can post questions in the forum. Also, because the Internet is a fluid place, check my blog—www.trishussey.com— for updates since this book was published. By the time this book hits the shelves, there will be several updates to plug-ins and even blog engines themselves. Although these updates won't change the mechanics of how you blog or set up a blog, they are helpful pieces of information (and will explain if a screenshot doesn't match 100% what you're seeing onscreen).

Ready? Let's start out with as little history to give you some perspective on what we're doing here. On to Chapter 1, "Beginning the Story: Blogging Then and Now."

CHAPTER 1

Beginning the Story: Blogging Then and Now

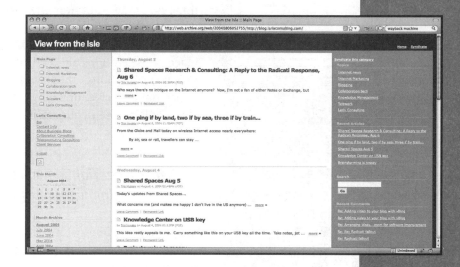

FIGURE 1.1

Derek K. Miller's blog, Penmachine.com, with his final post.

YOUR BLOG AS YOUR DIGITAL LEGACY

In May 2011, the Internet lost a great treasure, and I lost a friend. Derek K. Miller was just 41 when he passed away from cancer, leaving behind a wife and two daughters—and a blog. Derek's blog, Penmachine.com, was one of Vancouver's longest-running blogs and, if all goes according to plan, will continue to be so for years to come. Knowing that his time was drawing to a close, Derek made plans to help ensure that his daughters and the rest of us would be able to read his words and listen to the music he created—including a piece he wrote for me—for years. Derek felt that what he created should be a part of his digital legacy. In the past, we might have left behind boxes or journals or letters; today, we leave behind Facebook accounts, pictures on Flickr, and blogs as the fragments of our lives. I encourage you to visit Derek's blog and read more than his final post. His explanations of how cameras work, why you put only one space after a period, and some truly brilliant musings on life, love, and technology are why he has ensured that his blog will remain.

A Brief History of Blogging

Believe it or not, blogging has been around for more than 10 years—this is an eternity in the tech world. Remember that the computer mouse, the Internet, and email are just over 40 years old, which makes them ancient technologies in comparison. Yes, contrary to what the mainstream media (MSM) says, this blogging thing *isn't* a new fad from the geek set. In fact, if you think in terms of people writing in journals and recording their thoughts, the spirit of blogging is centuries old. The difference is that now you can publish these works not only on paper, but also electronically. Instead of only a few people reading your missives, the world can read them.

> *When you get right down to it, a blog is simply a website.*

Blogging started out with people making public lists of bookmarks and links, mostly for themselves, and putting up a page on their website to display them. New items on the website were added at the top of the screen, which gave us the accepted blogging style of items presented on the page in reverse chronological order. This style helped website visitors easily view new items instead of having to scroll down the page.

In those days, however, blogging *was* the world of geeks. Individuals created their own "blogging engines" to publish their content—certainly not a task for the faint of heart or faint of code. It wasn't until 1999, when the folks at Pyra Labs created the first easy-to-use blogging tool called Blogger, that the world of blogging could leave the geek set and start to be used by "normal" people.

In 2001, soon after the emergence of Blogger, Ben and Mena Trott started working with something that would become Movable Type. (Later, in 2003, they introduced the Typepad blogging service.) Movable Type was one of the first blog engines you could install yourself. This was an essential step to the birth of blogging because now people could not only sign up for a service, but also install a stable and extensible blog engine on their own servers. Because there were folks, like me, who quickly outgrew a hosted service (or who wanted to integrate a blog into their existing sites), being able to manually install a blogging engine on any basic website host was a giant leap forward.

By 2006, you could, in a short amount of time, buy a domain name, get website hosting from the same company, and install a blog. It became so easy that everyone was expected to be blogging. Blogging would be the next great thing in commerce, communication, and technology, saving everyone time and energy. Like nearly all tech pronouncements (like flying cars by the year 2000), blogging hasn't come to pass as it was expected; however, some pretty amazing things have happened along the way, most of which were not predicted.

The Blog Heard Round the World: Blogging Gets Mainstream Attention

In 2005, Canada hosted its first blogging conference (Northern Voice), and two Blog Business Summits were held—one in Seattle and another in San Francisco—and I was at all three of them. Back then, I would sit down at a conference session, fire up my blog editor, and

December 1997: Weblog coined as term for online journal "web log"

April–May 1999: Shortened to "blog"

April 1999: LiveJournal born

August 1999: Blogger launched by Pyra Labs

October 2001: Movable Type launched

2001: Drupal to open source

February 2003: Google acquires Blogger

May 2003: WordPress 0.7 released

October 2003: TypePad launched

November 2002: Technorati launched

April–May 2004: Tris starts his first blog

January 2005: LiveJournal purchased by Six Apart

January 2005: *Fortune* names "Eight Bloggers You Shouldn't Ignore"

January 2005: First "Business Blogging Summit"

August 2005: WordPress.com opened to private testing

Fall 2005: NowPublic starts crowdsourcing news

December 2006: *Time* names "You" person of the year because of rise of blogs

January 2007: Tumblr launched

November 2007: First BlogWorldExpo

December 2007: Six Apart sells LiveJournal to SUP

December 2007: Movable Type released as open source

Sept 2009: NowPublic Purchased by Clarity Digital

December 2009: *Create Your Own Blog* first published

August 2010: Tumblr hits 1 billionth post

September 2010: Six Apart and VideoEgg form SAY Media

January 2011: SAY Media sells Six Apart and Moveable Type brands to Infocom

July 2011: WordPress powers 50 million websites (~25 million on WordPress.com)

September 2011: Tumblr hits 10 billionth post

October 2011: Google Launches Google+ and integrates with Blogger start typing to beat the band. When the session was over, I would take lots of pictures. These were uploaded to the photo-sharing site *Flickr* for all to see. All my posts and pictures were "tagged" with the agreed upon *Technorati* tag for the event. I wasn't the only one doing this, either. At any given conference, 10 or more people might all doing the same thing at the same time.

> **NEW TERM**
>
> Technorati was launched in November 2002 as an index of the blogosphere. It added identifiers, called *tags*, as a way to categorize posts and group them together. Since then, tags have become ubiquitous not only for blogs, but almost all content online. Technorati is no longer the keeper of tags, and most bloggers today probably don't know that Technorati started it all.

> **NEW TERM**
>
> The Flickr photo-sharing site, born in Vancouver originally as a game, was later purchased by Yahoo! and is the preferred site for bloggers to share their photos.

> **NOTE**
>
> It was important that people all used the same Technorati tag for an event so that everyone's content could be searched and found together. Asking "What's the tag for this event?" was like asking where the coffee is at a conference. It was just one of those important things to know.

During this time, people were starting to think there was something to this blogging thing and that money could be made from it. Uh, oh. Blogging "purists" started to get more than a tad testy on this point. Could you have blogs written by a business? Could people blog for companies they didn't work for? Could a fictional character blog? These were the hot topics of 2005–2006. That probably seems naïve today, but eventually people moved on and realized that blogging was becoming the new "publishing," and we found new things to argue about.

Throughout 2005 and into 2006, businesses were told they had to start blogging or they would be left behind. It hasn't quite ended up like that, but technology-related and customer service companies have found that the personal connection that blogging allows has helped them reach their customers in new ways.

In 2006, *Time* magazine declared "You" its Person of the Year, saying on the cover, "Yes, you. You control the Information Age. Welcome to your world." Bloggers were clamoring for attention and wanted to be recognized as "new media" or "citizen journalists." The Consumer Electronics Show (CES) realized that bloggers couldn't be ignored and started giving them passes like other journalists and media in 2006. Many conferences started to offer blogger rooms for people to work, write, and socialize (sometimes called blogger lounges). Today, blogging has become so mobile that setting aside special rooms isn't needed.

With blogs, blogging, and Web 2.0, a lot of technologies were invented, but what individuals *were really doing involved creating better and better ways for people to connect and communicate.*

In 2007, people started talking about the "blog bubble" and Web 2.0 getting overinflated. There were serious discussions that "blogging was dead," and several a-list bloggers publically gave up blogging (a few "gave up blogging" several times). The blog bubble, if there ever was one, passed, but the pragmatists won in the end. Blogging matured into a stable form of online writing and expression.

It could be said that blogging, having a blog, or even just expressing oneself online has become commonplace. Not passé, but commonplace—something that could be taken for granted, if it were not for the fact that

we've come to expect that we'll be able to learn about and read about the news, hobbies, movies, culture, and so on online through blogs. The question of whether a website is or isn't a blog isn't important here, because I'm referring to the posting of frequent, interesting, timely articles.

Here's a quick example: Over the past few years I've become friends with Gillian Shaw, lead tech reporter at the *Vancouver Sun*. I've been interviewed by Gillian, featured in her stories, and I've returned the favor for her on several occasions. I also read her pieces on tech as they cross my (virtual) path. So Gillian might write several stories a week about some piece of technology or tech news, and a few of those pieces will make the printed version of the *Vancouver Sun* (see Figure 1.2). The *rest* of the pieces are posted on her portion of the *Vancouver Sun*'s website and her blog. There isn't room in the *Vancouver Sun* to *always* publish Gillian's articles on dead trees, but there is *plenty* of room to publish them online.

FIGURE 1.2
Gillian Shaw's columns on the *Vancouver Sun* website.

By the way, Gillian isn't unique at the *Vancouver Sun*. Many of the other reporters and columnists do the same thing: They publish daily, but what gets printed is only a fraction of their actual output.

That, folks, is blogging in action. We expect that all the news on a topic will be covered online. The tools that came about as part of the blogging revolution (the *Vancouver Sun*, by the way, runs its larger online presence on a blogging engine) have made this possible, not just for giant mainstream publications, but for anyone with a voice and a story to tell.

As far as giant leaps forward in blogging and blogging technology, those days might be over (we're just making all the tools better now), but the importance of blogging is greater than ever.

Blogging Comes into Its Own

Blogs and blogging aren't what they used to be. Right now you're reading the second edition of a book started in the fall of 2008 and completed about a year later. This second edition is being written in the fall of 2011 (the pattern of working on this book in the fall isn't lost on me), and the intervening couple of years since I signed off on the last pages of the book have been "interesting" to say the least in the blogging world.

For the most part, it's safe to say that blogging has become an accepted form of online discourse and publishing. Using "accepted" instead of passé or "dead" is *essential* here— and not because I want to sell more books— because blogging's death knell has been

sounded many, many times (and shall be many more times, I'm sure), yet blogging as a tool remains.

Blogging isn't a niche activity any longer. Bloggers aren't considered odd fringes of society by the media (or anyone else). Bloggers have become…normal. Blogging isn't just mainstream, it's mature. Throughout this book, I'll still refer to all blogs as part of "the blogosphere," although, in truth, people don't use that term as much as they used to even a year ago. I think it's because now that CNN correspondents have blogs, journalists have blogs, reporters have blogs, even some blogs have stopped calling themselves blogs, we just think of blogs as part of the World Wide Web itself, not as a special segment of it.

This is a wonderful thing.

Having your own website where you talk about your own stuff, even if you just post links, photos, and videos on Tumblr or Posterous (I'll talk about those in more detail in Chapter 2, "Installing and Setting Up Your First Blog") is just normal.

This isn't to say that blogs aren't considered a little different from other websites. Blogs are about content, written or visual; when people think about blogs, they think about opinion pieces, information, reviews, and information sharing. You will hear and read in the media mention of "what the blogs are saying," but that isn't stated (as it once was) in terms of niche or fringe content but rather what pundits and regular folks are saying about issues.

Like I said, blogs are the new normal. Welcome to the return to normalcy.

Culture of Sharing, Connecting, and Caring

"Social Media is nothing more than what you'd do at a cocktail party…but online. And in your pj's." —Erin Kotecki Vest (Queen of Spain)

The funny thing about blogging is that although its boom and heyday might *seem* like bygone times, in reality, people are still happily blogging away like nobody's business—we're just not making such a big deal of it anymore. What has remained a constant over all these years is a culture of connection and sharing. People write about the things they are passionate about, and other people who are passionate about the same thing eventually find them and—boom—connection! You share, we connect. Along the way, another interesting thing happens—we start to genuinely, truly *care* about the other person. Even when you're reading "professional" blogs, if something has gone off the rails for the author, you feel bad. It's not called "social media" for nothing. It's this larger, deeper community that you're about to join…hold on, because it's a fun ride.

There was a lot made of being transparent and authentic during the early days of blogging. We talked about it as if people wouldn't naturally write like that. Funny thing is that over the years, I've found that when people start writing and sharing and connecting with people who share their passions and interests, transparency and authenticity seem to naturally happen.

As blogging was being born and shooting into the mainstream, in the background "social media" was emerging as the greater, more important trend. Blogging certainly was the catalyst for social media and is not just a part of social media, but intertwined with it as well.

Blogs, Society, and the News

I can think of no other field or industry that has been changed more since the advent of blogging than how people create, consume, and disseminate the news. The news had been "revolutionized" when publications started to put articles online, but when bloggers were scooping newspapers, TV, and all other forms of media on breaking stories, the real change began. Suddenly CNN was playing catch up to bloggers, and it wasn't amused. Newspapers were criticized for not reporting fast enough, and the idea emerged that they were becoming irrelevant in the era of instant news. Bloggers were the new "investigative journalists," except they often only investigated what Google brought to them in search results. They were breaking new ground. They were, well, just mucking things up all over the place and having fun doing it.

Bloggers are often quoted in the news as expert sources—because often they *are* the experts on particular topics. Some bloggers have made the transition to mainstream media, and many journalists are blogging—some very well. Newspapers have blogs for columnists so they can report on news in their area of expertise on the days they don't have a column in print. What's the future, then?

FIGURE 1.3

Vancouver's NowPublic.com, Crowdsourced news.

NOWPUBLIC TURNS JOURNALISM ON ITS HEAD—WE'RE ALL JOURNALISTS

What about reporting? A few years ago, a "citizen journalist" was a nosey person who wrote a lot of letters to the editor. Today, they are bloggers. When it became apparent that bloggers were just as agile and deft at reporting the news as any news outlet on the planet, people wanted to leverage that. NowPublic was born in Vancouver to do just that.

Built on an open-source blogging engine, NowPublic made anyone a journalist. A member of the NowPublic site could post text, audio, video, and images of anything he or she thought was news. This is when things started to get hairy. People who have spent their lives being journalists bristled at bloggers calling themselves "online journalists" or "news media journalists." Bloggers didn't generally follow the rules of journalism. They were biased and freely gave their opinion and spin on the news. Bloggers accepted free things from companies to try. Some people were better at disclaiming these potential conflicts of interest than others. But then, as in all things, some bloggers are better citizen journalists than others.

In 2008, major newspaper and media chains filed for bankruptcy protection (like Tribune Media Group) and reduced home delivery (*Detroit Free Press*). CNN sourced whole shows from bloggers and social media and during the elections of 2008 (not just in the United States), blogs and social media played a tremendous role in all facets of the campaigns. It is plain to see that what has happened since 2005 has changed how people think about news and information, even if you don't know about blogs or blogging.

The lines aren't getting blurry, they were buffed out—and bloggers are drawing new ones. Today, having people contribute their own pictures or videos to news broadcasts is pretty common. Even if you don't consider that "blogging," the rush to tap into citizen media or crowdsourced news is no myth. Unlike pronouncements made around the time this book was *first* published in 2009, the mainstream media hasn't gone belly up or completely changed how they do things. Rapid publishing technologies—inspired by blogging engines—have made news more responsive to new updates than it was a few years ago. The advent of tablets like the iPad has made news more portable again and has brought back the idea of the "newspaper." What have blogs and blogging done for news?

They made it better. They made it more interesting and faster. Perhaps, blogging even *saved* the traditional media by forcing them to change and adapt to new threats. Regardless of anything else, the news media, blogs, and blogging are very much intertwined now, all thanks to people just writing and speaking their minds.

Gaze into the Looking Glass and the Future of Blogging

If you step back and look at what blogging is all about, it's really just a set of technologies that makes communicating easier. These technologies have allowed individuals to publish information rapidly. Text, images, video, and audio are so quickly available online that the world can know about an earthquake, tsunami, or disaster within minutes of it happening. That isn't going to change. People expressing themselves online with words, images, and audio, and enriching our lives with their stories, knowledge, and opinion won't change either. Neither will how politics and protest are now organized online. That has been changed forever.

> *If you step back and look at what blogging is all about, it's really just a set of technologies that make communicating easier.*

Blogging, however? Blogging like how I started in 2004, with the blog shown in Figure 1.4, is changing. So I want you to think about self-expression and technology as you read this book. If you're writing a personal blog, what do want to tell the world? As a business, what do you want people to know about you? What do you want to know from or about your customers?

I'm going to talk and write about blogging throughout this book, but while I am doing that, I'm also going to paint you a bigger picture. I'm going to show you why, when I started this book, I started a new blog. I'm going to show you why I have my photography portfolio online and why I encourage professionals, such as lawyers and writers, to have blogs. I'm going to show you how to build and design a blog now that is based not on jargon or the latest thing, but on the essential human fact that individuals like to communicate and share with each other.

FIGURE 1.4

My blog circa August 2004. Stop laughing—it was state of the art for the time.

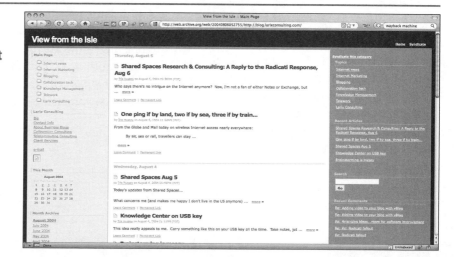

Another trend that is new to this book is very important to understanding how blogs, blogging, social media, and technology are changing. In the past few years, blogs have become almost the "standard" for long-form online writing. When you write a blog post, it's about 300–500 words. However, people found that often they didn't have *that much* to say about something, and they wanted a way to share a little bit but in a way that was also bloglike. That desire is what fueled services like Tumblr and Posterous and later Google's Buzz, Wave, and Google+ (Google Buzz and Google Wave were both discontinued), which provide the capability to write something longer than a tweet on Twitter (140 characters) and shorter than a standard blog post. Technology to the rescue.

The other facet to Tumblr, Posterous, and Google+ is the idea that your online presence might not just be a blog, but a blog, a profile on Flickr (photos), Google+, and a Tumblog (what a blog on Tumblr is called). You share different kinds of content on different places. It isn't one tool to fit all uses now, it's a tool that is best suited to the kind of content you'd like to share.

As you work your way through this book, keep that in mind. Don't think that you have to have your blog do it all, or that you can have only one blog, or that you can't have a blog where you write longer posts as well as a place on Posterous or Tumblr to gather and share interesting things that you may (or may not) write more about later.

Today, the world of blogging is much richer, more flexible, and more interesting than it was a couple of years ago when this book first came out. By the end of this book, I hope you're as excited about the new developments as I am.

Summary

By now, you are well on your way to having a blog. I know it still seems early, but that first idea of "I could write about…" is all it usually takes to get someone going down the blogging path.

With a short history of blogging in your head, I hope you understand how *rapidly* everything changed for blogs and bloggers. Blogging went from a niche thing that geeks did to something every company had to have almost overnight. Although it is safe to call blogs mainstream now, the sense of what a blog is has changed and matured to a point where I think most people surfing the Internet don't realize or think they are looking at a blog; it looks like a website to them. Honestly, I'm pretty happy about that because the days of considering blogs as some strange and unique part of the Internet was getting tiresome.

We're ready now to make the next jump— setting up your first blog. Chapter 2 is probably the most techie and geeky chapter in the whole book. Don't worry, though, you can take it slow; nothing is all that complicated. If you get stuck, help is only a few clicks away on my blog: www.trishussey.com.

CHAPTER 2

Installing and Setting Up Your First Blog

Starting Your First Blog

Now that you know a bit about me, the history of blogging, and a bit on where blogging is headed, let's dig into the meat of things and get going. You need to think about only four things when you're starting a blog, and after you've set up one blog, the last step becomes second nature.

- What are you going to write about?
- What are you going to call your blog?
- Which blog engine will you choose?
- Who are you going to write as?

I'm going to introduce you to thinking about your blog's topic here, but will cover writing good blog posts in Chapter 3, "Creating Content for Your Blog." By the end of this chapter you'll be all set to start blogging!

Choosing a Topic for Your Blog

Choosing a topic is one of the most important steps for starting your blog. If you're thinking, "I don't know, I just want to blog," stop now and think it through for a minute. What do you do for a living? What are your hobbies? What are your passions in life? No matter what you might be thinking, all of those are interesting and great topics for blogs. I've started blogs on cooking, fountain pens, coffee, technology, photography, business blogging, and even men's grooming. I haven't kept all of them running, and some have died slow and painful deaths, but they were all fun and, yes, people did read them.

No matter what you might think, there is an audience for almost any topic you can write

about. I'll add a note of caution here: Don't write for readers. Don't write for traffic. Write for you. I didn't start writing to be famous or get a book deal. I wrote because I had opinions I wanted to share and nowhere else to do it. If you want to write about knitting beanies for baby bunnies, more power to you. Just do it.

When my friends have told me they wanted to blog, I always start with that question: What are you going to write about? Just as often, I start with saying, "you should have a blog about that," because I can see the passion in their eyes when they talk about it. I see how excited it makes them to delve into the minutia of a topic. Those people always make great bloggers. Blogging is about passion and storytelling. You can learn storytelling, but passion? You either have it or you don't.

Another great way to find a good topic for your blog is finding a gap in the information you can find online about that topic. Suppose you have a particular medical condition; writing about your trials and tribulations can be very therapeutic, but you also have an opportunity to educate others about the condition. A friend's husband contracted MRSA (Methicillin-resistant *Staphylococcus aureus*), and she started a blog about it—how to prevent it and current treatments. That blog and her other blogs on health and beauty became a career for her. Another example is that I found that few men were writing about men's grooming (like shaving, hair products, and skin care), so I started a blog about it, and it became very successful very quickly. I took advantage of an opportunity to write about something I liked *and* that no one else was really talking about.

Picking a Name for Your Blog

Picking a name for your blog sometimes just comes to you. Mine was "A View from the Isle" for about four or five years (an eternity in the blogging world). Why "A View from the Isle"? When I started blogging, I lived on Salt Spring Island, BC, followed by Pender Island, and then Victoria, BC. Luckily, Victoria is on Vancouver Island, which, although huge, is still an island.

But now I live in Vancouver, and that's not an island at all. Eventually, I decided, after a lot of teasing and questions, to change my blog to just TrisHusseyDotCom. I was sad to see the name go, but its time had come and gone, and I needed to better reflect my current status more than I needed to be tied to a name. So, just a word to the wise—if you are really specific about your blog's name (where you live, your marital status, whatever) you might run into the same "problem" that I did. A time may come when your blog no longer reflects who you really are in life. Because your blog is *really* about you, you need to make sure that its name reflects you as much as the writing does.

Lots of people use their online moniker, like "Queen of Spain" from Chapter 1 (see Figure 2.1). Other people have a fun name, but use their name for the domain name of the blog. Regardless of what you choose, put some thought into it.

FIGURE 2.1
Queen of Spain Blog by Erin Kotecki Vest.

TOP 10 WORST DOMAIN NAMES FOUND AROUND THE INTERNET

Who Represents—www.whorepresents.com

Experts Exchange—www.expertsexchange.com

Pen Island—www.penisland.net

Therapist Finder—www.therapistfinder.com

Italian Power Generator—www.powergenitalia.com

Mole Station Native Nursery—www.molestationnursery.com

www.ipanywhere.com

www.speedofart.com

Lake Tahoe—www.gotahoe.com

Not all of the domains remain active—for obviously good reasons.

As you think about names for your blog, first consider whether the name is long or hard to spell. If you put it all together as a domain name, does it spell something you'd rather it didn't? (Don't laugh. Several companies have made this mistake.)

Here's my history (and this is *not* the best way to pick a name, by the way): My consulting company's name was Larix Consulting, so I had larixconsulting.com. This makes sense because a company should try to own a domain as close as it can to its real-world name. As you can figure out, my website's URL was www.larixconsulting.com and my blog became blog.larixconsulting.com. So, people typed blog.larixconsulting.com into their browser to get to my blog, which I called "A View from the Isle." I soon realized that my blog was becoming my calling card because it hosted the best examples of my work. I ditched my old website and went forward with just the blog alone.

NEW TERM

A domain name is the word or words that are used to easily remember website addresses. The domain name is made up of two parts: the name itself and the top level domain or TLD. For example trishussey.com is one of the domains that I own. The ".com" is the TLD, trishussey is the actual domain. The TLD is an important part here because trishussey.com and trishussey.ca are different domain names and could go to different websites.

Eventually, I dropped larixconsulting.com as my primary URL in 2008 because I found that, regardless of what my business name was, it was *my* name that had become paramount. This wasn't ego as much as branding, not to mention I was tired of spelling "larix" for people. (You get bonus points if you know what "Larix" refers to.) As you can see, you can have a domain that people will recognize (trishussey.com) and a blog that maintains a sense of branding. I could have also bought aviewfromtheisle.com and used that all along (it would have been smart to do that), or do both.

Here is what I'd suggest that you do. Start with a clever name for your blog. Got it? Awesome. Go to a *domain registrar* like NameCheap.com and see whether it is available as a domain name (see Figure 2.2). Yes? Super—buy it. No? What about your own name? This is a bit of a long shot for most people, but try it. Keep working at it.

NEW TERM

A domain registrar is the site/service where you "buy" your domain name. Buy is in quotes because when you register a domain name you typically have to renew the registration in a year. So maybe "rent" or "lease" is a better term.

FIGURE 2.2

A basic domain name search at NameCheap.com.

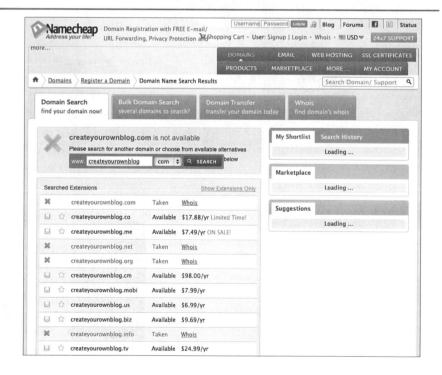

Here are some of the blogs that I think have great names and URLs:

- Lifehacker.com
- AskDaveTaylor.com
- Miss604.com
- GlobalNerdy.com
- DoItMyselfBlog.com
- Copyblogger.com
- ProBlogger.net
- Digital-Photography-School.com

TIP

You're probably wondering why I'm suggesting you buy a domain name when you might start out with a service like Blogger or WordPress.com, where you don't need a domain name to get started. Although it's not free, for just $10 a year you can reserve that name for yourself. More to the point, this helps you plan ahead so that if you start with myreallycoolblog.wordpress.com you can switch to myreallycoolblog.com if you want to later. This is just insurance. You don't have to buy the domain, but I think it's a good idea.

Notice the domains and blog names I've listed here. You can probably guess what the blog is about, can't you? This isn't an accident. Another important consideration in choosing a name is *search engine optimization (SEO)*. The previous domains use the keywords I want the search engines to index. Keyword-rich names don't have to be long, and they can be clever; it just takes a little more effort to get the right name.

NEW TERM

SEO is a process by which you attempt to improve your site's traffic by optimizing its content so that it's more likely to appear higher in the results a search engine generates.

If you're talking about knitting, writing, painting, or collecting action figures, the name should reflect that. Hold on, you're saying, I don't really *care* about SEO; I'm just doing this for fun. I know, but it's just like buying a domain name ahead of time. It's about planning ahead. Many of my friends started blogging for fun or just to test it out, or someone said, "Here, start a blog," and then found themselves suddenly popular. These are people who are now sought out as consultants and speakers. However their blogs have some goofy, off-the-cuff name, or they didn't buy the domain when they should have. The blog is now "stuck" at .blogspot.com or .wordpress.com, and they can't move it because of the links to that URL. Moving to a domain of their own would break all the links to the old blog, or at least they'd have to keep redirecting people from your "old" blog to your "new" blog.

NOTE

Okay, saying you "can't" move your blog is a little harsh. You *can* switch to using a new domain for your blog and *some* services (WordPress.com) will help you with the process. However, it's still a pain to do.

Yes, redirecting people is technically easy, but it's like riding a bike uphill—when you have momentum, you want to keep it. Stopping in the middle of the hill to change to a "better bike" might be a good idea, but you are going to lose all the momentum you built up with the previous one. That momentum is all the SEO value you've built up, all the links, and all the branding.

At least by buying the domain and thinking about SEO early, you're being prudent. You're planning ahead.

How are you doing on that name?

Remember:

- ▶ Think about what you are going to blog about.
- ▶ Think catchy.
- ▶ Think about branding.
- ▶ Think about whether it spells something you don't intend.

Choosing a Domain Name

I'm going to get a little more into the choosing of a domain name now by dispelling a couple of myths first. One, all the good domain names aren't gone. There are lots of great names; you just might need to be a little more clever about it. Two, the TLD (top-level domain, such as .com, .net, and .org) *does* matter, but you don't need to buy all the variations of your domain name unless you are a business or organization.

Personally, I try to buy a .com domain first. If I can't get my first choice of .com, I might explore variations of the name before I try adding a hyphen to the name (such as

manscaping-101.com) or even consider using the .net domain. If all else fails, you could try one based on your country. For example, because I'm Canadian, I could look for a .ca domain. I'm not a fan of .org, .me, or .info. Avoid .info domains like the plague. Yes, it makes a lot of sense to have knittingpatterns.info, but the problem is that the majority of .info domains are spam sites, and the search engines are blocking them from their indices. Getting indexed by Google with a .info domain isn't worth the hassle when you can opt for a good .com, .org, or .net in the first place.

> *Getting indexed by Google with a .info domain isn't worth the hassle when you can opt for a good .com, .org, or .net in the first place.*

What about the other domains like .tv? If you are doing a video blog, sure—grab it, but .tv domains are *much* more expensive than a regular domain. (It is the country code for Tuvalu, like .us is for the U.S. or .ca for Canada). Unless you're reading this and really planning to make a go of it online, hold off for now. Buy an inexpensive domain, maybe two, and leave it at that.

Choosing a Blog Engine

This is the geekiest section of the book. Don't be scared. While I am fluent in geek, I also speak regular human as well. I'm going to make this as jargon free as possible. No, there won't be a quiz at the end. I begin with the decisions about which blog platform to use and where your blog will "live," and then I get into the tweaking and tuning part. Think of this as first choosing between Ford, Toyota, or GM, and then picking what kind of car and adding the options. Start with the big picture and work down.

First, decide whether to start a hosted blog or do it yourself (self-hosted). What this boils down to is who is responsible for setting up, installing, and maintaining the "backend" of your blog. The backend of your blog is not where all your bad ideas go; it's the files, settings, and databases that make it work. When your blog is hosted, making sure stuff works and generally keeping the lights on is someone else's problem. If you can't get into your blog to post, you have someone else to scream at. When you have a self-hosted blog, it's *mostly* just the opposite. Although you'll probably have to do the installation and database setup yourself, making sure the server (the big computer) is running and working is the responsibility of the web host.

NEW TERM

A web host is a company that provides a service hosting websites for people. A typical web host will maintain hundreds of servers and host thousands of websites. Web hosts charge a monthly fee for being able to host your website there.

I've done both hosted and self-hosted blogs, and I prefer to host the blogs myself. I have more control, and I can test new technologies as they come out. However, if you don't like having to mess around with the technical aspects of running a blog, running updates, and so on, then hosted is what's right for you.

TIP

Don't rule out a self-hosted blog because you don't think you're "techie" enough. Many web hosts automate the most technical aspects of hosting for you!

Hosted

There are three kinds of hosted blog solutions: free, paid, and "freemium." Freemium is a bit of an odd duck in the Internet world, but I'll get to that in a moment. Remember, with the hosted model you're trading flexibility for having less to worry about. This is not a bad thing. I used hosted systems for years and made the switch to self-hosted/DIY only when I started to need more flexibility. That was *years* down the road for me. The following are some of the hosted platforms that you might have heard of:

► Blogger

► TypePad

► Tumblr

► Posterous

► WordPress.com (the .com is important here)

There are certainly more than these services, but these are also the "big players" in the market. These are the blog hosts that have the best infrastructure and would be least likely to have problems with uptime (that is to say, working). Will they give you the best support? That is a completely different question and one that often depends on the individual.

Let's get into the three types of hosted blog solutions. Free solutions are, as you might guess, free. Because nothing is ever really free in this world, your blog is sometimes supported by ads around your content that the blog host owns and runs. Running the ads helps them recoup the cost of the servers, people, and such things that keep the proverbial lights on and the blogs running. Yes, if you have an incredibly popular blog, you are potentially making a lot of money for the host. Consider this as the cost of having a free blog. Blogger, owned by Google, generally doesn't put ads around your blog, just a navigation bar to guide you to the next related blog. On Blogger you can put your own ads on your blog to earn money from it.

> **CAUTION**
>
> Read the terms of service (TOS) carefully when you sign up for any free service! Sometimes you are restricted to the kinds of topics or things you can do with your blog.

Generally, free solutions don't let you have or use your own domain name for your blog. If you use your own domain with Blogger, you honestly might as well go self-hosted. With free services, your domain name is something like myawesomeblog.blogspot.com (if you are using Blogger). Is not controlling the domain really a bad thing? Yes and no. Having your own domain name gives you more legitimacy and a professional touch. It looks like you're taking your site seriously. There is some debate about the search engine benefits of having your own domain versus .blogspot.com, but I think that can be overcome with simple search engine optimization techniques. So why go free?

Frankly, free is a great way to start out. There is no monetary risk to it. You can practice and

experiment, and get a good feel for blogging, before committing to something larger. I have free blogs set up for teaching or when I want to have an anonymous blog to experiment with different writing styles. Before you stop reading and go sign up, I have to give you the "but…" part of having a free blog: You don't own the URL.

If you'd just like to learn and experiment a bit, or even do some anonymous blogging, go with free. Just keep in mind that if your "experiment" starts getting some attention, you should think about switching to something else. From Blogger, shown in Figure 2.3, you can "easily" move to another blog platform or even have a hybrid solution where you have a blog on your own domain, but run by Blogger.

> **TIP**
>
> If this blog is for your band, you should have a MySpace page. MySpace is still the leading blogging platform within the music world.

There is a step between free and paid that I do recommend, and that is "freemium." Freemium means that you can sign up for a service, in this case a blog with no fee, but if you pay a fee (generally reasonable) you get more features. In the blog world, the stand-out leader is WordPress.com (see Figure 2.4). In the interests of full disclosure, I know the people at Automattic, makers of WordPress.com and I think that not only is the service awesome, but the people are, too.

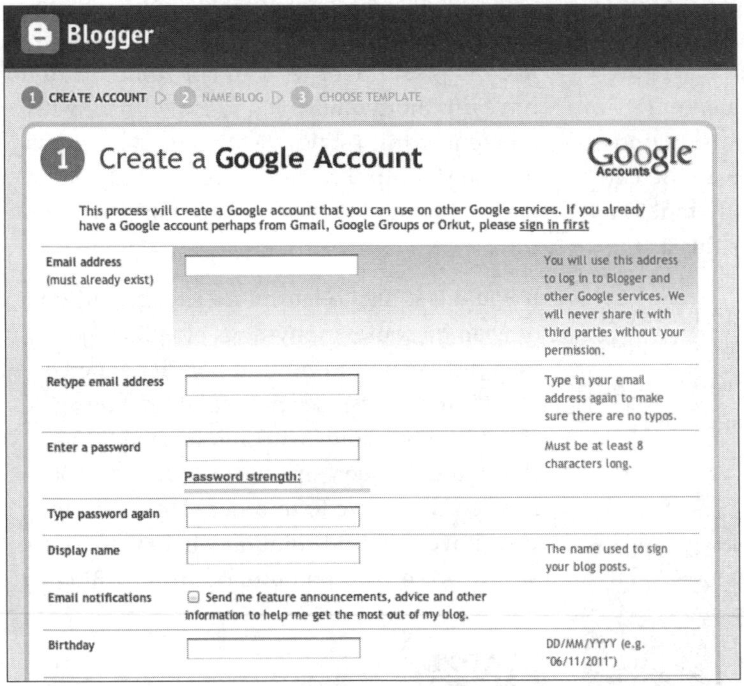

FIGURE 2.3
Many new bloggers find that Blogger.com offers the best balance of free and freedom.

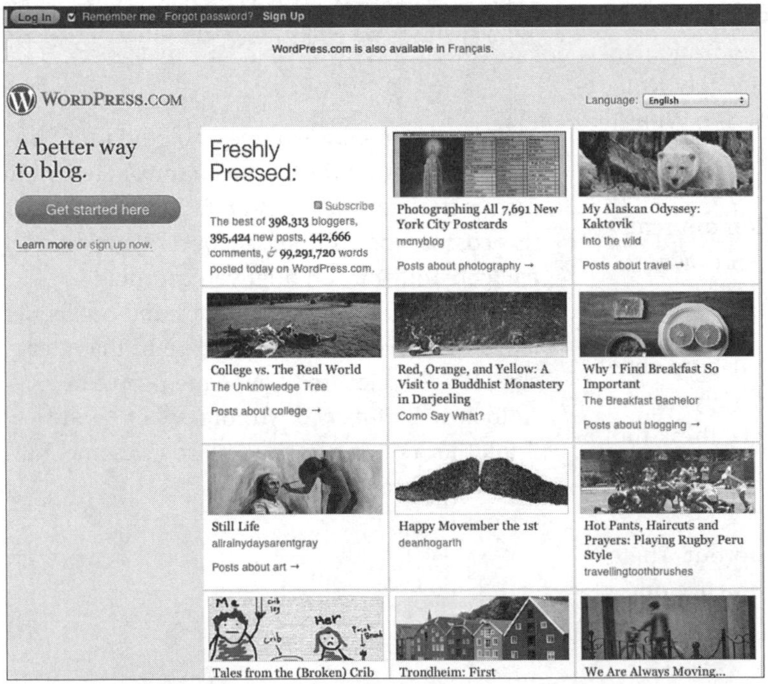

FIGURE 2.4
The WordPress.com home page, where you can sign up and explore other WordPress.com-based blogs.

With WordPress.com, you can sign up for a blog and have trishussey.wordpress.com. Later, if you decide that you want to have trishussey.com, just pay a small fee to map that domain to that blog. Done like dinner. All the links to the old blog work, but they just point to the new location. This is the best of both worlds. If you decide that you'd like to have more control over your blog, or if you have already used domain mapping for WordPress.com, you can switch to your own host without worry or penalty.

Although WordPress.com is better than a purely free host, they do have some of the same limitations. You have a limited number of theme choices on WordPress.com, although the number of choices is extensive as far as hosted services go. You also cannot put adver-

tising of your own on your blog or use all the *widgets* that people add to their blogs (more on this later).

Moving on to the "paid" group, the leader of the pack is TypePad (see Figure 2.5). TypePad is purely paid (after a free trial) with differing cost levels related to the number of features you want to have. The basic service probably suits most people (and even includes being able to use your own domain if you want), and the bigger packages are geared more toward business than personal bloggers/users. Some for-pay services give you a one-price-fits-all model where you get everything for one price. I think that is a good choice if you are pretty sure about what you want and what you're willing to pay, but if you're not, the flexibility of a service like TypePad is invaluable.

FIGURE 2.5

The TypePad home page, the leader in the "for-pay" hosted blog solutions.

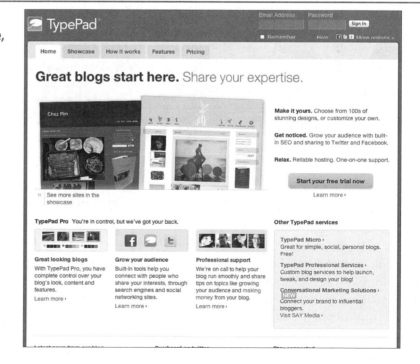

Which should you choose? My recommendation is the freemium model as used by WordPress.com. You can start out free and move up as you're reading. If you want to go self-hosted in the future, you have a clear upgrade path. For the free services, I like Tumblr, not only as a blogging engine, but also a *complement* to a WordPress or Blogger blog. Yes, I'm saying you can have more than one blog for different reasons. As far as paid services, although TypePad is always getting better, I am hard pressed to recommend TypePad for the first timer. TypePad is a great blogging engine and one of the most popular online. It is stable, secure, and efficient. Personally, however, the configuration and system for changing templates drives me crazy. Yes, it's a personal thing, but because I've tried just about all the blogging engines around, I have a basis for comparison. If you want to go free, go WordPress.com.

TIP

Don't take my word for it! Try all the engines in this section and see which you like the best. Even with TypePad, you get 30 days for free.

Self-Hosted

Self-hosted is the way to go if you want to have control over all aspects of your blog or if you already have a website (and therefore a webhost) that you'd like to add a blog to or convert your website to use a blog engine—that's what Chapter 7, "Creating a Website," is all about. Going the self-hosted (or DIY) route gives you control and flexibility, but also a measure of responsibility. The great thing is,

today going DIY isn't very hard, and you'll be well armed with the information you'll need to get going by the end of this chapter.

When you host your own blog, the hosting provider is responsible for making sure the server is running, configured, and secure. You are responsible for installing, configuring, and maintaining your website or blog. It can be challenging at first, if this is an entirely new experience for you. After you get your feet under you, it isn't that hard or that big a deal to install and maintain your own blog.

Picking a good web host is easy, right? Just ask your geekiest friends who they use and do the same. Yeah, except bloggers all use different hosts and overall they hate them all. No matter which web host you use, someone is going to love them and someone else will hate them. I have used great hosts, terrible hosts, and mediocre hosts in the past. To help you choose a web host, here are my tips for finding one:

▶ Ask your geek friends who their preferred hosts are. Just don't be surprised if you get conflicting answers about the same host. Geeks are like that. Sorry.

▶ It's not always about money. Yes, I try to get the best deal I can when I pick a new host, but cheapest isn't always best. Look for the features you need (more on features later in this chapter).

▶ Look for discounts for paying for months or a year at once.

▶ Look at their support area (if it's open to the public). See whether the forums and FAQs (Frequently Asked Questions) seem helpful. The support areas should be the first place you check when you have a question, so they need to be good.

▸ Make sure you'll have room to grow. You'll start off with a "shared hosting account," which means lots of sites are going to be running off the same physical server or computer. If your blog starts to get bigger, make sure you can upgrade to more storage space, bandwidth, or a dedicated server without hassle.

NEW TERM

When you use a dedicated server, you have an entire server (the whole computer) to yourself. This gives you more flexibility if you want to run specialized software for your site, but also more responsibility if something goes wrong (often you have to fix the problem yourself).

Without a doubt, there is always a bit of a leap of faith when you pick a web host. Moving from one host to another isn't a fun thing to do. What if you pick a bad host? How will you know?

Ultimately, you'll know good hosts from bad because your blog will be unavailable often or your host will do things like shutting down your blog with no warning because it is "using too many server resources." Most blogs on well-run hosts shouldn't run into that problem, so if you do have that problem it's a sign that something *could be* wrong with your blog or that the host isn't doing a good job at managing resources. If you run into problems, don't jump ship right away. Give the host (and your trusty geeky friends) a chance to fix it. If it happens once, fine; work out the issue and stick with your host. But if it happens a couple more times, start shopping around for a new host.

FEATURES TO LOOK FOR WHEN SHOPPING FOR A HOST

When I'm looking for a web host, these are the things I look for:

▸ **Unlimited disk space**

▸ **Unlimited bandwidth**

▸ **Unlimited add-on domains and subdomains**

▸ **Unlimited MySQL databases**

▸ **One-click installers for popular tools like WordPress, wikis, shopping carts, and forums**

Although the difference to you will be largely transparent, my preference is also to choose a UNIX or Linux-based host over a Windows-based host. I've found that WordPress and other blog engines work better on UNIX hosts than Windows hosts. UNIX hosts are also most likely to have all the prerequisites for installing WordPress by default.

Moving to a new host is beyond the scope of this book, so I'll give you the best piece of tech advice you'll ever get: Geeks love baked goods, chocolate, and coffee. Yes, geeks can be bribed. Asking a geek friend for help and bringing a treat for him or her with you—yeah, you're in good hands. This is why you'll never see a "please don't feed the geeks" sign in a tech company. Oh, and for the record: chocolate chip cookies, milk chocolate, and strong coffee with cream.

TIP

Finding helpful geeks is as easy as going where they are! Search the Internet for blogging and tech meet ups or groups in your area. Events like BarCamp, DemoCamp, and local computer conferences are great places to meet all kinds of helpful, friendly neighborhood geeks.

Getting Started

By now, you should have a good idea of whether you're going to use a hosted blog solution or be self-hosted. Let's crank that geek-o-meter up a couple notches and get you set up with your blogging platform.

In the interests of keeping this simple, I'm going to walk you through the setup of both a WordPress.com blog and a do-it-yourself WordPress blog (that is using software downloaded from WordPress.org). Why WordPress? For simplicity's sake, I need to pick just one platform to use for this book, and I've gone with WordPress because I think it's the best overall choice if you're just starting out. It's easy to use and flexible to grow. I've used

almost all the blog engines out there, and WordPress (WP) is the one I always come back to.

NOTE

If you've already decided to use one of the other options, don't worry. In terms of getting your blog set up, some of the details and visuals will differ from what I show here, but you should find enough parallels here to guide you.

In the end, all the major blogging engines do the same basic things. The content is stored in a database, and the layout is in a template. The differences are in how easy the administration part (the backend) is to navigate, how flexible it is, and how easy it is to grow with you. Posting is very easy in all the platforms, so I'm taking that out of the mix right now.

Signing Up for a Blog on WordPress.com

Signing up for a blog on WordPress.com is fast and easy. From the time you get to the WordPress.com home page to when you can put up your first post should be less than five minutes. When you sign up for a blog, you can pick just a username or a username with a blog. The key here is that for most people the username they choose and the blog name/URL are the same. Something like billswoodshop would be billswoodshop.wordpress.com. You can get just a username (like trishussey) and then set up a blog to go with that name that is different from your username.

NOTE

WordPress.com and WordPress.org are related but very different sites. WordPress.*com* is where you sign up for a free, hosted blog. WordPress.*org* is where you download all the files to install WordPress on your own server.

Confused yet? I know it seems rather odd, doesn't it? Let's look at the process step by step.

First, go to WordPress.com (this is different from WordPress.org) and follow the link to sign up. You'll get a screen to pick a username and URL for your blog (see Figure 2.6). This is a relatively important decision. You might go with something like kristieskurtains.wordpress.com or autobodycentral.wordpress.com. Both are good and both are descriptive. As a business blogger, you will want to tie your business name to the

blog. The blog name and administrator email address can be changed later, so don't stress over these. Do make sure that the email address you enter works, because your blog won't be activated until you click a link in a confirmation email.

Second...oh, wait—there really isn't a second step, because after you've clicked the email activation link you're ready to start posting.

This is the great thing about using a hosted blog service like WordPress.com. After you've gone through the set-up process, which is usually just one form, you're done. Yes, you should do some tweaking, pick a spiffy theme, and maybe add some nice widgets, but as far as posting, you're done. We'll walk through the major sections of WordPress.com to get you familiar with them in the "Tweaking Your Blog's Setup" section later in the chapter.

FIGURE 2.6
Signing up for a WordPress.com blog.

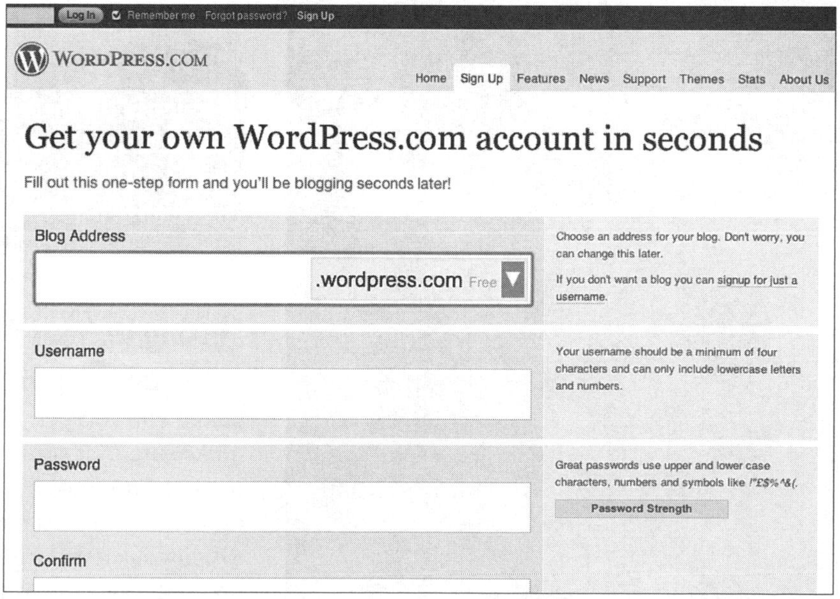

KEEPING YOUR SELF-HOSTED BLOG SECURE

Several times a month, a high-profile blog is hacked by someone, and the results are predictably catastrophic. What can you do to protect your own blog?

▸ **Keep your installation up to date (which is much easier now with one-click updates).**

▸ **Change your default admin password.**

▸ **Create a *new* account with administration privileges, then disable the default admin account (in WordPress you set its role to "none").**

▸ **Create a good, strong password that is not a word or name and contains a couple of numbers or characters in it (for example, ! or @).**

Just the step of creating a new administrator account can foil basic hacking attempts, but if creating a new account seems daunting, changing the admin password, especially if you were emailed a default one, is essential.

Remember, if you choose to go the hosted route, make sure that you can move or upgrade to be able to use your own domain in the future. I would venture that you own the domain name for your business already. I would also venture that you might want to pay the small additional amount to use your own domain with your WordPress.com blog. Strategically, using your own domain name ensures that you own your "name space" online and would have the greatest influence on searches for your business name.

Setting Up a Self-Hosted Blog

Okay, you have a domain, you have a host; now what? Now the fun stuff begins. Yes, this is fun, and yes I do get out often, thank you. Think of it this way—you are about to *create something all your own*. You are carving out your own piece of the Internet. Yours, all yours! See? It is fun.

> **NOTE**
>
> Because of the sheer number of hosting options and flavors out there, I'm going to try to keep this as general as I can, but still give you a decent roadmap to follow.

Setting Up Your Domain Name to Work with Your Web Host

Before you can get your blog up and running, make sure that your host and your domain are matched up to work together. This is about a 6 on the geek-o-meter; don't worry, it's not bad. When you signed up for your new host, you probably were asked whether you have a domain to use with it. Hopefully, your answer is yes. Often, web hosts include "one free domain registration" with a hosting package. This is good, except after the first year, sometimes their renewal fees can be steep. A domain should cost you about $10 a year. If the host is going to charge you $15 in your second year, don't bother with the "free" domain.

After you tell the host in the sign-up process that myawesomeblog.com is what you'll be using, they start the wheels in motion for that to work. Now here is the geeky part—you're going to have to update the *domain name server (DNS)* address for your domain to point to your web host.

NEW TERM

Think of the DNS as a phone book. It matches each name (domain) to a unique number, called an Internet Protocol (IP) address. For every domain you need a "master" DNS record. This is the place that says, "No matter what anyone else says, I'm right and know where this domain lives."

Your host gives you DNS addresses in your "welcome" email when you sign up (such as ns1.areallyawesomehost.com and ns2.areallyawesomehost.com), and "all" you have to do is go to the website where you registered your domain (your domain registrar), find in your account where you can update the name servers for your domain, and do it. Really, the hardest part is finding where your registrar has hidden that function. I almost always have to hit the help file to find it on a host I'm not familiar with, so don't feel bad if you have to look at the help section or email the registrar's support team. The support team at your registrar will be able to help you make sure that your domain is updated with the right settings.

When you're changing your DNS settings, what you're doing is telling the Internet that your domain's master record can be found at this (new) location. Your host has already edited its DNS server to add your domain and the address of the server where it will be "living." Figure 2.7 shows what it looks like when I update the DNS settings at NameCheap.com. I'm just putting the name server addresses in the boxes and clicking Save. The arcane Internet magic all happens in the background.

After the name servers are updated on your registrar, it can take up to a day before that information has propagated around the Internet and you'll be able to get your blog set up. Sometimes I've been lucky and had it all up and working in a few hours, but don't bet on it. Typically, the change should be made in about 24 hours. The best way to test if the change has been made throughout the Internet is to type your domain name into your browser and see what comes up. If the page is something still from your registrar, it hasn't. If it's the default holding page for your web host, it has. Don't worry, there's plenty to keep you busy in the meantime.

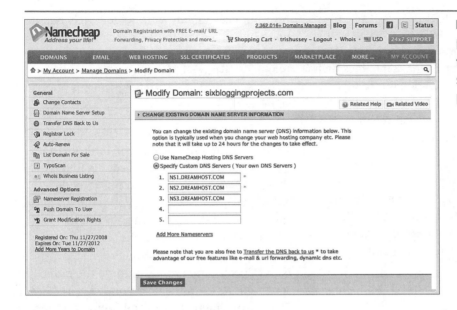

FIGURE 2.7

NameCheap.com's panel for updating my DNS settings for sixblogging-projects.com.

NOTE

DNS records on servers look like large spread-sheets. They aren't even very interesting, or arcane, or geeky.

probably lots of other cool tools as well). Why an easy install and not going old school with doing *everything* yourself? Simple. It's faster and nearly foolproof. Yes, it's a good idea to know what is going on behind the scenes and how your blog engine works (in general), but this isn't a requirement any more. I've found, especially in recent years, that new users can get started with less fuss and less muss if they use the easy install functions with their hosts.

Remember that if your blog is hosted (for example, TypePad, Blogger, and WordPress.com), you don't have anything to install. If you're using your own domain, they help you with the previous DNS steps. Now if you're rockin' it geek style and doing the self-install, let's get to it.

Installing the Blog Software

First, log in to your hosting account's control panel (see Figure 2.8).

The next step is going to be to look for the "easy install" method for WordPress (and

NOTE

Depending on your host, what you're looking for might be called "easy install," "one-click install," or "Fantastico." Because installing blog engines—and WordPress especially—is so popular, most hosts will try to make it easy for you to find (and use) this function.

FIGURE 2.8

The control panel for Dreamhost, where all my blogs and websites are hosted.

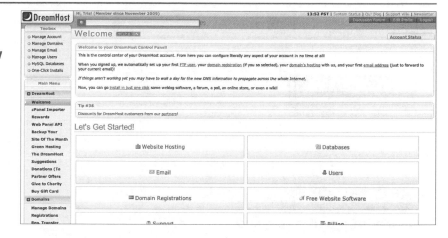

FIGURE 2.9

Easy, one-click installs on Dreamhost.

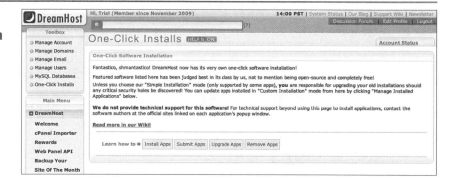

Look for WordPress in your choices of what to install. On Dreamhost it looks something like Figure 2.9, and when I choose WordPress I get a screen that looks like Figure 2.10.

The next step is to pick the domain to install the blog on—for this book I'm going to use techplanations.com—and create a database for the blog. Each host manages these steps a little differently, but because the goal is an *easy* install, you should be able to walk through the steps with ease.

For some hosts, you'll receive an email that the install is complete and you can just log in with a username and password. Other hosts, like Dreamhost, let you know that the final step is ready (the actual install process) and you should go to a link and proceed. Don't worry when installing WordPress; the final install process is painless and is just filling in a simple form (see Figure 2.11).

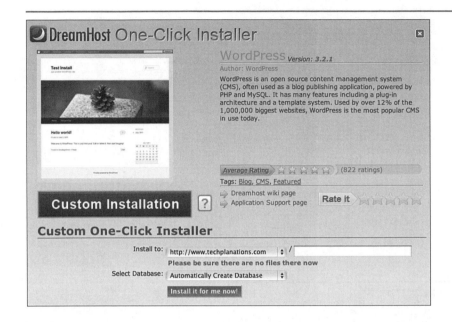

FIGURE 2.10
Dreamhost's WordPress install selection.

FIGURE 2.11
The Install screen for WordPress.

Congratulations, you have now installed WordPress and have a blog!

That wasn't so bad, was it? Right now, you have WordPress installed and ready to go. Sure, it's running default settings, and the default theme isn't the most attractive site in the

world, but it's *running* (see Figure 2.12). You could stop now and blog away, but there's a lot more fun to be had. Let's tweak and tune this baby now. There is going to be a little geeki-ness, but you can handle it.

FIGURE 2.12

A brand-new blog ready for posting and customizing!

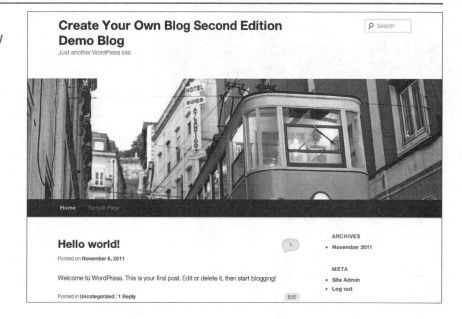

If you didn't want to go with WordPress, use another engine install, one that isn't listed in your one-click installs, or even do a WordPress install completely from scratch, the following are the basic steps to install any blogging engine:

▶ Visit the main site for the blogging engine.

▶ Download the install package (usually a .zip file).

▶ Unzip and read the instructions for installing.

▶ Using an FTP program or your host's web-based file manager, upload the files to your hosting account.

▶ Set up the database as recommended in the install instructions.

▶ Install the engine and test.

One-click installs automate this entire process. The files are already on the server and are unpacked where you need them. The databases and configuration files are created and edited as needed. All you have to do is fill in the form: setting the username, password, and administrator's email address (that would be you). Another benefit of one-click installs is that when you need to update or upgrade the install, often these are done and managed for you.

Touring Your Blog's Dashboard

The Dashboard is the central hub where you adjust the settings for your blog, write posts, and do other administrative tasks. I'm going to use the Dashboard for WordPress 3.2.1 as the example. For other blog engines, or even later versions of WordPress, things might be named differently, but you should be able to follow along.

In Figure 2.13, we have the basic, standard WordPress Dashboard; I haven't added anything or made changes to it.

Because I will be showing you the various sections of the WordPress administration area as we tweak and tune the blog, I'm not going to show you every screen in the administration section, but I will tell you what each of them do. For the sake of consistency, I'm going to call the sections "blocks" and subsections "tabs." I know they don't look like tabs, but sections doesn't sound right either (and they used to be tabs in previous versions of WordPress).

Content Block: Posts, Media, Links, Pages, and Comments

This block deals with all the content on your blog—the posts, static pages, images, links, and comments. All the tabs function similarly in that when you click the tab you see the most recent items in a table. As you pass your mouse pointer over the title of the post or other content, you see options to edit, delete, view, or in some other way manage that content.

FIGURE 2.13

The standard WordPress Dashboard as you'd see in almost any WordPress or WordPress.com blog.

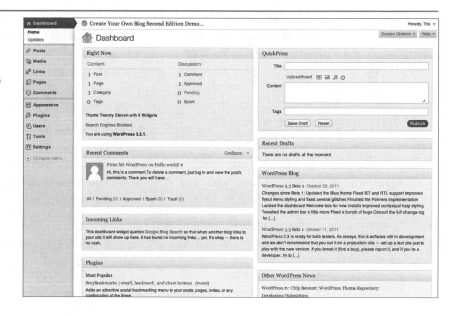

The Posts tab is where you manage the posts on the blog, as well as tags and categories. As you can see from Figure 2.14, when you click Posts you see a list of the latest posts, newest first, and can manage these posts (edit, delete, or view) or create a new one (by clicking the Add New link).

Clicking Add New brings up the post editor, all set to start writing your next brilliant post. Clicking Post Tags or Categories allows you to set the sitewide post tags and categories. I'll talk about tags and categories later in this chapter.

Under the Media tab, you have access to all the files you have uploaded through WordPress, as well as the ability to upload additional files. This area is handy because, as you start to build a library of graphics, you can review the images you have stored and see what might fit into a new post (for example, a picture of a person or product).

FIGURE 2.14

The Posts tab showing the latest posts as well links to add sitewide tags, categories, and create new posts.

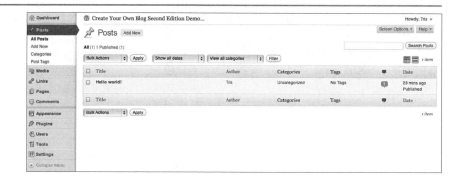

Under the Links tab, you manage your blogroll. You have a list of current links to other blogs and websites, a link to add more links, and a link to create groups of link categories. For example, you might have a group of writing links and group of graphic design links that you could display separately.

The Pages tab is just like the Posts tab, except you have links only to Edit and Add New. I'll be covering the difference between posts and pages in greater detail in Chapter 3.

Finally, the Comments tab allows you to edit the comments that come into your blog. You can approve, delete, mark as spam, or even edit the content of the comments here.

Administration Block: Appearance, Plugins, Users, Tools, and Settings

This is the section of the administration part of the blog where you change how it looks, behaves, and who can do what on the blog. You use the Appearance tab to change themes, add new themes, manage your blog widgets, and adjust any settings specific to your theme.

> **NOTE**
>
> Newer themes under WordPress 3.2 and later have the capability to have their own easy-to-manage settings. These settings take the place of having to edit the code in the theme itself.

Chances are that after you pick the theme for your blog, get the basic widgets in place, and adjust any theme settings, you won't be coming back to this tab very often—unless you're like me and like to change your blog template every few weeks just because you can.

Next is the Plugins tab, where you manage the various plugins for your blog. Plugins are little add-ons you install (upload to the web host) and activate here. In Figure 2.15, you can see a list of all the plugins I have installed for the book blog.

As you can see, under this tab you can add new plugins, and *occasionally* there will be plugins configured here (like the antispam plugin Akismet). Editing plugins through the Editor link isn't something I recommend unless you have been given specific instructions to do so. I've edited a plugin only once or twice in the more than three years I've used WordPress, so I doubt you'll have need to edit one ever.

The Users tab, as you can guess, is where you manage the users, or accounts, on the blog. If this is just your blog, there will be one or two users. One is the admin user and the other is an account for day-to-day use of your blog. I'll talk about why you should have two accounts on the blog when we get to tweaking this blog later in the chapter.

You use the Tools tab, shown in Figure 2.16, to get to the import-export functions of a WordPress blog, as well as the very handy Press This bookmarklet.

FIGURE 2.15

The plugin management area under the Plugins tab, administration block.

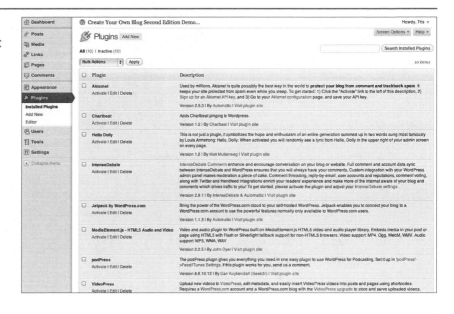

FIGURE 2.16

The Tools tab showing the Press This bookmarklet.

"Press This" is a bookmarklet, a special kind of link that you can drag to the Bookmarks or Favorites toolbar of your web browser to make blogging faster and easier. This is a cool tool, and I'll talk about it in Chapter 3.

Use the Import and Export links if you need to import content from another blog into this one or when you need to back up your content or save it locally to then export into another blog. Chances are you aren't going to do either of these things very often.

The Settings tab is where most of the tweaking, tuning, and configuring is done on your blog. Figure 2.17 shows what you'll probably see when you first turn on and set up your blog (using WordPress).

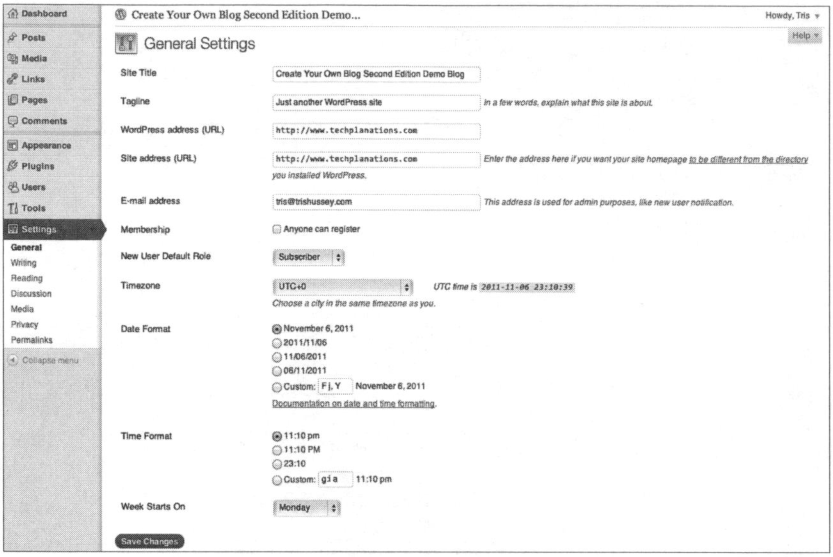

FIGURE 2.17

The list of settings and options under my Settings tab for the blog for this book.

Tweaking Your Blog Setup

It's taken a long time to get here, but we're at the part of the chapter where we're ready to start making your blog sing; now is the time for tweaking and tuning. Here we'll go through and set up things on your blog so it will look great, work fantastically, be found by search engines, and be protected from the dark side of the Internet. Although this sounds like a very geeky undertaking, it isn't. All these steps are simple, straightforward, and make sense even to non-geeks. You have my permission, however, to brag to all your friends how difficult and technical the whole process is when you're showing off your blog.

Rather than get into the minutiae of how to tweak WordPress or Movable Type or Blogger specifically, I'm going to hit them all in broad strokes. Just as before, screenshots and examples will be from WordPress-based blogs, but

the concepts are, generally, applicable to all blogs.

Tweaking and Tuning a WordPress.com Blog

The entryway into the administration of your WordPress.com blog is the Dashboard—remember from earlier in the chapter (see Figure 2.18). This is the place where you can get a bird's-eye view of your blog. I know you're dying to start posting, but let's configure a few of your blog's settings, choose a theme, look at widgets, and edit your About page first.

When you click the Settings button in the left column, the first screen you come to is General Settings, where you give your blog a name and set your time zone (see Figure 2.19). When you're done, click Save Changes.

FIGURE 2.18
The WordPress.com
Dashboard for the
demonstration blog for
this book.

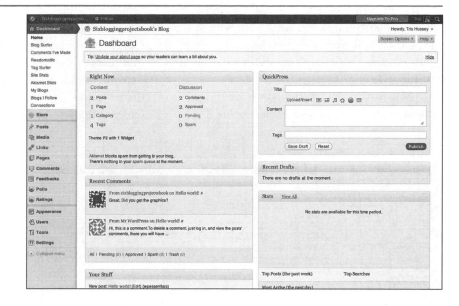

FIGURE 2.19
The WordPress.com
General Settings page
where you give your
blog its name.

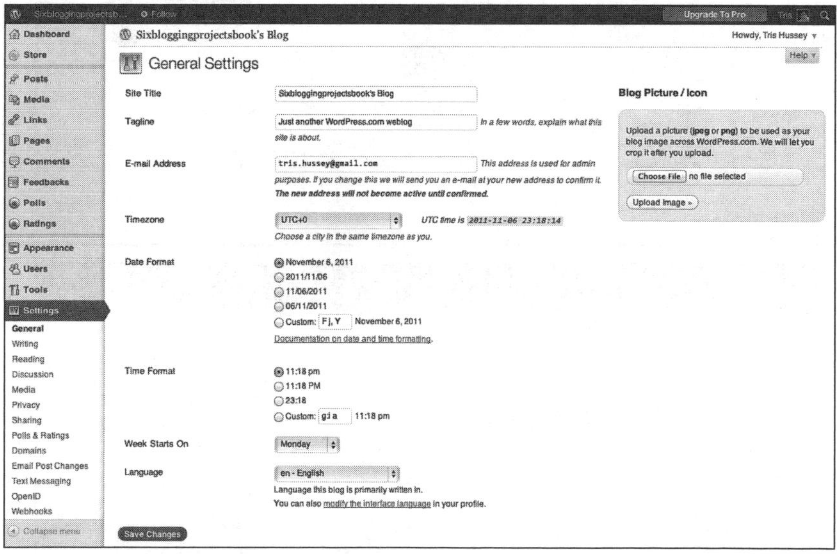

Now that your blog has a name, let's make it look cool with a nice theme. As I'm writing this, 170+ themes are available on WordPress.com, with a huge range of colors, styles, and special features. To change your theme, click Appearance on the left side, and you'll come to the Manage Themes section (see Figure 2.20).

Browse through the themes, and when you find one you like, click the thumbnail and you'll see a preview of what your blog will look like with that theme applied. If you like how it looks, click Activate [name of the theme]. That's it—the new theme is applied to your blog (see Figure 2.21). I told you this was going to be easy!

FIGURE 2.20
The WordPress.com theme manager and a few of the 170+ available themes.

FIGURE 2.21
Previewing the Bold Life theme for the book's WordPress.com blog.

A WORD ABOUT SIDEBAR WIDGETS

Now that your blog has a name and a spiffy new look, let's add some nice touches to the sidebar of the blog. When you visit websites and blogs these days, you see all sorts of things off to the sides (left and right). These sidebar widgets either add some cool function to your blog (like showing the latest pictures you've uploaded) or provide a way to see the most recent article you've posted. Adding sidebar widgets on a WordPress.com blog is a simple matter of dragging and dropping (see Figure 2.22). An impressive number of widgets are available to you by default; I usually add Recent Posts, Recent Comments, Tag Cloud, Categories, and Pages to my sidebar. Because you can add and remove sidebar widgets easily, I recommend trying them out and seeing which *you* like best. This *is* your blog after all, not mine.

The last thing to do is to edit your About page. This is a short page telling readers about the blog and you as the author. You can provide as little or as much information as you like—just edit the default content of the page (and not with "coming soon"). To edit the page, first click Pages on the left side, then mouse over below the title About and click Edit (see Figure 2.23).

There are *tons* of widgets you can add to your blog. You can have tag clouds, Twitter feeds, polls, rotating pictures from Flickr, or even movies from YouTube. The sky is the limit. Well, almost. Just don't overdo it. Pick the ones that most benefit your specific blog.

Most of my favorite widgets come from the services I already use, like Flickr, Twitter, and Google+. When you sign up for these services, they often point you in the direction of their latest widget. If all else fails, a quick Google search for "blog widgets" will get you on your way to widget bliss (or overload).

Widgets can add great features, color, and interactivity to your blog, but they can also slow down how quickly it loads and sometimes cause the blog to not load at all for some browsers. The add-on widgets I'm talking about here shouldn't be confused with WordPress sidebar widgets that come as part of the core install. These widgets, such as Recent Posts, Pages, Recent Comments, and Categories, run straight from the WordPress core and are just fine to add. The same goes for similar widgets on Movable Type/TypePad. These widgets won't slow your blog down very much, but they can lead to eyeball clutter, so just see how things look before you go nuts.

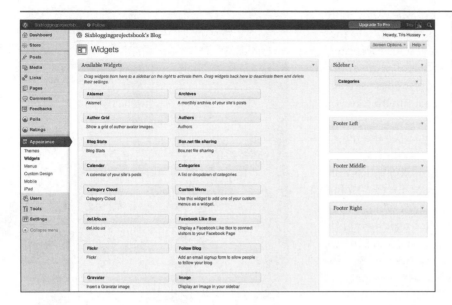

FIGURE 2.22
Drag a sidebar widget from the left side to the sidebar space on the right to activate it on your blog.

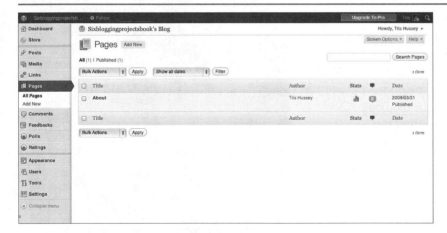

FIGURE 2.23
The Edit Pages screen on WordPress.com.

The next screen, shown in Figure 2.24, is the standard WordPress editing area (the editing areas for Pages and Posts look almost identical and work in the same way) where you can edit the content of your About page (remember, "coming soon" doesn't count!). When you're done, click Update Page, and that's it!

TIP

Some things you can do right off the bat that show you're serious about blogging are changing the tagline Just Another WordPress Blog, editing your About page, and deleting the first Hello World post.

FIGURE 2.24

The WordPress.com web-based Page editor, where you can make changes to your About page.

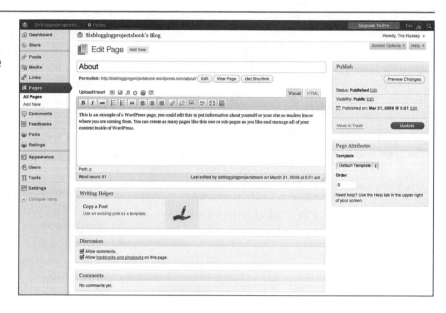

I'll get into writing posts in Chapter 3, but at this point your WordPress.com blog is ready to go! In the next chapter, I'll talk about adding categories, working with tags, editing your blogroll, and other details. These things can all come later, but right now it's time to start thinking about those first posts. You can think while you read the rest of this chapter.

These steps I've outlined for WordPress.com can be followed, in general, for all hosted blog systems. TypePad follows a lot of the same logic in their blogging system as WordPress does. Blogger is a bit of an odd duck when it comes to themes and widgets, but it's not hard to figure out. Again, I choose WordPress.com for a hosted blog solution because I believe that it is the best and most flexible blog engine available. There are certainly more powerful blog engines, and maybe engines that are even simpler to use than WordPress.com, but I think WordPress.com has the right balance between power and ease of use.

CAUTION

For the remainder of this chapter, I'm going to cover various important settings and tweaks for blogs in general. Some of them don't apply to all blogs, especially WordPress.com and Blogger blogs. I will make a note of this in each section.

Setting Good Permalinks

When websites first started to use databases store content (as blogs do), the URLs for each page were generated when someone clicked the link to go to the page. After the person left, that URL was discarded. You might remember that when you bookmarked a page on a site, but went back to the site using that bookmark, you either got a different page or an error. This wreaked havoc on how those sites were indexed and ranked by search engines (they weren't at all). So, as the first blog engines were being developed, the idea of the *permalink* came about.

NEW TERM

Permalink is short for "permanent link," which means the address or URL to a post or page on a blog that can be bookmarked in a browser.

The idea of a permalink is that every page, post, category, and tag on a blog has a corresponding permanent link that can be bookmarked *and* indexed by search engines. Although this is great, the problem is that often the default permalink for many blog engines doesn't give readers or search engines much of an idea what that page is about. Some blog setups, like Blogger and WordPress.com, do a good job of this by default, whereas others need some coaxing. For example, the default permalink for a post in a self-hosted WordPress blog is something like www.trishussey.com/?p=102. Not very interesting, is it? From looking at the URL, there isn't an indication of the post title (and no indication of what the post might be about). Yes, the post title is in the title portion of the page and would show up in a bookmark; however, search engines pay attention to the permalink URL as well. A good permalink is a good thing for everyone.

My personal preference is something like www.trishussey.com/2009/01/mypostrocks/ or /2009/01/10/mypostrocks/. The "mypostrocks" part is the title of the post that gives search engines an idea of the content (if you are writing good titles, which I'll get to), and if people mouse over the link to the post on

another site, they can get an idea of what it's about, as well. In these two examples, I include the year and month with the title; in the second I also include the day. Using the post date in the permalink helps to make sure there is no confusion around the links. You could, for example, write a birthday post to yourself every year. If the title is always "Happy Birthday to Me!" then having the year lets you and your readers know right away which year you are talking about. For self-hosted WordPress (downloaded from WordPress.org) folks (not WordPress.com—you can't change your permalink structure), you change your permalinks under the Settings tab, and then click Permalinks.

Antispam

Just like email, blogs are susceptible to spam. Interestingly enough, you see the same kinds of things in email spam as in blog spam. Blog spam comes in the form of comments and links back to your blog (trackbacks). The comments and links, as you might expect, often contain links to online pharmacies, pornography, scams, and the other dregs of the Internet. To combat this scourge, antispam plugins were developed to block these comments and trackbacks from appearing on your blog at all.

So, the next step is to make sure the antispam plugin is turned on and working. Because WordPress is my engine of choice, I use Automattic's Akismet. Matt Mullenweg wrote the first version of Akismet, and it is now maintained by Automattic, the company he helped found. Akismet is free for personal use, and the license fees for commercial sites are reasonable. There is a version of Akismet for

Movable Type as well, and it's one of the platform's most popular plugins. Akismet works by using a database of known spammers and common spam keywords to proactively block spam as it comes in. Akismet also "learns" how to identify new spam as bloggers mark comments and trackbacks that are spam that Akismet missed. The details of exactly how Akismet works is a closely guarded secret for obvious reasons.

SEO Tuning

Next, tune the blog for SEO using plugins designed to make life easy in that respect. The first and foremost thing that needs to be changed is how many blog engines write the titles of posts and pages. By default, WordPress, for example, makes the title of the page (what would show up in a bookmark) as [Blog name] | [Post name], so for this book's blog it would be: Six Easy Blogging Projects Blog | My blogging process-The 2012 edition. This *isn't* what you really want. You don't need Google (or other search engines) continually indexing with your blog name first when that *never* changes!

What you want is this: My blogging process-The 2012 edition | Six Easy Blogging Projects Blog. Which is exactly what you'll see when you visit the blog for this book: [Post name] | [Blog name]. This way, Google indexes the *new* thing *first* (the post title or page title) and the static thing (the blog's name) last. This simple switch turns out to make a *huge* difference to Google.

There are lots of ways to achieve this result. We *used* to have to edit our themes to make the switch manually, but now themes come with

Plugins are like little programs that you add and install into your blog engine to allow it to do something new (like serve audio files) or better (like create pages that are more search engine friendly).

Think of plugins like this: You buy a car and it didn't come with a sunroof. You really *wanted* a sunroof, but for whatever reason, your new car doesn't have one. So you go down the street to a place that sells and installs sunroofs in cars and have one put in later. That sunroof in your car is like a plugin for your blog. And just like sunroofs in cars, there are plugins that work well and plugins that don't (like sunroofs that leak in the rain).

the tweak already done, or bloggers use a plugin designed to tune and manage your SEO for you. My favorite for WordPress is All in One SEO Pack, a great plugin that does 90% of the work for you. It also comes with a couple side benefits, such as being able to have a title, keywords, and description that are unique to the blog's home page, but not other pages. For other pages, the keywords and description data are automatically generated from your post. All in all, it's a slick plugin that I highly recommend.

Categories and Tags

Next up are categories. I'll get into the differences between categories and tags in Chapter 3, but for now, think of a category as your silverware drawer (it's a big container) and tags as the utensils themselves (knife, fork, and spoon). When setting up categories, and this isn't something that you do only once, think about the big topics you might be writing about—for instance, Product Reviews, Social Media, Press Releases, or Thought of the Day. These are large containers that hold lots of different posts, but all generally about the same thing. Yes, a post can have more than one category, and I encourage that kind of broad thinking.

Categories are about classification. They help you and your readers place posts into some kind of context that they can relate to *and* be able to use to find similar posts. If you visit my blog, you will quickly see that I usually categorize a post several ways. As your blog evolves over time, you might add or remove categories; categories are intended to be fluid and organic, adapting to your blog as *you* need them to. I find if, after about six months, a category has

only one or two posts in it, I delete it and make sure those posts are filed in other categories. In that case, the category deleted probably should have been a tag, but at the time you might have thought it would be a larger bin. No problem, just deal with it now. As a general rule, try to keep to about 10 or 15 categories. Remember that you're thinking large bins here, top-level stuff.

Blogrolls

Your blogroll is a list of links to other blogs that you read, like, or want to help promote. WordPress blogs have a small default blogroll to a few key WordPress sites, and most themes will display this blogroll unless you change the theme widgets. The blogroll used to be *the* way to find other blogs. Getting listed on a major blog's blogroll was a *huge* thing, and it could vault a blog into a whole new level of traffic. Now, however, my opinion is that the blogroll has become superfluous. I find most new blogs through microblogging-micromessaging services like Twitter, RSS feeds, or links within posts. However, I do still maintain a small blogroll on each blog. I link to my other blogs, my current job, my photography portfolio, and a couple of friends.

At one point, there was a whole social etiquette around blogrolls and reciprocal linking. Sometimes not getting on a friend's blogroll led to hurt feelings and even minor feuds—seriously, as strange as it might seem. Given the needless politics involved, I eventually decided to cull mine. I link to my friends in my posts, meet them in person (gasp, I know a shocker), and chat via IM to show them I like their work.

Comments and Trackbacks

Two of the essential connectors in the blogosphere are comments and trackbacks. Make sure these are turned on by default for all your posts. It may sound strange, but sometimes people turn comments off or make people jump through hoops to comment. I moderate comments, but only if it's your first comment on my blog or if it has a lot of links in it (lots of links in a comment is a red flag for a spam comment).

Trackbacks are on by default, and you're not likely to ever have to worry about them. A trackback is when someone links back to your post. The link shows up in your post like a comment a person would make, but often above or below the "human" comments. Trackbacks also suffer from the scourge of spam. Spam blogs are pretty easy to pick out, so if you're unsure, follow the link to the post and check it out. If the blog and post look funny, it's probably spam, and you can safely mark it as spam in your moderation section.

Security

As I mentioned in the tip earlier in the chapter, it is very important to, at the very least, change the default password for the admin account. It's better to disable it entirely and use a new account with administrator privileges. When you take this step, you deny potential hackers the first step in trying to break in—the username of the administrator account.

The next essential part of security is keeping up on security updates for plugins and your blog engine. If you're using TypePad, Blogger, or WordPress.com, you don't have to worry about this, but if you have a self-hosted install of WordPress or Movable Type, you need to stay on top of when updates come up and update your blog as soon as a security update is released. When updates are released, the blogging community is very good about helping each other out, making sure people who are less comfortable with tech get the update in place. As you become more a part of a community of bloggers, you'll know who the generous souls are who are happy to lend a hand now and then.

About Page

Create or update your blog's About page to tell people about yourself and the blog. One of the most important parts of your blog aren't the posts, but the About page. Really. Your About page gives your readers insight into who you are and what the blog is about. You can go into as much detail as you want. You can add contact information if you want—I highly recommend you do add some kind of contact info, especially if you are a business—but a little about yourself is essential. One of the signs of a "real" blog is a "real" About page—something that sounds like a real person is behind the blog, not a computer program automatically generating the content. Figure 2.25 shows a look at my About page from my blog.

FIGURE 2.25
My About page on trishussey.com.

Themes and Colors

One of my favorite things about blog engines is the capability to change the look and feel of a blog in a click or two of the mouse. Because the content is divorced from the design, you can change the design and not have to worry about "breaking" anything you've written. I've shown people who have paid thousands of dollars on a website redesign how I can "redesign" my blog for no cost in a few seconds. Let's just say that I shouldn't repeat what they said.

Picking a theme is like having carte blanche to wander through a store and just pull awesome clothes off the racks and walk out. Most of my favorite themes are free, just requiring keeping a link to the designer's website in the footer. There are some amazing premium themes that do cost some money, but usually they're less than $100. I've purchased these themes before, and yes, they *are* worth the money.

I've shown people who have paid thousands of dollars on a website redesign how I can "redesign" my blog for no cost in a few seconds. Let's just say that I shouldn't repeat what they said.

For hosted blogs, you'll often be given a set choice of themes, or limitations on how you can edit them. Blogger is somewhat of an exception to this rule, but I'm not a fan of trying to edit Blogger templates. I still have coding nightmares about it. If your blog is self-hosted, you'll be able to download and install/load most any theme available for your blog engine. Themes are engine specific, so a Movable Type theme doesn't work for WordPress, or a WordPress theme for Blogger. Picking a theme, its layout, and color scheme is up to you, but the following are what I look for when picking a new theme:

- Is the text easy to read? Too small, too crowded, maybe not enough contrast? Remember that you want people to be able to *read and enjoy* your blog, not have to pull out a magnifying glass.

- Are the colors nice and pleasant or do they make you want to claw your eyes out? One of the most criticized things about MySpace are the eye-jarring layouts. Do us all a favor and pick something that looks nice.

- Is there good use of white space? You know when you see a simple, clean layout and things just seem to fit and flow? Look for that.

- Can you tweak and edit the theme easily? How hard is it to place an image of your choosing in the header?

These are just a few suggestions, but look at the free template sites for the blog engine of your choosing—this assumes your blog is self-hosted—and pick several that you like, load them all up, and try them out.

TIP

Some of my favorite places to find themes are www.wordpress.org/extend/themes (for WordPress themes) and www.smashing-magazine.com (mostly WordPress, but some for other blog engines as well). If you don't find something you like there, I suggest giving Google a try. Search for your blog engine with the word "theme" and maybe something like a color or style. For example, "wordpress themes blue magazine style" should yield some good results to start with on your hunt for the perfect blog theme.

Tracking Your Blog's Stats

I love to look at the general traffic statistics for my blog. I like to know what posts are popular, what search terms are used to get to my site (the number one or two is "yam fries recipe"), and all the other tidbits I get from great web stats. Yes, I am a web stats junkie. Truth be told, web stats have been my bread and butter for about a dozen years. I used to spend a whole morning processing log files through arcane programs (with manually configured settings files that were oh-so-easy to mess up) just to see what the last day or two had been like. Because it often took so long to process all the data, I didn't do stats runs more than once a week, unless there was a big event I needed to keep track of. Today, I glance at my stats whenever I feel like it. I have real-time live stats and stats that update once a day. And I don't have to lift a finger to make it all happen.

My stats are gathered, tabulated, and reported (and even emailed to me!) automatically using Google Analytics. Google Analytics gives me great info and details from my blog, and if I put Google Ads on my blog, they can be tied to it as well (see Figure 2.26). Google Analytics gives me easy ways to slice and dice the data so I can really understand my traffic.

The best part about Google Analytics is that it's free. Just sign up with a Google account, visit https://www.google.com/analytics/ and enter the basic information about your site. There are simple plugins for Movable Type and WordPress that enable you to add these services without having to mess around with pasting code.

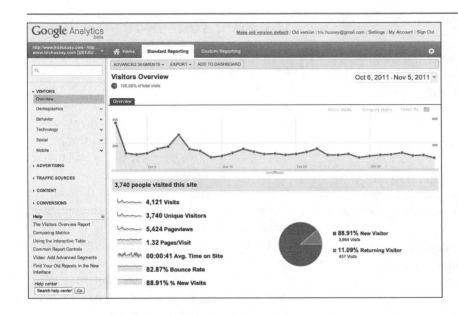

FIGURE 2.26
My Google Analytics Dashboard for my personal blog.

If you have a WordPress.com account, you can use WordPress.com Stats on your self-hosted WordPress blog using the WordPress Jetpack plugin. WordPress.com Stats don't replace Google Analytics, but are a nice, quick complement to them.

Summary

By now, you've gone from having an idea about a blog to actually having a blog. Even if you decided only to dip your toe in the water with a WordPress.com blog, you're off to a great start. If you've jumped in with both feet and have your domain, a web host, and a freshly installed WordPress blog, I hope you're well on the way to getting it set up, tuned, and tweaked.

Next up is the section that most people tend to be the *most* afraid of—writing. Chapter 3 is all about writing and creating compelling content. My goal in the next chapter is to inspire you to start writing—maybe even before you have decided whether you want a personal blog, a business blog, or even a portfolio blog. I hope that you finish Chapter 3 dying to have your say, so let's get down to business.

CHAPTER 3

Creating Content for Your Blog

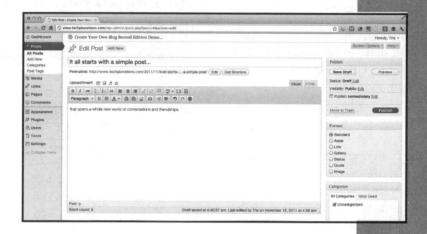

Chapters 1 and 2 focused on "the easy stuff." As much as technology can confound and frustrate you, it's pretty easy after you have a few tricks up your sleeve. Plus, there are always people who can help you with the techie stuff if you feel lost or stuck. Writing, however, is completely up to you. It's your voice, your words, and your story. I can't tell your story for you, but I *can* tell you what I've learned about writing, blogging, and conversing online.

What is exciting, fun, and scary is that your blog is your own place to say and write what you want. It's your soapbox to stand and shout to the world. Although blogs started off as mostly personal journals, after people could leave comments on posts, blogs became *conversations*. You tell your story, people read it, sometimes they will add to it, maybe with their own experiences, and in the end you have something richer and bigger than you did before. The result is that you have something more than what you started with.

In this chapter, we explore all the aspects of writing a blog post: finding your voice, whether to be anonymous, and making your life public or keeping it private. Although no hard and fast rules exist about how to write a great blog post, there are some things you can do to make your writing more engaging to an online audience. There isn't a lot of "this is good" or "that is bad"; instead, I give you tips on how writing online is *different* from, for instance, writing a book on blogging.

Let's not waste any time getting into the nitty-gritty of writing a blog post.

> *You tell your story, people read it, and sometimes they will add to it, maybe with their own experiences. The result is that you have something more than what you started with.*

Turning an Idea for a Blog into Blog Posts

After reading Chapter 1, "Beginning the Story: Blogging Then and Now," you should have the general topic for your blog. After reading Chapter 2, "Installing and Setting Up Your First Blog," you should have a blog to start posting content, but you might be stumped for how to get some posts going. This is fine; don't worry because *everyone*, including me, has moments of "Okay, what am I going to write about today?" This section is going to help you get the post ideas flowing.

No, I'm not going to suggest strange creativity exercises or rituals to help you get inspired. I have tried so many of these tips and tricks that I lost sight of one very important fact—inspiration is like a flock of birds. Sometimes, it's a lovely thing to watch and marvel at, and sometimes it's an Alfred Hitchcock movie. You just don't know until you stop and look at it for a while. That's a mixed metaphorical way of saying that inspiration often just hits you, and often at inconvenient times, so the trick is being ready to take advantage of it when it strikes.

Capture Inspiration Whenever and Wherever It Strikes

I get most of my news and information online through *RSS* feeds and social networks like Twitter, Facebook, and Google+. I am extremely lucky to know a lot of gifted, brilliant, off-kilter, funny, silly, and cool people. I try to read as much of what they write and produce as I can. Their creativity fuels my creativity, and at the same time I hope my creativity doesn't make them run screaming down the street. Because I don't really know when one of my friends is going to say something brilliant online, I have several tools to help capture those nuggets of brilliance when they come up.

NEW TERM

RSS stands for Really Simple Syndication and is a computer-readable (not intended for people to read) version of the latest posts of a blog or website. You subscribe to RSS feeds using an RSS reader (which makes the feeds human readable), like Google Reader, which then lets you know whenever the site has new content for you to read. Using RSS feeds and a good reader, you can read through the recent posts of all sorts of websites in a fraction of the time needed to visit them one by one.

As I've gone through the process of writing this book, I've been testing and trying new software, helpful hints, and other things that fall under the heading of "Research." (They could also fall under "Making Surfing the Net Look Like Work," but I'm not going to talk about that.) Research is something that in the

Internet age is a lot different from what it was even a couple of years ago. The scale of information you can have at your fingertips with just a Google search is nothing short of mind blowing. For this reason, some very brilliant folks created note-taking apps—or as Shawn Blanc calls them, "anything buckets." I use two programs for anything buckets to keep track of quotes, links, pictures, and any other interesting online piece for review later.

The first app, pictured in Figure 3.1, that I've been using for years to gather notes and track projects is called Evernote (free and paid versions, Mac/Windows/iPhone/iPad/Android/BlackBerry/Web). Evernote is an application that lets you keep (and find) notes, links you find online, documents, even pictures in notebooks. You can organize however works best for you. You can even share notebooks with other people or over the Internet to collaborate with other people. You might be interested in *My Evernote* from our sister imprint, Que, to learn more about Evernote.

The next tool is a service called Instapaper that allows me to save articles to read later. Although Evernote is more for *storing* information for later, Instapaper is for all those times you see something great online, but just don't have time right then to read it. Instapaper is a free service (with a paid option unlock searching on the iPhone and iPad app) that is geared toward saving those things to read later (see Figure 3.2).

FIGURE 3.1

A clipped reference page of Evernote for the Mac.

FIGURE 3.2

Instapaper on my iPad with articles I'd like to read later.

For saving—and sharing—links to sites, articles, and pages that I want to refer back to, I use Delicious.com (free) for making sure I'll have a bookmark later (see Figure 3.3).

How do these apps work for capturing inspiration? Simple—whatever I'm doing on my computer, I can quickly capture it one of these tools. If I see a great website I'd like to note for later, I don't bookmark it in my browser, I put it in a "post fodder" or "book research" folder in one of these programs. When I'm looking for something to post or for that site when I get to a section of the book, it's right where I can find it: alongside any other related items I've previously found.

Of course, keeping things straight (where did I put that link?) can be hard, which is why consistency is important. I put notes, clippings, and details in Evernote. Posts I want to read later, but might not want or need to keep go into Instapaper. Links I know I'll want to refer back to later (maybe I already read it after saving through Instapaper), go into Delicious. I also use Delicious to create *stacks* of links to share with other people. For example, this book, or classes I teach, might have stacks with more detailed information on a topic.

The idea is that when you see a site, get an email, or whatever else you might come across, you can quickly jot a note to yourself to save it for later. Evernote wins hands down in the "whenever and wherever" department because there are versions of Evernote for pretty much any kind of computer or device out there, and, best of all, Evernote keeps your notes in sync *across all the devices.*

FIGURE 3.3

Delicious.com and some of the links to articles that I might need later.

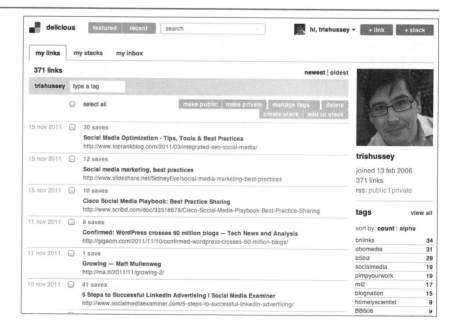

Regardless of the electronic tool, or even pen and paper (I always have a pen and small pad in my pocket), you should be ready to jot ideas down because you don't know when an idea or inspiration will hit you. I've lost count of the number of potentially great posts that never came to be because I forgot them before I could note them. And, yes, I even have a pad and pen on my nightstand to jot middle-of-the-night ideas down, too.

Finding Your "Voice"

The hardest, and the most fun, aspect of starting a blog is finding a tone and style that expresses "you" in written form. How do you find your voice? You just write until your style comes out. There are no shortcuts, no easy tricks. Even working on the second edition of this book, I've noticed how my "book voice" has changed and improved (I hope) since I started the first edition in 2008. Finding your writing just takes time. Just write, and it will come out. And no one can tell you if your voice is good or bad. Because your voice is you and you is who you are.

Is this stiff and formal writing? No, this is not English class all over again. (Write a two-page essay on the role of Google in today's info-centric society....) Just write like you're chatting to a friend or a favorite professor or teacher. Let me give you a couple of examples from my own writing (not that you don't have a really good idea of what my "voice" is like). The following is a section from my personal blog:

You combined the persistence of a solid RSS reader with the immediacy of a dashboard or ticker? Have your ginormous list of feeds, but mark a select few as HUD feeds? Feeds that maybe could be pushed to Twitter or tapped into by HootSuite or Tweetdeck. Like your top 20 "I don't want to miss a single thing" feeds, while in the background the "reader" part is building a relevancy-linked reading list? Find a way to consolidate articles on a topic, meme, headline, or concept into streams of articles. Sure be able to read your feeds like we do now (an interface like FeedDemon or NetNewsWire is good I think), but also have this information stream pulled together.

Looking for the day's posts on RSS or Facebook or social media or H1N1? Then they are already consolidated for you. Yes, you can build "smart folders," but you have to know the topic first to do that. Sure you can have a folder with big concepts that you're interested in, but when news breaks, wouldn't it be good to have something like your own Techmeme based on the sources you follow?

The following is from a business blog I contributed to:

Is social media a fad? Yes, using the term social media is a fad. Just like "internet marketing," "new media," "business blogging," were all "fads." The terms fade away, thankfully, but the ideas remain. We still have websites (more and more actually), write (aka blog), and continue to find more and more ways to interact with each other, our customers, clients, and business partners.

So while none of these 15 best mindsets are magic bullets to success, if you don't employ them your chances of success are greatly reduced.

Neither of these sections are all that different, but the tone is more corporate or professional in the second, and the first is more informal. My voice is the tone that I use to write with when I write a post (or a document). It's my choice of words (informal or formal), it's my tone (serious, funny, ironic, or sarcastic), and it's my phrasing. All put together, these give you a mental picture, or a feeling, on the post you're reading.

I don't have one voice I use in writing—and neither will you. I change and adapt my voice to the writing task at hand. You wouldn't write a business proposal like you write an email to your best friend. The audience is different, so the tone is different. However, regardless of your audience, the best voices I read are all natural; they aren't forced, and that takes practice—a lot of practice. And switching voices isn't easy. You'll notice subtle differences in voice throughout this book—and probably where I edited something for the second edition. This book was first written over the course of a year, and the second edition over a few months (I told you it gets easier). So one day, I might have been feeling serious and philosophical and another day more funny and sarcastic, and these moods *will* and *do* come out in your writing. As you're reading the book, keep an "ear" out for how my writing voice changes. Sometimes it was accidental, and sometimes it was on purpose (like when addressing a serious topic), but it's always there.

The only way to develop your voice is to write—*a lot*. It might help to try to write as another person (say one of your parents). What would your dad sound like if you were trying to portray him in words? Or create a character, maybe your alter ego, someone you want to *pretend* to be and see how you would make that character come alive.

Your voice will come on its own. You might even think about writing an anonymous blog under a pen name, which might free you to experiment with different styles and topics that you might not be comfortable tackling under your real name. Who knows? Maybe your pen name might become popular.

BELLE DE JOUR

Belle was crass, frank, gritty, brazen—and real. The stories of Belle's life as a high-end London call girl fascinated people. Even if some might have been offended at her frank and open discussions of sex, sexuality, and the sex trade, you couldn't ignore her vulnerability or humanity. Her writing pulled people in because it was so real, not to mention that it laid bare (couldn't resist the pun) the sex trade. She didn't name names, but the look into her life was enthralling.

Her blog became a TV series and a series of books, not because she wrote about sex, but because her writing gripped us. Her writing struck a chord with people. We all understood the need to love and be loved. We understood that sometimes you have to make hard, unpopular choices. Belle chose to become a call girl, and she doesn't paint a rosy picture of it. She paints a *real* picture of it.

This isn't career day at school mind you; she doesn't advocate a life in the sex trade. Even if her topic isn't your cup of tea, you should read a few of her posts to see how she pulls you into a conversation and makes you feel like she is talking to you across a café table. I bet you'll go back to read more. All good writers, like Belle, leave you craving *more*.

To Anonymously Blog or Not: The Line Between Public and Private

This has nothing to do with the length of your post. It has to do with depth. How much information about yourself do you put out there for public consumption? Family? Pets? Your hometown? Spouse? Love life?

These are difficult questions—I know you're thinking that you would not talk about your spouse on your blog or about the date you had last night. Yes, all bloggers think that, too, but as you become more comfortable blogging and as you build an audience for your words, it gets easier and easier to let personal details slip—details you might not otherwise want to share. Sometimes it just happens and sometimes that's okay. Other times, it can blow up in your face.

Although it is assumed that most people blog as themselves, and use their real names, some of the best and most famous blogs are written anonymously. Washingtonienne and Belle de Jour were both written by women who chronicled their sexual escapades online and became very famous for it. Washingtonienne was revealed to be an aide to a U.S. senator, and Belle "outed" herself just before a British tabloid did it for her. That, however, didn't stop a TV series and two books based on her blog. Although the names are not revealed, the writing is real. There was a blog penned by "Fake Steve Jobs," who wrote as if he were Steve Jobs, but in a mock parody of all that is Apple. It was witty, biting, and damn good stuff. People loved it, and in the tech world, the discussions about who Fake Steve Jobs really was were almost as good as Fake Steve's writing.

It was an interesting day, almost anticlimatic, when Fake Steve revealed himself to be Daniel Lyons of *Newsweek* magazine. All the speculation was over—no more guessing who might be behind the satirical and funny posts. Sadly, I was never considered to be one of the possible people behind the blog.

Washingtonienne and Belle de Jour might be two extreme examples, but they aren't alone. People pen blogs for many reasons (and books and articles) anonymously. Maybe they don't want their friends to know they write; maybe the topic clashes with their public persona. Maybe, like Fake Steve Jobs, they wanted to write some parody or satire that could be done only behind the safety of a pen name. Whatever the reason, nine times out of ten, it's a good one.

What can happen if you blog publicly or if you blog anonymously and you're outed? I've seen friends I've known for years fired from their jobs. There have been court battles where blog posts have been used as evidence against parents in custody fights. That doesn't even start to cover the standard libel suits that have been filed (and some have been successful).

CAUTION

Anonymous or not, you have to stand by and live with what you write. There are real consequences to telling tales out of school, speaking ill of someone, or any other unsavory thing. You can't hide behind "oh, it's just a blog" because a public blog on the public Internet is just like any other publication. As Gillian Shaw of the *Vancouver Sun* reminds us: If you wouldn't want what you post online printed in the paper, don't post it at all.

Now, what about you? Are you going to write as you or under a pen name? Before you decide, you don't actually have to decide. I'll tell you right now that I have a couple anonymous blogs out there. I have anonymous blogs to explore different sides of my writing. Writing about different topics stretches my creativity. Stretching and pushing yourself is a critical aspect of being a writer.

When you're deciding whether to be anonymous, think about whether you would mind someone from your job, church, or local watering hole reading your posts and knowing that you wrote them. None of that should necessarily stop you from writing about what you want, but it just might stop you from writing about these things so openly. You might also not want the whole Internet to know exactly who you are, where you live, or the names of your family members. Although I do blog as myself, my children don't choose to (my daughter has a private blog), so they are mentioned only by initials (if at all), and I don't post their pictures publicly. The same goes for other people in my life. They didn't ask to be dragged into the wide-open land of the Internet, so I keep a lot private. I also make a lot public.

I've taken strong stands on mental illness, education, learning disabilities, my own health, and sometimes politics. I take those stands because sometimes it's the right thing to do; sometimes, individuals need that chorus of voices calling for change. I feel I've been given a tremendous responsibility by having an audience. Even if it isn't a huge audience, I know it's a far-reaching one. So, I take a stand. Sometimes, it isn't popular; sometimes I cringe as I select Publish, but I haven't had many posts that I regretted posting. If nothing else, anonymous or not, always write from your heart, be proud of what you write, and stand by your words.

> ### If nothing else, anonymous or not, always write from your heart, be proud of what you write, and stand by your words.

There are degrees of anonymity. You can blog as Jane Smith, but not tell all about where you live, or blog as Bob the Delivery Guy and use a pen name. It's your choice. One of my friends is a "Daddy Blogger" and blogs under the name "Genuine." His family members are Mrs. Genuine, Genuine Girl, Genuine Boy 1, and so on. There is a layer between the world at large and his family. Is he anonymous? Nope. His name is Jim Turner. He and I were business partners in a company together. Oddly enough, he's far more famous as Genuine than as Jim (at conferences he writes "Genuine" below his real name). Just mull that over for a minute, because now you're getting to the really fun stuff.

So the question is, "Where does your public life end and private life start?" This isn't a question I can answer for you. Bloggers usually find out by crossing the line. In doing so, you'll learn from experience what topics you want to keep off limits.

Write Until You've Said Your Piece

One of the most common questions I'm asked is "How long should a blog post be?" I often give a rather impish answer of "as long as it takes for you to say what you have to say," but that is a cop-out answer. Generally, a blog post is short, about 200–500 words or so. I think it became that way because geeks have notoriously short attention spans. That's not to say that people, including myself, don't write longer pieces. It's just in general, blog posts are short. The short-form post is something that seems to fit in well with today's fast-paced society; however, there is a *huge* drawback to it: People often just regurgitate the same ideas and links without adding anything to the conversation. Trying to squeeze some original analysis into 200 words isn't the easiest thing to do, but it is worth it when you really pull it off.

I've read great posts that are around 6–10 words long (a single sentence) as well as epics of thousands of words. One isn't better than the other. When you're writing a post, just write it out. Don't worry if it's too short or too long. Say what you want to say and when you're done, see what it looks like. You might want to split a longer post into a part 1 and part 2 (or 3, 4 …); series posts are *great* ways to keep readers coming back (don't forget the age-old cliffhanger!).

CAUTION

I do place one caveat on longer posts (500 words or more): People find it hard to read a lot of text onscreen. If you have long paragraphs without breaks, readers might skim through the post. The solution to this is easy: shorter paragraphs!

If You Post It, They Will Come: Posting Frequency Answered

How often should I post? This might be the number one question people ask about blogging, along with "How do I post links and images?" The honest answer is that it's up to you, but if you are trying to build traffic and a profile for a professional or business blog, you need to post *at least* three times a week, and not all in one day. Honestly, a post a day should be your goal if you want to build a readership and traffic. Yes, that might seem difficult at first and it does require a significant time commitment, but once you get going you might not be able to shut up.

If you feel like you have to post more than once a day, I suggest spreading the posts out over the day. You can do this two ways: One is to just hold off on posting, and the other is to use the Post to the Future feature available in most blog engines (see Figure 3.4). I recommend the latter, because it gets the post out of your system.

In addition to gaining *readers* by posting every day, search engines index your blog more frequently if you post frequently. Each post ties into the previous ones and strengthens the association between your blog and the keywords you use. After a solid month of posting five times per week (or more), your ranking in the search engines will increase significantly.

FIGURE 3.4

Part of the WordPress post editor showing the time-date adjustment panel.

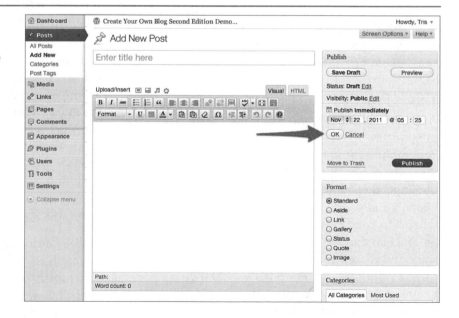

Your First Post

So, your first post. The "Hello world, here I am. Time to listen up" statement.

Uh huh.

Right.

Chances are your first post will suck. Yeah, it is pretty much guaranteed that you're going to look at it in month or so and die a little inside. You'll want to delete it. Expunge this dreck from the world.

Don't.

Your first post is something of a birthday statement. It's what you're going to look back on and smile after your blog has been around for a year or so. But, yeah, it will still suck and really that's okay. Just get the first post out there and out of the way. No, you don't have to write some great expressive post about what your blog is about; just a "Hi, yeah this is the first post, I'm going to talk about [insert topic], hope you enjoy it…" is great. Don't worry or stress about post number one.

This Is Practice

As you're writing remember that these posts are practice. You might hesitate to post them. You might want to read and edit them over and over again. You might think that they aren't good enough. Well, they *are* good enough and you *should* post them. Sure, check for spelling and grammatical errors, but don't go and edit the post over and over. Don't try to work and rework your post for just the right turn of phrase. It isn't worth it. I've said it before and I'm going to repeat it again. Ready? Listen. Seriously, this is important:

Your first post will suck, and that's okay because all first posts suck.

I think my first post, which I wish I could share, but I lost it in a blog move, was something like this:

> *Here's a cool thing I found today. I think this collaboration tool is cool. [Link]*

This is a riveting piece of writing, isn't it? This is a post full of passion and depth, inspiring you to think in a whole new way about collaboration tools. Yeah, not so much. This is why you just keep writing. It gets easier, and eventually you find a voice to write in that expresses who you are. Experiment with short posts, long posts, lists, reviews, a brain dump of links, and so on.

Your first post will suck, and that's okay because all first posts suck.

At the beginning, writing and posting might seem like a struggle, especially if you're not used to writing on a regular basis. It *does* get easier—I promise. When I talk about sources of inspiration, you'll see that I don't just pull ideas out of thin air. Nor do I think my writing needs no improvement. I appreciate the feedback I get on my posts, and especially this book, because often a gentle critical look can help bring out the great writer that you are.

Before you get worried or excited about the content of your blog posts, remember that blogging isn't rocket science. There aren't rules that you must follow to make a good blog post. When my friends and colleagues ask me, "Is this an okay post?" I generally say that it's fine. If it's a post trying to make a point, I'll read and offer suggestions for clarity, but that isn't often. Sure, I might help them fix a link or move a picture around, but generally that's it. Why? Because it's *their* story, not mine.

I hope that you are more inspired and think that I'm dead wrong about writing. Stop shaking your head, because it's absolutely true. I want to get you *thinking* about *your* voice and story, and if you don't agree with me about my take on writing, that's great. It's your blog, not mine.

Writing Your First Post

Let's get into the nuts and bolts of posting. The following examples use the WordPress post editor, but many blog engines use the same components and icons in their editors, so it shouldn't be too difficult to make the transition.

> **CAUTION**
>
> Although it is the word processor of choice for most of us, regardless of platform, Microsoft Word *sucks* as the tool for you to write your posts. Why? Because when you copy and paste from Word into your post, Word brings along a ton of extra "stuff" in the formatting code that makes it not display properly when someone views it in your blog. You can avoid this problem with a couple extra steps, but frankly everyone forgets to take those steps, so just write in a simple text editor like Notepad or TextEdit.

The post/page editor in WordPress should look familiar to you if you've used a web-based email service like Hotmail, Yahoo Mail, or Gmail (see Figure 3.5). All these online writing tools share similar icon sets sometimes and even background technology!

FIGURE 3.5

The post editor in WordPress, which is similar to other online writing tools.

THE "MAGIC" PASTE FROM WORD BUTTON

If you're like me, you have a love-hate relationship with Microsoft Word. Sure, you *have* to use it (because everyone else does), but you don't have to *like it*. I mentioned how copying text from Word to your blog engine brings along extra stuff. This extra code changes the font of that post from all the other posts and the rest of the blog. The extra codes could even turn the whole layout of your blog into a jumbled mess. Don't do it.

But wait. "I like or even need to write in Word," you say. Whether it's a dictate from the boss or a personal preference, there are valid reasons to use Word, and it's because of them that the Paste from Word button was created (I call it magic).

Here's how you find it.

In WordPress, look in the post editor for an icon that looks like two lines of colored squares (it's the last button in the top row—or only row until you click it; it's called the Kitchen Sink). Click it. You should see a button that looks like a clipboard with a very familiar "W" on it. That's it.

Select your post in Word and copy it to the Clipboard (from the Edit menu select Copy, or you can press Ctrl+C). Next, click in the post area where you want the text to start (usually the top) and click the Paste from Word button to paste your post into the window that pops up. Finally, click Insert. If the little window doesn't go away after you click Insert, click its close box in the upper-right corner.

If your text has underlines, italics, or bolding, that formatting will be preserved in the post and put in as proper HTML code.

The layout should be pretty easy to follow. The title goes in the skinny bar at the top, the post itself goes in the larger box below the formatting buttons, and the tags go to the right in their own box. Categories are also set on the right, chosen with check boxes (or created ad hoc by clicking the Add New Category link).

When you are ready to post, click the Publish button, and you are done! If you are worried about losing your work, or want to finish a post later, click the Save Draft button. The draft post shows up in the post list noted with "Draft" next to the title. WordPress has a handy autosave feature that stores a copy of the post as you write it. The default is to save every five minutes, so if you accidentally close your browser tab or window (that has happened to me more times than I like to remember), your browser crashes, or your whole computer crashes, WordPress will have a version (the last saved one) for you. I, however, don't trust autosave functions. I still proactively click Save Draft if I'm working in the browser, and you should, too.

Let's pull this all together now. There is a menu item called Add New located close to the name of your blog (see Figure 3.6). When you hover over the menu, you will see the option for a new post. If you fast forward in your mind, after you've written something to post, it will look something like Figure 3.7.

FIGURE 3.6

WordPress Dashboard and the Add New menu.

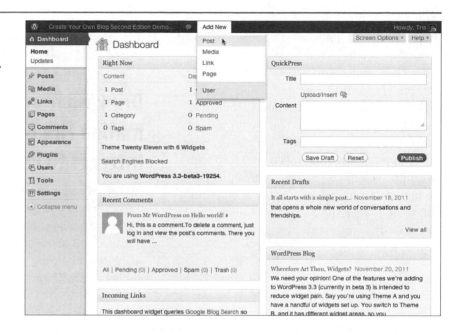

FIGURE 3.7

A brand-new post ready for publishing.

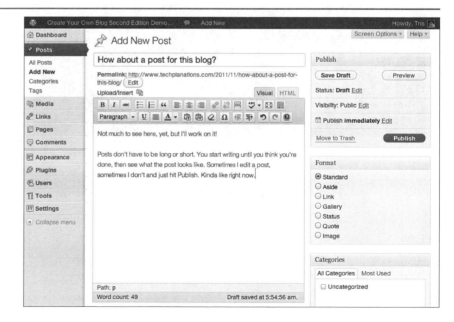

This post is ready to go. I put in a simple title and a little text. I'm not going to worry about Categories or Tags at the moment. I'll talk about how those work when I talk about SEO (search engine optimization). I also skipped putting an image into this post because for your first post, you should just write and get something out there—I will talk about images in Chapter 5 "Creating a Personal Blog with WordPress.com." If you are confident enough to include an image, go for it. The only thing left to do is click the Publish button and make the post live on the Internet, as shown in Figure 3.8.

That's it, really. Keep your first post simple; don't overthink it—just do it. It is as simple, and as hard, as that.

Drinking from the Information Fire Hose: Using the Internet to Power Your Posts

"But what should I write *about*?" I'm asked that over and over, and sometimes when I suggest topics I even get, "Oh, no one would want to read about *that*." No, you're right. I suggested it because I want to see you write really bad stuff (sarcasm).

FIGURE 3.8
The post is now published and live on the Internet.

In seriousness, getting that spark of inspiration is something that is hard to explain. The bolt from the blue *does* happen, just not often. I get most of my ideas from other people who intersect with me. Sometimes it's an electronic intersection; sometimes it's in real life (IRL). The key I've found is when you become inspired, don't dismiss it. Run with it for a bit in your head, on paper, or electronically. Just see where it takes you.

Now, let's get to those intersection points.

Other Bloggers

I can't speak for everyone's friends, but I am lucky enough to be surrounded by some of the most brilliant, creative, and scary-smart people I've ever known. Looking at the things *they* create, share, and link to always gets something going in my head.

I talk more specifically about building your online community in Chapter 4, "Building a Community Around Your Blog," but within your community, there are always people who send you interesting links and such directly. Many of them inspire you with a comment they leave on your blog. The great stuff from you often comes from all the other "stuff" readers do online.

The question you'll now ask is, "Where, oh great sage of blogging, can we find this 'stuff' of which you speak?" This is a *very* interesting question. We've (*we* being us geeky, early-adopter types who try *every* new product or service that we come across online) tried, and failed, to find ways to coalesce all our "stuff" into single places. The problem, ironically, became that we wound up with *more* fragmented conversations. In the end, everyone fell

back to interacting and sharing their posts, pictures, videos, and so forth where the most people they knew would be able to find them. For some people that's Facebook; for others it's Google+ or Twitter. Savvy folks will have their Twitter feed also on their blogs, and maybe Facebook or Google+ as well.

Let's start small, though. My two favorite ways to get inspiration from the community (and just small segments of larger lifestreams) are Twitter and Google+.

Twitter is a *microblogging* service where people share "tweets" of 140 characters or fewer with people who follow them (like being friends on Facebook) and read the tweets of the people *they* follow. I follow and am followed by several thousand people right now.

> **NOTE**
> You can follow me, too, on Twitter. Go to www.twitter.com/trishussey to find my Twitter profile.

> **NEW TERM**
> Microblogging emerged in 2006 to describe services like Twitter, where you post content that is very short in length (in Twitter's case, posts can be no more than 140 characters).

I read the tweets from the people I follow using a service called HootSuite (www.HootSuite.com), which enables me to segment people into groups (such as Friends, News, and Folks) so I can read more and not miss something that is important to me (see Figure 3.9).

FIGURE 3.9
Organizing tweets using HootSuite.

Along with the wit and news my friends share, I also get updates from sources such as CNN, CBC (Canadian Broadcasting Corporation), and a myriad of tech websites. Combined, this makes for a lot of potential inspiration, but it doesn't end there. Google launched a service (and alleged "Facebook killer") called Google+, in which, like Twitter, people follow your shared items. The larger and more diverse the number of people you follow, the more varied kinds of things you will see. Google+, like Facebook, allows you to easily share links, videos, and images. Unlike Twitter, Google+ doesn't cap your update to only 140 characters. For the information junkies, Google+ is the new must-watch place for news and analysis. Interestingly enough, Twitter has become the best tool for breaking news, and Google+ for *breaking down* the news.

It doesn't matter what time of day or night, what the topic is, and so on, the community of people I follow and who follow me as well are a *constant* source of inspiration and support. So, if your community doesn't inspire you, come visit mine—we'd love to meet you.

"Real" World

Contrary to popular belief, geeks do have lives and do venture outside. Sure, geeks often carry laptops, cameras, iPhones, and iPads, but they're out in the "real" world. As you would expect, the real world can always provide something to write about. Going to a conference, a store, the local coffee place, and even walking down the street can provide you with much-needed fodder. If you aren't inspired by real life, you need to get out more.

Geeks like to share what they know and have learned. To do this, they like to hang out together and generally geek out. In Vancouver, they have regular meetups for bloggers and people interested in PR and social media, and photowalks to just wander around and take pictures. There are even tweetups, which are meetups organized through Twitter. Often, meetups are purely social—just spending time after work in a pub. But meetups, like Third Tuesday, bring in guest speakers to talk about blogging, social media, and society. These semistructured social times are only *part* of the inspiration the real world brings.

> ### The world around you is inspiring— remember to open your eyes.

How about a good or bad encounter with someone at a store? Did you get awesome, over-the-top service, or something that makes you want to never go there again? How about something you see on the street that strikes you as funny? Take a picture of it with your cell phone, if you can, and use that as the seed of a post.

The world around you is inspiring—remember to open your eyes.

Reader Comments

Chapter 4 goes more in depth with comments, but here is a short bit on how comments inspire me and my writing. As a reminder, part of blog posts and blogging is the capability of people to leave comments on the posts you've written. These comments can be everything from "That was awesome" to "You're completely wrong!" to "Yes, but have you thought about this angle…" and all of these can be sources of inspiration for your writing.

Sometimes, there is nothing more inspiring than people reading your post and taking it in

a whole new direction. It's very gratifying to me when someone reads what I wrote and then sees something else in the post that is *more* interesting than what I wrote about. When that happens, and it will, build on it by writing a follow-up post. You might even think about asking the commenter to contribute to the post. This kind of writing symbiosis is one of the greatest parts of blogging. When your readers feel that they are also *contributors* to your blog, it only serves to strengthen your larger community. You also start to build a loyal following who will cheer you on when you get that book deal!

Great comments like that are amazing gifts. Don't waste them!

Writing with Search Engines in Mind

"Well, just look it up on Google…."

How many times have you heard or said that? If you're like the majority of North Americans, you've probably said it a lot. Looking up information through a search engine—Google being the reigning champion—has become standard practice. The take home of this idea is that if you want people to get to *your* site/blog/whatever, you need to make sure that not only Google knows about you (that isn't very hard), but that you're *writing* so people will find your content when they are looking for your topic.

How do you get to this search engine nirvana? Believe it or not, just by starting off with a blogging engine, you're already ahead of the game. Search engines love blogs because they automatically link all your site's content together. Even better, as you link to your own work, use categories, and tag your posts, you build connections that search engines can use to better understand and index your content. As great as blog engines are at the basics of SEO, you can do some really easy things to dial your SEO up to an 11. Now let's get you the rest of the way there with a few tips.

> **TIP**
>
> Did you know that Google does math? Oh yeah, and that's not all. The following are some of my favorites, which can be entered into Google's search field:
>
> Who is [put in a name]?
>
> What is 30c in f (converts from Celsius to Fahrenheit)
>
> What is $1 CAD in USD (converts from Canadian dollars to U.S. dollars)

For the moment, you're going to take for granted that Google and the other search engines have found you. Yes, I know it doesn't happen overnight, but most blog engines automatically inform all the search engines when you post, so within a few weeks to a month you're being indexed.

> **TIP**
>
> If you've gone the DIY/self-hosted route for WordPress, I recommend that you install these plugins: Google XML Sitemaps and All In One SEO Pack. These two plugins help all the tips I'm going to give you work even better. WordPress plugins can be found at www.wordpress.org/extend/plugins/.

One of the key parts to having people find your blog via search engines is understanding how people actually search for things: *keywords*.

> **NEW TERM**
>
> A keyword is the term used for the words people use to find something through a search engine.

Keywords

Put yourself into the shoes of someone searching for your topic. What words would you use to find a topic? What words in the title or the excerpt will get you to click that result? Don't just think, "Oh, of course someone will search for x." If you follow that track, very often you'll be wrong. It's okay. Initially, your gut will be wrong, but you can use some tools to check how often certain words are used. These tools include the following:

▶ Google Adwords keyword tool (https://adwords.google.com/select/KeywordToolExternal)

▶ WordTracker free keyword tool (http://freekeywords.wordtracker.com/)

For example, Figure 3.10 shows what Google's tool shows for the term "blog."

When you're writing posts, it's a good idea to learn what keywords people use to look for information on your topic. Because so many people use the word "blog" (and variants), using a term like weblog might not bring many people to my site. However, you can use the variety of search terms people use to your advantage.

FIGURE 3.10

Using Google AdWords Keyword tool to see how often people search for "blog" and similar terms.

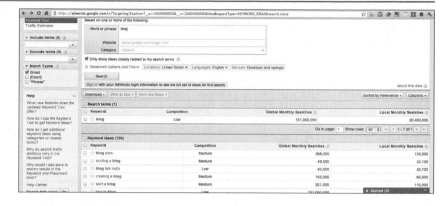

After you have your keywords, run a few searches with them. What results do you get? What catches your eye? Follow the links to those sites and see how the content is written. I bet you'll notice how important terms are repeated often in the text, not in a strange way, just often. You should also notice how the authors use synonyms and variations of the keyword terms as well. This is because Google and the other search engines are putting more weight on the *content of the page* than they were in the past. It isn't a battle between who could write better code for pages; it's between who can *write better content for pages*.

Writing for Search Engines

Diversity is critical to your success with search engines. How many different ways do you know to express an idea? How many words do you know that mean pretty much the same thing? Can you distill an idea into a short sentence?

These are all key to writing for search engines.

It isn't a battle between who could write better code for pages; it's between who can write better content for pages.

The operating principle is to write keyword rich. The title of any blog post you write should have the words that describe what the post is about. If your post is about investments and the stock market, then those words should be in the title. By the same token, the content of your post should include words like investing, stocks, securities, and so on. Write normally, but write *diversely*. Flex that vocabulary. Use different words and phrases in the post to explain the point. This makes your copy keyword rich. Your post will be indexed for the breadth of those keywords, which means that when people search for something like investing, your post is strongly associated not only with investing, but all the other shades of meaning. Search engines will take this to mean that your site might be more *relevant* to the searcher.

Google and other search engines strive to learn human language and shades of meaning. They try to tie words to ideas and concepts, so the more words you use to describe a concept, the more accurately your post will be indexed in terms of the rest of your site and other sites.

Categories and Tags

Blog engines, like WordPress, use categories and tags to help you organize your posts into topic areas. Categories and tags are very similar, but easy to differentiate by just thinking about your kitchen's silverware drawer.

A category is like the silverware drawer itself; the drawer holds a lot of similar and related objects. In the drawer you have those metal objects you use to eat. If you were writing a post about those objects, you would put it in the category of "silverware drawer" but then tag the post with "utensil, fork, stainless steel, dessert fork, Oneida."

I'm betting that you have figured out the post is about stainless steel dessert forks made by Oneida. The tags help readers and search engines connect all the dots to put your post into *context* with other posts on your blog and blogs all over the Internet. You can see by extension if the tags for another post were "utensil, knife, stainless steel, steak, serrated, Oneida" you'd know what that was about. If someone wanted to see all the posts you wrote about your vast collection of Oneida silverware, clicking the tag name in any of the posts with that tag brings up *all* the posts with that tag (knives, forks, and even spoons).

So, categories are big buckets for content. When you're thinking of good names for categories, think of the major concepts you'd use to look for your topic and what you're writing about. Categories might be the keywords that are *almost* too general, but still enough to get you in the right direction. You don't want to have too many categories on your blog. My rule is around a maximum of 10.

Summary

This has been a very diverse chapter, hasn't it? A lot goes into writing good blog posts—finding sources of inspiration *and* remembering them for later, and then going through the process of just writing, getting that idea down. Posting is, really, just a small step, just one click. Then you need to think about how people will find you and your nascent blog.

It's not about learning tricks for search engines, but rather *habits*. Writing, creating categories, choosing tags, and even writing titles are all *proven* ways to help search engines find and index you properly.

The next chapter focuses on writing to encourage discussion and on reaching out to other bloggers in your area of interest.

CHAPTER 4

Building a Community Around Your Blog

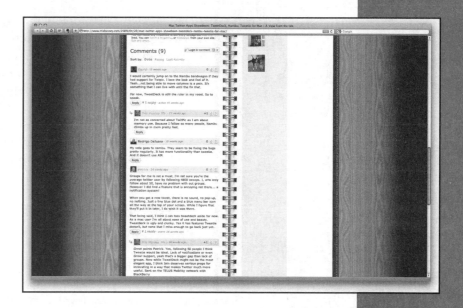

Although the framework of social media and blogging is supposed to be built around ideas of openness and transparency, sometimes things can get a little *too* open. As a general rule, I keep comments turned *on* for all my posts and *off* for all my pages. Comments for posts are on because I want commentary on what I've written. I have them off on pages because that's information I've put up for reference and I don't want commentary or feedback.

However, there are good reasons to turn comments off on a particular post. If a post is controversial, often the comments can get out of hand quickly. Even if the comments are civil, just the sheer number can become a management problem! So, closing off additional comments (and putting an update in the post) can be the only way to stem the tide. People also close off comments if comments in a previously written post turn nasty, which is a painful thing to see. This is often a last resort if moderation and deleting comments isn't working.

Finally, closing off posts on a topic that is sensitive or painful might be a choice you make for yourself. Although I've often received my best and most fulfilling comments on my most heart-wrenching posts, you might not want that. It's up to you. It is your blog.

If you are a business blogger and afraid of having comments on your business blog, the *worst* thing you can do is close off all comments. This shows to other bloggers that you aren't really serious about having conversations; you just want to talk *to* people not *with* them. Keep the comments open and moderate all comments for a while until you are comfortable with the kinds of comments you get. Closing them off entirely can only backfire on you.

Even from the beginning, blogs weren't something that existed alone on the Internet. They were connected to each other. Bloggers linked to each other's posts and left comments. The world of blogs, bloggers, and blogging was very much, and still is, a *community*. Even as the world of social media and blogging has become more complex and diverse, it is still the sense of community and friendship that keeps things together.

This chapter is about more than getting people to leave comments on your posts—which, believe me, is sometimes like pulling teeth—it's about how to use *all* the tools within the realm of social media to build something bigger and more satisfying—a community of friends. We'll start off together talking about how to encourage people to leave comments, and then move to all the *other* ways to build community.

Encouraging Comments and Discussion

Comments keep blogging going. The dialogue and feedback you get from readers not only helps you grow as a writer, but also ensures that you stay on track. Through comments, you learn, interact, and gain inspiration. I've written entire follow-up posts based on a single comment. I've also received cease-and-desist letters from lawyers because of comments (more on that later).

Part of getting comments is writing to encourage comments. First, make sure comments are enabled (that is, turned on) for all your posts. Usually, the default setting for blog engines is to have comments on, but sometimes they get turned off, so it's important to double-check. Whether or not just anyone can post a comment or whether there is some kind of moderation in place is up to you, and I'll get to that shortly.

With comments turned on, the next part is subtler: getting people to leave comments. There isn't a magic formula for you to get lots of comments. Sometimes I pull it off; sometimes I don't. In any case, the following are simple things you can do to help encourage comments:

- Leave examples out on purpose. People love to feel that they are contributing by adding to your post.

- Ask open-ended questions.

- Ask for comments directly.

- Take a contrary or controversial stance to the status quo. (Just make sure you believe in it. Few things in the blogging world are more annoying than a blogger whose only stance on anything is that he believes the exact opposite of what everyone else thinks.)

Even with these tips, including soliciting for comments, sometimes a great post just doesn't get any comments. This happens regardless of how much traffic your blog gets, and it happens to the very best of posts. Sometimes it's the posts that you don't expect to receive any comments on that are the ones that get the most commentary. You just never know.

When you do get comments, to keep the flow going, you have to respond to the comments you receive. Be open and willing to be proved wrong or challenged, and never lose your temper. Some commenters are just *trolls*. Don't take the bait.

NEW TERM

As discussed later in this chapter, a troll is Internet speak for someone who posts obnoxious or inflammatory comments with the intention of stirring up trouble. The intent of a troll is not healthy dialog, but to provoke a hostile response.

ARE BLOGGERS LIABLE FOR THE COMMENTS LEFT ON THEIR BLOGS?

Yes, to an extent. If a blogger is exercising due care and not allowing clearly libelous comments, the remainder should fall under the purview of free speech. However, this has not always stood up in court. The safest thing to do for a questionable comment is to hold it in the moderation queue until you can talk about the comment with the commenter. Sometimes, a person might be willing to edit the comment. Remember, this is your blog, and you don't have to accept any comments that you feel cross the line.

I mentioned receiving a cease-and-desist letter because of comments on a post on one of my blogs. The post was about accusations of wrongdoing at an Internet-based charity. The accusations were pretty serious, including things like tax issues and how much people were paid to do things for the company. The comments started to raise some disturbing questions. The story didn't seem to be as cut-and-dried as I thought. (When is it ever, really?)

At one point, the comments started to become ad hominem attacks on the founder of the company and his personal integrity. I received a letter from his lawyer demanding that I take down the post and all comments. Lucky for me, I was working for a blog network, and they stood behind their bloggers. In the end, we (within our company) agreed that there was some merit to saying that as a blogger, if I allowed a potentially libelous comment to be published, I could be liable for that.

The compromise was easy, actually. I reviewed all the comments. Any comment that I thought was borderline, I sent to the management team to review. Together, we made a decision on keeping it or pulling it. In the end, I had to remove only one comment. Nothing ever went to court, and everything worked out in the end.

Engaging in a healthy dialogue makes your blog a place where people will go for ideas and inspiration, which means that you will gain inspiration as well. Every blog, no matter what the topic, is made better with comments.

Commenting on Other Blogs

There is another way to help increase the comments on your blog: Comment on other people's blogs. Yes, it might seem odd, but this is the community aspect to blogging. You should be reading blogs on a regular basis, and when you find a post you enjoy and feel you have something to add to the discussion ("great post" doesn't count, sorry), leave a comment.

The trick here is that there is a space in the comment form for the URL to your blog. See where I'm going here? Yes, leave a good comment, with your name linked to your blog, and you can bet that the author of the post is going to check out your blog. It's almost 100% guaranteed that you'll get a visit from the author, but only if it's a good comment.

To get good comments, you need to give good comments. It is simple as that. Conversations take two people, so start your conversations off on the right foot with good comments. As you get to know more people through your blog, make sure you support what they are doing with comments (and links) on their posts.

Remember, though, that just like real life, some people like to stir up trouble and leave comments that aren't just off topic, but malicious as well. These folks are the aforementioned trolls, and they don't just live under bridges anymore.

Spam, Trolls, and Other Vermin: The Comments You Don't Want

Although commenters can be a source of support, gratification, and inspiration, they can also be a royal pain in the, well, you know. Often, the problem isn't really a "person" but a computer sending out "comments" filled with links to the dreckiest dreck of the Internet. People run these charming little programs to leave thousands of spam comments on blogs. These comments are full of links to porn, online pharmacies, cheap car insurance, generally the same things you see in your email. There are also people who get a lot of enjoyment from making other people's lives miserable—these are trolls and they are some of the worst vermin online. Like their fairytale counterparts, they don't like the light of day and can be managed. Both comment spam and more human vermin can be managed if you employ some pretty simple tricks and techniques.

Spam

Dealing with comment spam isn't as bad as it used to be. When comment and trackback/pingback spam first hit the blogosphere, it was just a trickle. It was nothing that you couldn't manage with a few minutes a day, and then the storm hit. When the first blog spam storm hit, bloggers were caught off guard. It was so big that many blogs and entire hosted blog platforms (such as Blogger) ground to a halt. Yeah, imagine if a newspaper was flooded with so many letters to the editor that the printing presses overheated and shut down. That's pretty much what happened (see Figure 4.1). Bloggers were not amused.

> **NOTE**
>
> Why is it called spam? This term comes from the Monty Python skit and song "Spam, Spam, Spam." It's about a restaurant where you can get anything you want, but with Spam, and you couldn't order something without Spam. So email and blog comments that you didn't want or ask for became—wait for it—spam!

Being just as smart as the spammers, the blog community quickly figured out ways to combat them. Plugins were written, server rules were created, blacklists were made, and it was under control. Today, you don't have to "deal" with spam as much as be aware of it.

If you're using a hosted service like TypePad or WordPress.com, these services have antispam countermeasures already set up—it's in their best interest to. If you are self-hosting, you'll need to install the antispam plugins yourself. With Movable Type and WordPress, you can use Akismet. For other blog platforms, anti-spam countermeasures are available. Because comment spam can be a huge problem if it isn't managed, all major blogging platforms have ways to manage it.

Managing spam means that you have to look at the comments and trackbacks you get with a bit of a critical eye.

FIGURE 4.1

A selection of typical comment spam from my personal blog.

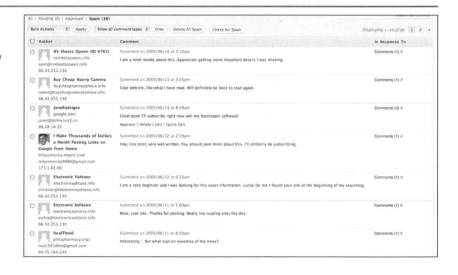

Managing spam means that you have to look at the comments and trackbacks you get with a bit of a critical eye. Legitimate ones stand out clearly, as well as spammy ones (services like Akismet learn over time, so when new styles come out, you have to help by marking them as spam). It's the subtle ones that you have to watch for. The following is how I separate the wheat from the chaff:

▸ Follow the link in the trackback. The spammy sites are obvious for their copious advertising and just posting excerpts from other blogs without original content.

▸ Sometimes comment spammers probe blogs with seemingly legitimate comments to get a comment approved. Generally, after commenters has been approved, they can comment without moderation. Look at the email address and site the commenter links to, which are often the giveaways. If the email address looks a bit odd, you can probably bet it's a spammer testing the defenses.

▸ Don't worry if you accidentally mark a legitimate comment spam, because you can get a commenter or site off the blacklist easily. As a community, bloggers would rather people be overcautious than overly kind.

Like email spam, comment spam thrives because there are people who let it get through. The spammers can make profits even if an infinitesimal fraction of blogs let spam through. So the fewer blogs that allow it through, the better off bloggers will be.

Trolls and Other Vermin

One of the facts of human nature is that no matter where or how people communicate or gather, there is always a jerk to be found. These are people who bait others into a fight or say something wholly inappropriate just to get attention or make people uncomfortable. You know who these people are in real life, and if you see them at a party or meeting, you groan and try your best to avoid them. Sometimes they get the hint, sometimes they don't—and sometimes the bouncer tosses them out of the bar on their tush.

In the online world, the virtual equivalent is the troll. A troll is a person who just likes to stir things up and make trouble. They are often vulgar, insulting, and hateful.

Trolls are usually out for attention. Some people get their kicks being a jerk because the anonymity of the Internet makes it very easy to "be" someone else online. Although it's best to ignore them, that's easy to say when someone isn't personally attacking you. Sometimes it is not enough to ignore the troll; you might have to go beyond that. Blocking the person from commenting can be tricky because it is hard to isolate a single person on the Internet all the time. Most often, you need to keep deleting their comments. It might not be an automatic solution, but it is certainly a deterrent. The majority of the time, trolls are just royal pains who will go away after they realize no one's taking their bait, but sometimes they cross the line, and when they do it often gets ugly.

Although you want to encourage conversation, you want to encourage thoughtful, witty conversations—not personal attacks, rants, or diatribes. (Okay, if you're the one ranting, that's different.) Having a comment policy is a first step, but better is just standing firm when someone crosses the line (or maybe strays a wee too close to the line). Remember, feed the conversation, but Do Not Feed The Trolls (DNFTT).

How does one feed the conversation? Ah, that is easier than you think.

Finding Other Blogs in Your Niche

One of the most fun and gratifying parts of being a part of the blogosphere and social media is connecting with people all over the world who share interests and passions. Whether it's technology, books, pens, cameras, or cooking, I have met some truly amazing (and inspiring) people through my various blogs. Many of these people are close friends, even if I only get to see them once a year at most. So, how did I find these people? The answer is only a click away.

Part of blogging is reading other blogs. If you're into fly tying or indie neo-classical music, you want to read what other people are doing and saying. So, do what everyone else does: Google it. Specifically, Google Blog Search it.

IDEA GALLERY

http://headrush.typepad.com

KATHY SIERRA STORY

One the blogosphere's most (in)famous cases of trolls crossing the line surrounds blogger and technologist Kathy Sierra. Kathy was writing amazing and influential blog posts and, like anyone who starts getting attention, there is always a dark side to fame (I've had my share, as well).

In March 2007, a line was crossed, and the technology blogging community was aghast and horrified. Comments on Kathy's blog started to go from nasty and insensitive to threatening and downright scary. There were pictures of her posted next to a noose, and worse. Personal information, including her home address and Social Security number, were posted online, in addition to (perceived) threats to her life. Kathy abruptly canceled all her speaking engagements, closed down her blog (although it still exists online), and withdrew completely from public life.

continues

This incident highlighted not only the problem of trolls and other online vermin, but also the role of women in technology. In the end, the people who made the comments were called out and apologized. About a year later, Kathy returned to blogging and is stepping slowly back into public life.

This is an extreme example of the dark side of the Internet. Since 2004, comments on my blogs have been positive and on point 99.9% of the time. A few of my friends have regular trolls, but often their comments are more laughable than anything serious. The point is to remember that it's your blog. Yes, there is an ethos of allowing all comments through if they aren't spam, but just as you have rules of conversation in your home, you have rules on your blog. If someone crosses the line, just delete, edit, or mark the comment as spam.

Google Blog Search is a subset of Google that focuses solely on returning results from blogs. So if you're interested in opera and do a search, it might look something like Figure 4.2.

Some of the entries might not all be from blogs, but a lot are. Follow the links. Read the posts. Bloggers usually have links on their blogs to other blogs that offer similar content that they respect; follow their links to the other blogs. Now you've got the idea.

Using an RSS reader like Google Reader, FeedDemon, NetNewsWire, or Reeder, you can subscribe to a virtually unlimited number of blogs and easily keep up with particular bloggers' posts. If nothing else, bookmark them to come back to regularly read their new posts. To learn more about RSS and RSS Readers, visit the Google Reader help section at http://www.google.com/support/reader/.

As you amass a list of sites that you follow, leave comments, write posts based on the ideas you get from them (giving credit and linking, of course), and build a connection. After you start finding blogs in your niche, you will find many, many others.

As Twitter, Facebook, and Google+ have become mainstream, you can also find new blogs just by connecting with people on social networks. When I start following and interacting with new people on Twitter, for example, I always check out their blogs. Even if I might not *think* I'm going to be interested in the topic they write about, reading their blogs gives me a new sense of who they are. And often, it turns out, I *am* interested in what they are writing about! Reading these blogs leads to other blogs because bloggers link to bloggers. I've lost hours just reading and clicking and clicking. I guess I shouldn't say I "lost" the hours, because I generally leave enriched, better informed, and sometimes with nifty new techie toys to play with.

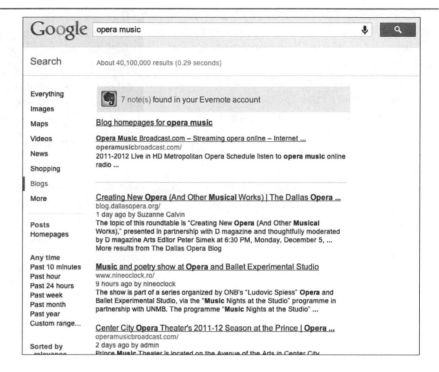

FIGURE 4.2

Searching for opera music on Google Blog Search.

Linking to Other Blogs

It is essential to link to other blogs if you want to be successful and noticed. Linking to others shows appreciation to others, gives credit for the inspiration, and gives your readers more background or information on the topic.

Bloggers know when you link to their posts because they get a pingback on the post, and most bloggers have searches send them results for links to them, mentions of their names, or mentions of their blogs (these are called "ego feeds").

Like getting a great comment, getting a link back is a great feeling. The more you link out, the more the search engines will love you.

Search engines love sites that are content rich, updated frequently, and link to a lot of other relevant sites. When you link to someone, make the text of the link something descriptive—for example, "as John said in his brilliant post…" instead of "click here." Beyond giving your readers some context for the link, you also give search engines context for your post and the other person's post. This amplifying effect helps both of you get better search engine rankings on a given topic.

Yes, at times you want to write a long post to stand on its own. This is perfectly okay. I do this when I'm feeling a little more academic or verbose, but just make sure that you do link to other blogs in the majority of posts.

The easiest way to include other blogs in your posts is with the "Blog this…" *bookmarklet* that all blogging platforms have, and many editors as well. All of them work in the same, simple fashion. When you're on a page that you'd like to blog about, just click the bookmarklet on your bookmark bar and a new post will be opened for you with a link to that original post (see Figure 4.3). If you select some text from the post, that becomes part of the post as well, along with the link to the post. Nothing could be easier. It's how I started blogging with Blogger back in the day and, for the most part, I haven't changed that workflow substantially in more than five years.

> **NEW TERM**
>
> A bookmarklet is like a regular bookmark, but it contains a little JavaScript script instead of a link to a website. This JavaScript tells your browser to go to a certain site and perform some action. In the case of Posterous or WordPress, these bookmarklets help you quickly create new posts.

So remember, no blog is or should be an island. You need to link out, a lot. Remember to keep it relevant to the topic at hand, or not only will your readers be confused, so will the search engines.

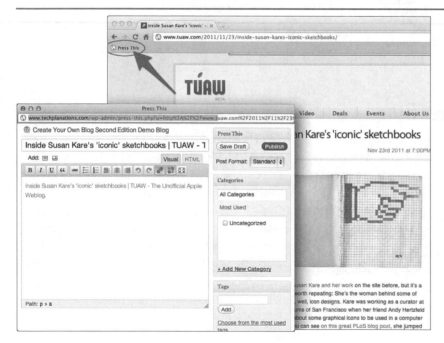

FIGURE 4.3

Using the WordPress Press This bookmarklet to start a post on how classic computer icons came to be.

Connecting with Other Bloggers

As you might have gathered, commenting, linking, and reading other blogs are the foundation to connecting with other bloggers. After a few comments on my blog, especially if they have been good comments, I'll often email the commenter, in addition to reading his or her blog, linking to it, and commenting. The blogosphere isn't really any different than the world as a whole. You start friendships one step at a time. Emails move into instant messages that, distance or timing permitting, move into meeting in person over a coffee. Because blogging is global in scale, there are a lot of people I consider friends whom I've never met in person.

> **NOTE**
>
> The blogosphere isn't really any different than the world as a whole. You start friendships one step at a time. Emails move into instant messages that, distance or timing permitting, move into meeting in person over a coffee.

Regardless of the distance, the key is a global meeting of minds and common interests. This is what gives bloggers the strength in numbers. It's the friendships and professional rapport that builds up over time that gives bloggers the ability to call on friends and colleagues to repost, retweet, and otherwise get the word out on a particular issue or topic. Public relations crises aren't created by just one blogger; it's one blogger tapping into his or her network that can cause giant corporations stand up and take notice.

When it comes down to it, a certain kind of person is attracted to this medium, and that person is inherently social. People like to chat, engage, and share. Yes, many people prefer to stay at home with the safety and distance the virtual world brings, but would enjoy social interaction and company.

So, no matter how you reach out and connect to other bloggers, do it. Send that email, follow them on Twitter, connect, and engage. There are a lot of amazing people out there.

Twitter

In case you hadn't noticed by now, the topics and sections of this book are more like a tapestry than a linear set of steps. Comments are for connecting with other bloggers, for conversation and inspiration. Linking isn't just to improve your SEO standings, but also to show appreciation and give your readers more depth and insight.

The phenomenon of Twitter is no different. Twitter is in a class by itself in how it connects, inspires, brings the world closer together, and spreads news faster than anyone could have imagined. Twitter can be very hard to explain. It started off as a service where you told your friends what you were up to by answering the question: What are you doing? For the first six months of its life, Twitter was something only the geekiest of geeks paid much attention to. In March 2007, it exploded and hasn't stopped yet.

GROUPING INFORMATION LETS YOU MANAGE IT

Without a doubt, Twitter can dump an unfathomable amount of information into your lap, but only if you let it. Even though I follow about 6,800 people on Twitter (some Twitter accounts are just news feeds from BBC and CNN), I can manage the flow of information *and* still keep up with my friends (which is what Twitter was originally designed to do). How? Simply by grouping people together and having an application that lets me look at those groups easily.

HootSuite is a free, web-based application for Twitter (and other social networks like Facebook and LinkedIn) that enables me to use Twitter's list feature to display lists of people in columns. For example, I have a column for news sources and a column for tweets that mention me. I have columns for friends and one for colleagues. I also build columns for searches of interesting topics. These let me search through all the tweets posted on Twitter, not just from the people I follow.

I think looking at the deluge of content that Twitter can unleash makes it pretty obvious why bloggers need tools to group, filter, and search through Twitter.

Now if I could only do this for email.

So, what good is it? Your messages can be only 140 characters long. The more people you follow, the harder it is to keep in touch with your friends.

You'd be surprised at how much you can say in 140 characters. In fact, it's a great exercise in brevity to distill a complex idea into a few words. As for the fire-hose effect—having too many comments from too many people you follow coming through seemingly at once—that is handled with good applications that help you manage your Twitter stream.

> *For the first six months of its life, Twitter was something only the geekiest of geeks paid much attention to. In March 2007, it exploded and hasn't stopped yet.*

Fine, it isn't so bad, but still, why?

Because Twitter has become an online nexus of information and communication. Twitter is where people come together and not only update people on their thoughts, but share links, pass on headlines, and just chat. Twitter is one of those you-have-to-get-it-to-use-it things, and even then a lot of people don't like it or get it. That's okay. It is like trying to talk with a flock of hummingbirds on amphetamines (and you're one of the hummingbirds), but after you get the knack of it you might find that it is one of the best places for news and conversation.

> **NOTE**
>
> Twitter started as a side project for the folks at Odeo to break a creative slump and have a way to let each other know what they were up to. Today, Twitter is growing by leaps and bounds and even celebrities of all stripes use it. So, what are you doing?

Facebook, Google+, and Other Social Networks

I'm going to tell you right now that I'm a certified Facebook curmudgeon. If I know you, I'll accept your friend request, but I don't necessarily participate in a lot of the reindeer games that go on there. Sure, I'll respond to an event, but ask me to play Farmville? Thanks, I'll pass. However, Facebook and the myriad of personal and professional social networks are great places to connect with people and their blogs.

Facebook has become one of *the* most important tools for large and small businesses. It's so important that businesses ignore Facebook at their own peril (of losing marketing opportunities). For "regular" folks, Facebook has become such a powerful worldwide water cooler that if you can't find something interesting on Facebook at any given moment—you're not really trying. The first way you're going to start the connecting process is to make sure you have a link to your blog in your profile on these networks. If you have more than one blog (yes, sometimes that happens), add as many as you can, or just pick a blog to be your hub online.

Facebook has been and remains the hot thing right now, but other social networking sites, such as LinkedIn, are also going strong. Google launched its own social network tied in with all that is Google, called Google+. While Google+ is still a young pup as I'm writing this (nary six months old), it is gaining a large following and is certainly a place where I find lots of inspiration.

All social networks do one thing well: They connect people. Part of this connecting is giving people a little about yourself to not only learn more about you, but also match you with similar affinity groups. For example, if a social network asks in your profile what you do for a living (say, writer) and a hobby or two (reading and cooking), it will be easier for other writers to find you. Likewise, if you can add geographic info, you might be able to find other bloggers near you. In Vancouver, there are several social media-blogging groups, such as the Vancouver Blogger Meetup, Third Tuesday, WordPress Meetup, and Drupal Users Group.

I found all these through one social network or another. Maybe I saw a mention of it on Twitter or was invited through Facebook or read about it on a blog. Regardless of source, these groups are a lot of fun and a great way to meet like-minded people in real life.

Remember that it isn't the site or program or whatever that makes a social network; it's the people in it. Facebook might implode on itself (I can only hope so), but the desire to connect with each other will remain as strong as ever, and people will find (and build) a site or service to do just that. Count on it.

Summary

This chapter discussed the ways you can expand your readership and build a community around your blog. Whether it's leaving comments, linking, social networks, or meeting people in real life, the central premise is that what people are doing is social. Humans are social animals. We like to gather together. People like to find other people interested in the same things, whether specifically (the left-handed fly-tiers club) or generally (Vancouver Blogger Meetup), through that meeting and connecting, people's experiences, writing, and blogs become richer and more fulfilling to everyone.

It's about community, and community is one factor that can separate a blog from the crowd. Whether it's comments on your blog or another's, these are the first steps to building a community. After you start writing your blog, look for other blogs in your niche. Use these blogs as inspiration, as part of your community, and as connections to other social networks. Make sure you leverage the networks you're already a part of, like Twitter and Facebook, to promote your blog and connect to your community of readers in another place.

Like any society, the Internet and blogosphere has a darker side. Like your email, there is spam to handle, which is easy to manage, and also people who like to cause trouble. These trolls are best left ignored and comments either deleted or left to sit. If a troll crosses the line, you might need to take additional steps, but that is a rare occurrence.

Building a community around your blog is like building a community of friends; it takes time, but it is a very rewarding experience.

CHAPTER 5

Creating a Personal Blog with WordPress.com

Hi! My name's Kelly, and I'll be blogging about this later tonight.

It seems a little redundant to talk about creating a personal blog, because in the beginning all blogs were personal. To have a business blog was anathema to bloggers. Making a blog that is all about "you" is the heart of personal blogging. You is in quotes because, as you've learned, who "you" are online depends on how much or how little you want to reveal. Because this is a personal blog, it's intended to reflect your beliefs, hobbies, and family—essentially, who you are.

I think many people dismiss personal blogs as less serious than "professional" or "business" blogs, but I think it's just the opposite. Personal blogs are very serious, even if the subject matter isn't. What's more important than who you are? Because the origins of blogging center on the personal blog, it's important not to dismiss them out of hand.

I first started blogging to learn about it for professional reasons and to have an outlet for things I wasn't doing at work. My blog was the epitome of the personal blog. In my case, my blog was mostly about collaboration tools, software, and other geek esoterica. Still, it was personal, and, because I expressed myself well and made some local connections, my humble blog became a springboard to my present career. However, there is a strange hybrid here that is worth noting, the personal-business blog. My blog falls under that category because it is my personal blog, but it serves to drive and support my professional career and business life.

This chapter takes what you've learned in the previous four chapters and builds on it so you can go from a general blog to something that's more your style. Roll up your sleeves here and get to work.

I've written this chapter to serve as a quick start for a blog using WordPress.com. I could have chosen Blogger or a few other engines—Tumblr will get a chapter of its own—to serve as the example, but I've found that starting a blog on WordPress.com gives you a great foundation to build a blog, or a website (which I cover in Chapter 7, "Creating a Website"), with a clear and easy path to grow and expand over time.

Unlike the first edition of this book, I don't cover how to start podcasting or video blogging in this chapter—both of those topics are covered in Chapter 10, "Creating a Multimedia Blog." Over the years of teaching people how to blog and create websites with WordPress.com, I've found that people want to do the following:

▶ Post content

▶ Post images

▶ Embed videos from YouTube (and other places)

▶ Personalize the theme or design of their blog

That's pretty much it. This chapter puts the focus squarely on those goals. Technology will, for the most part, take a backseat to getting things done simply and easily.

Getting Started with WordPress.com

In Chapter 2, "Installing and Setting Up Your First Blog," I talked about setting up a blog on WordPress.com. I'm going to go into the process in more detail in this chapter to get more into the nitty gritty of things.

Before we get started on creating this new blog of yours, let's first create a place for it to live.

NOTE

Remember, WordPress.*com* and WordPress.*org* are related, but different. WordPress.com is a commercial venture run and owned by Automattic. WordPress.org is the home of the open-source version of WordPress that you can download and install yourself on your own servers. Automattic set up and supports the WordPress Foundation that runs and maintains things needed for WordPress.org to continue.

Creating Your Account

Creating an account on WordPress.com is fast, easy, and free. WordPress.com provides a tremendous number of features for free. In fact, it's pretty easy to start and stick with WordPress.com for years and years.

The first step is to go to WordPress.com and look for the big Get Started Here button (see Figure 5.1)

CAUTION

INTERNET EXPLORER 6 NOT WELCOME HERE

Microsoft's Internet Explorer 6 was, for a very long time, the most popular browser on the Internet. It was first introduced more than 10, yes 10, years ago. Although IE 6 was great for its time, its time has long since passed. However, many companies and users hadn't taken the time to update their computers to use newer versions of IE or other browsers like Firefox, Chrome, or Safari. Continuing to support IE 6 was keeping many sites like WordPress.com from taking full advantage of newer technologies, and supporting a decade-old browser just didn't make sense. So, if you try to use WordPress.com using IE 6, you won't be able to sign up until you come back with a "modern" browser.

Sure, it might be harsh, but IE upgrades are free, and sometimes, you have to let go of the past to move forward.

FIGURE 5.1

The home page for WordPress.com.

When you click the button, you'll see a screen that looks something like Figure 5.2. Note that I had to scroll down and shrink things down so you could see all the form fields in one image.

In Figure 5.2, you see that I've picked "createyourownblog2ndedition" for the name. The menu that is open shows that I can have createyourownblog2ndedition.wordpress.com for free, but other options, like createyourownblog2ndedition.com, for a cost. You don't have to decide right this minute whether you want to buy or use a domain for your blog. We'll talk about buying and using domains with WordPress.com later in the chapter.

You'll also note that my *username* for this blog is *also* createyourownblog2ndedition. On WordPress.com, you can keep your username and blog name the same, *or* you can put a different name in the field. Something shorter, like cyob2nded, might have been a good choice here. Why? Shorter URLs are easier for you, and everyone else, to type.

NEW TERM

A username is the word, phrase, or name you use to log in to a computer or service. It's different from your password. Some services use an email address as your username; others, like WordPress.com, ask for a different name to use.

I entered a password and confirmed it in the field, as well as an email address. It is *very* important that you enter your email address correctly because before you can start your blog, you have to click a link sent to that email address to confirm your account. When you click Sign Up, you go to a screen, like Figure 5.3, to put in a little information about yourself while waiting for that confirmation email to arrive.

FIGURE 5.2

The sign-up screen for WordPress.com.

FIGURE 5.3
The Edit Profile page on WordPress.com that you reach after starting the sign-up process.

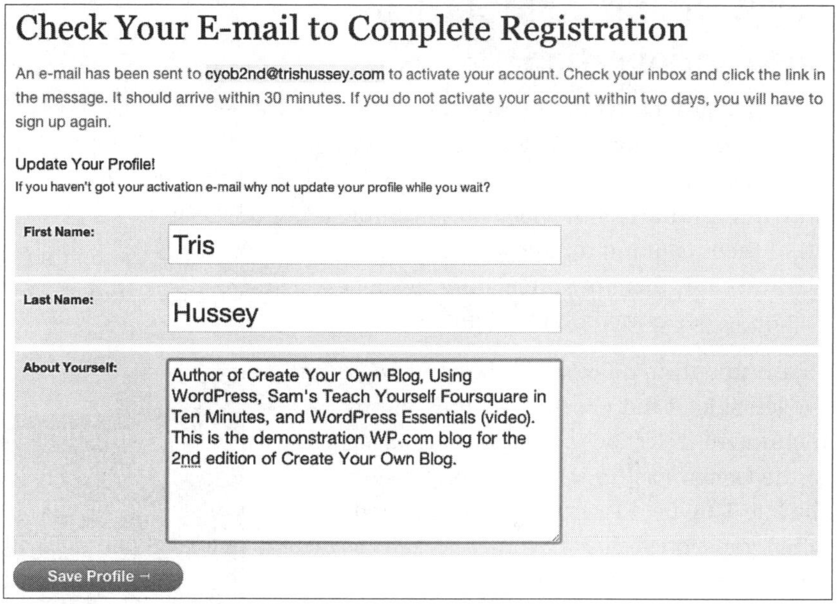

Check Your E-mail to Complete Registration

An e-mail has been sent to **cyob2nd@trishussey.com** to activate your account. Check your inbox and click the link in the message. It should arrive within 30 minutes. If you do not activate your account within two days, you will have to sign up again.

Update Your Profile!
If you haven't got your activation e-mail why not update your profile while you wait?

First Name:
Tris

Last Name:
Hussey

About Yourself:
Author of Create Your Own Blog, Using WordPress, Sam's Teach Yourself Foursquare in Ten Minutes, and WordPress Essentials (video). This is the demonstration WP.com blog for the 2nd edition of Create Your Own Blog.

Save Profile →

When the email arrives in your inbox, you need to click the Activate Blog button. When you do, you'll see a screen like Figure 5.4.

At this point, if you're ready, you can start blogging! But maybe you'd like to know what some of the import settings and configuration steps are before you dive into blogging.

FIGURE 5.4
Confirmation and success! Also, your Dashboard for your blog on WordPress.com.

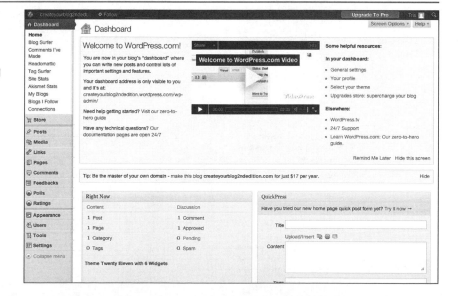

Key WordPress.com Settings and Configuration

Despite WordPress.com adding more and more features to the service, they've kept the number of things you need to do to get started to a bare minimum. Technically, you've completed all of them (signing up and confirming your account), but there are a few things I suggest you do to get started on the right foot.

First is updating a few of the basic settings. On the left side of the screen, click the Settings menu item (refer to Figure 5.4). This brings you to the General settings screen. You'll see that the Site Title field is the name you created when you signed up for WordPress.com. You'll also notice that the Tagline is "Just another WordPress.com site." In Figure 5.5 you can see I've updated those fields to things that are more descriptive and interesting. Try to keep

the site title reasonably short, but be more descriptive in the Tagline field. The Tagline is supposed to tell visitors a little about what they can expect to read when they come to your site. The last thing I change on this screen is the Timezone. Just pick your city from the menu.

Scroll to the bottom of the screen, click Save Changes, and you're done!

> **NOTE**
>
> Did you notice that on the settings screen, it doesn't say Blog Title, but rather Site Title? That change was made to reflect the fact that blogs have become synonymous with websites *and* that many people are creating traditional "websites" using WordPress as the engine to power them— as you will read in Chapter 7.

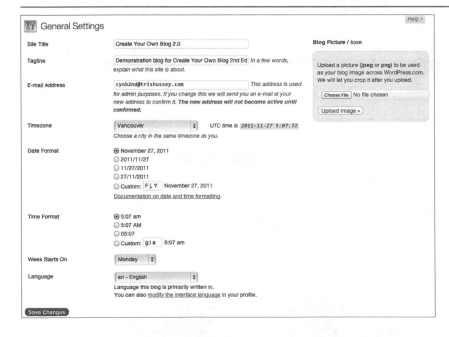

FIGURE 5.5

The WordPress.com settings screen.

Now that the basic settings are updated—yes, believe it or not, that's all you *really* need to do—let's fix up a couple other things that will help you get off on the right foot.

When you start any WordPress.com blog or install WordPress yourself, the software automatically creates a new post and adds a comment to it. This is great so that you can see that everything worked, but leaving the "Hello World" post on your site isn't needed. So, let's delete the post—which will delete the comment as well.

First, click Posts from the menu on the left side. This brings up a list of all (right now, all one of them) posts on your blog. Pass your mouse pointer right below the title of the post until you see the menu that has Trash as an option. Just click Trash and you're done (see Figure 5.6)!

One last thing, and then you are set to get off and running. Just like creating a default Post, WordPress also creates a default About page. Again, on the left menu (you're going to be clicking this menu a lot, by the way), click Pages and you'll see a list of all the pages currently available (see Figure 5.7).

Just like with the Posts listing, pass your mouse below the title, but instead of clicking Trash, click Edit. You can also just click the title About, and you'll get to the same editing screen (see Figure 5.8).

WordPress-based blogs and sites have two basic kinds of content: Posts and Pages (the capitals are intentional). A Post is just what you'd think it is, a blog post. But it's also more. A Post is a piece of content that is also connected to other pieces of content (that is, other Posts) through time and the post topic (based on the categories and tags you picked for that Post). A Page, on the other hand, is a more static piece of content that is more timeless and *isn't* connected to other pieces of content through time or subject. You can easily look at all the Posts in a category by clicking a category link in that post. You can also look at all the Posts from October 2010, for example, by choosing to look at posts by time.

You can't look at Pages in the same way. You can't easily have a list of Pages for your readers. Pages aren't meant for that. Most people use Pages for things like an About page, a contact page, or similar content that can stand by itself.

As a blogger, you will probably create 10 or 20 Posts for every Page you might feel the need to create. You won't need many Pages in your blog. Now, when we start talking about using WordPress to build a website, the whole discussion about Posts and Pages gets more interesting. Let's leave that discussion for Chapter 7.

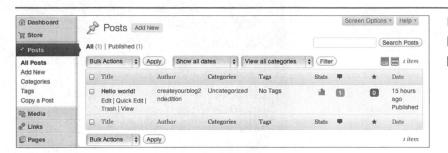

FIGURE 5.6

Deleting the first default post on a new blog.

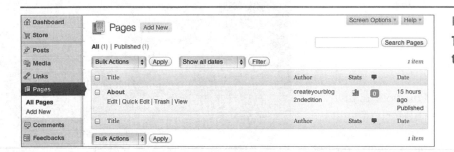

FIGURE 5.7

The list of the Pages for this site.

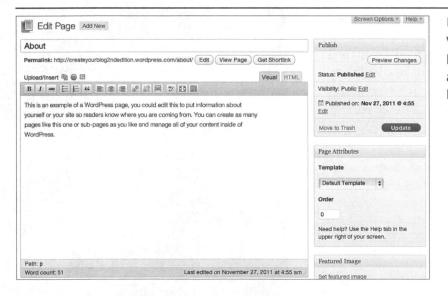

FIGURE 5.8

You'll soon see that the Post editing screen looks almost identical to this Page editing screen.

What you're going to do here is update the content. Maybe you'll change the title to something more than just "About" (about what?) and edit the content of the Page as well. Don't worry if you're not sure about what you're going to say; you can always come back and edit this Page as much as you'd like. Nothing is set in stone here. When you're done, click Update. If you want to see how it looks, click View Page and a new tab or window will open with the results. Figure 5.9 shows what I did for this demo blog.

We're ready to start with the next step of getting this blog ready for action. Are there more things you can update? Certainly. If you pass your mouse pointer over the Users menu item on the left, a menu will pop out. If you choose My Profile, you can update the picture that is connected to your account and edit other bits of information (see Figure 5.10).

FIGURE 5.9

My updated About page, as meager as it might be.

FIGURE 5.10

The profile page on the blog, where you can update more information if you want.

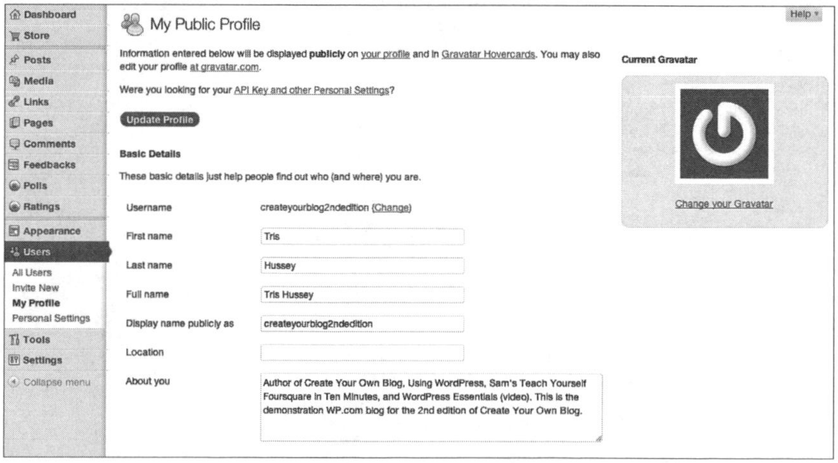

Do you *need* to update this? Eventually, but not right away. Right now we have more fun things to do. The next step is picking a cool and awesome theme for your blog.

Themes and Customizations

One of the best things about WordPress (and most other blogging engines) is that, on a whim, you can change the look and feel of your site with a click. Your content (Posts and Pages) isn't affected at all. You might have to put widgets and menus back in place, but the important stuff—the stuff you've written—will be safe and sound.

Choosing the Right Theme for Your Blog

To get started picking a theme for your blog, first click the Appearance menu on the left. You'll come to a page showing about 30 of the more than 190 themes available to you on WordPress.com. If you see what you like on the first screen, that's great, but most of us want to browse around a little first.

> **NOTE**
> ## WHAT ARE "PREMIUM THEMES"?
>
> When WordPress.com first launched, it offered a selection of some of the best themes available—the best *free* themes available. If you use self-hosted WordPress you can use one of the thousands of other free themes *and* have the option to buy a *premium* theme to use on your blog. Automattic felt that WordPress.com users were missing out on some great themes, so starting in February 2011, WordPress.com users could make a purchase from a selection of the best Premium themes. They cost about $45–$100, but often they offer more flexibility and professional polish than the free themes. The choice is yours, and choice is grand.

To try to narrow down your theme choices, you can put a term into the search box (for example, "blue") and click search, but you still might find yourself faced with a large number of theme choices. What I prefer to do is use the feature filter, as shown in Figure 5.11.

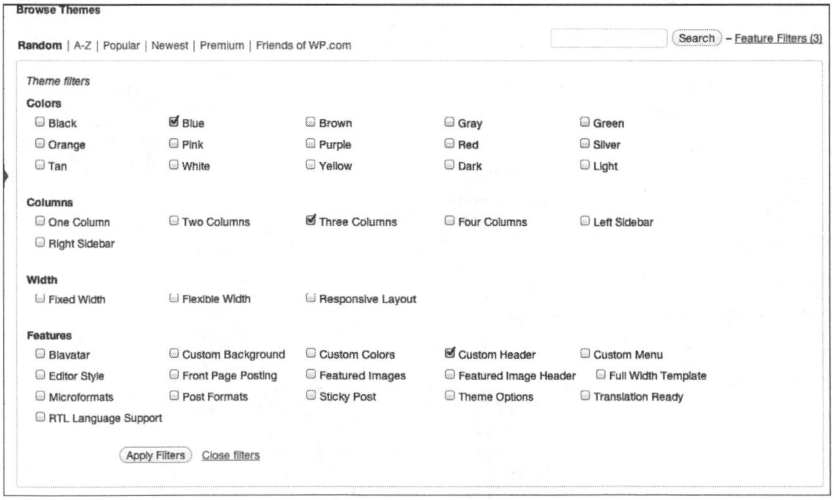

FIGURE 5.11
The feature filter with a few choices made.

After you've made your selections, click Apply Filters; you should see a few themes to pick from, like in Figure 5.12.

It is possible you'll see no results at all. Why? Well, because you might have narrowed the field so closely that there are no themes that appear to fit those criteria. Theme designers put in their own keywords and features, and sometimes they don't do the most thorough job of it. So, the best suggestion when you get no results is to reduce the number of filters you're applying and try again. Sometimes I'm reduced to looking for things like "three columns" or "blue" or "light" when looking for the perfect theme for the job. It just depends on what catches your eye for the task at hand.

After you pick the theme you're interested in, you can select Preview to get an idea of how it looks (but there isn't much to see, because you haven't posted anything yet). Click Activate if you like what you see—at least for the time being—you can always change your mind later and pick a new theme.

Headers and Backgrounds

Many themes allow you to set a custom header image. Themes like Twenty Eleven and Twenty Ten come with several images that you can choose from (or have chosen at random). The theme I'm using for the examples here is called Dusk to Dawn and doesn't come with any images, but you can easily add your own. You start by clicking the Header submenu under Appearance. In Figure 5.13 you can see that if you upload an image that is 870×220 pixels it will be used as is; if it's larger you'll be able to crop it (very handy that you can crop the image right within WordPress!). I made an image for this demo blog, uploaded it, cropped it a bit, and you can see the result in Figure 5.14.

FIGURE 5.12
Results of my feature filter selections (more choices are offscreen).

Mystique

Activate | Preview

Packed with six layout options, six color schemes, a spot for you to link to four popular social network profiles, and support for aside, image, and quote post formats, Mystique can meet the needs of many types of blogs. Further customize the design by adding a custom header and background.

Tags: dark, light, white, green, blue, red, pink, purple, two-columns, three-columns, one-column, fixed-width, right-sidebar, left-sidebar, custom-background, custom-colors, custom-header, custom-menu, featured-images, full-width-template, post-formats, sticky-post, theme-options, rtl-language-support, translation-ready, blog, journal, nature, one-page, outdoors, single-page, travel, bright, colorful, outdoorsy, photography

Comet

Activate | Preview

A very classy, lightweight, and content-focused theme, customizable to your liking. Includes seven color schemes, four layout options, and a full-width page template.

Tags: light, white, gray, red, yellow, green, blue, purple, one-column, two-columns, three-columns, fixed-width, right-sidebar, left-sidebar, custom-colors, sticky-post, custom-menu, custom-header, custom-background, full-width-template, rtl-language-support, theme-options, blog, journal, conservative, faded, simple, traditional

Delicious Magazine `Premium`

Purchase ($45.00) | Preview

An elegant and versatile magazine-style WordPress theme by WooThemes.

Tags: blue, custom-colors, design, full-width-template, generic, green, journal, left-sidebar, modern, orange, pink, purple, red, teal, three-columns, blog, business, magazine, news, professional, clean, elegant, light, minimal, simple, white, yellow, two-columns, right-sidebar, fixed-width, custom-background, custom-header, custom-menu, featured-images, rtl-language-support, sticky-post, theme-options, translation-ready

FIGURE 5.13

The custom header image screen within WordPress.

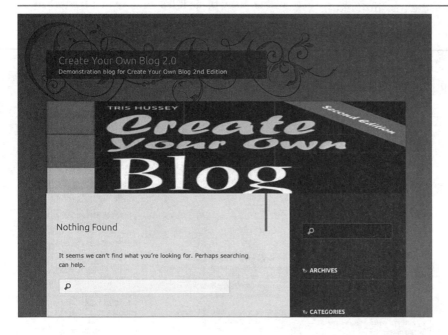

FIGURE 5.14

The result! The custom header in place on the blog.

Although the ability to have a custom header is built in to WordPress, not all themes take advantage of the functionality. I particularly like being able to easily have a custom header image (and one that I can change easily), so I make sure that's one of the features I select in the feature filter.

Some themes go even a step further and allow you to use a featured image on a Post to be the header for just that Post (like Twenty Ten and Twenty Eleven).

Being able to change your header as easily as uploading a new image makes updating your blog with a fresh look very, very easy. Changing things around doesn't just end with the header; many themes allow you to choose new background images and colors as well.

Dusk to Dawn is one of those themes that allows you to mix things up a bit. Start by clicking Background under Appearance and, just like the Headers section, you'll be given options for what to do next.

You can see what that default background looks like in Figure 5.14, but in Figure 5.15, you can see that I've picked a lighter shade of blue (if you're reading this in black and white, trust me, it's a lighter shade of blue). Figure 5.16 shows the result, which I think makes the details of the default background image stand out more.

Headers and backgrounds are nice window dressing, but what about something a little more useful, like a navigation menu? That's our next stop.

FIGURE 5.15

Custom background screen in WordPress.

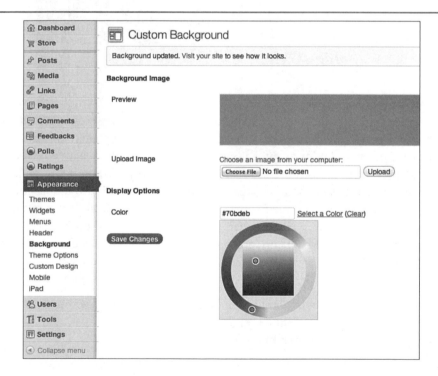

FIGURE 5.16
The new background color on the demo blog. Much nicer, I think.

Menus

Another feature built in to WordPress that themes can take advantage of is the custom menus function. Not long ago, editing your navigation menus was more than a bit of a chore. WordPress Menus allow you to create, edit, rearrange, and manage menus by just dragging and dropping. Like Headers and Background, choose Menus under Appearance to get started (see Figure 5.17).

This particular theme uses menus, but has them only on the sidebar. Other themes have menus horizontally across the top, either above or below the Header (sometimes even both places).

Working with Menus is easy. The first step is to create the menu by giving it a name in the Menu Name box and then clicking Create Menu. We don't have a lot to add to our menu

right now, but I added a custom link to my home page (trishussey.com) and added the About page we edited earlier in this chapter to my navigation menu. After I clicked Save Menu, I also made sure to pick the name of my menu from the menu in the Theme Locations box (and then clicked Save). This ensured that my menu would appear on my blog (believe me, I've missed that step before and wondered what was going on).

You can see the menu on the sidebar in Figure 5.18.

The last bit of fun we're going to have here in the themes department (and before we get to the good stuff—writing!) is talking about widgets. I talked a little about widgets in Chapter 2, but here I'm going to show you how they are used on a WordPress-based site.

FIGURE 5.17
**The custom menu config-
uration screen.**

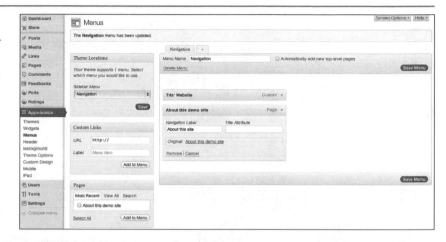

FIGURE 5.18
**My custom menu in place
on the sidebar.**

Widgets

Like everything else theme related, you'll find the Widget screen under the Appearance menu by clicking Widgets. In Figure 5.19 you can see what the default widget screen looks like *for this theme.* Like headers and backgrounds, each theme can define which and how many widgets are displayed at first.

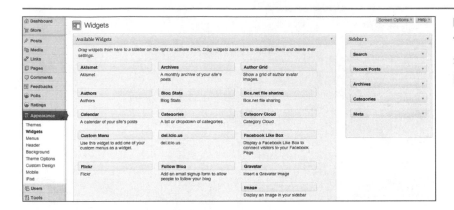

FIGURE 5.19
The default Widget screen. Oh, the possibilities!

Adding a widget to your sidebar is very easy—just drag and drop it into place! In Figure 5.20 you can see a number of widgets that I've dropped onto this theme's sidebar. I left the configuration area for the Facebook Like widget open so you could see how that looks.

Some themes have widget areas only in the sidebars, but other themes have them in the header, footer, and even in the middle of the page. In Chapter 2, I said that a widget is just an easy way to contain extra code to display things like Twitter feeds, Facebook Like buttons, a list of your recent posts, or all the pages on your blog. Because the widgets move in and out like little boxes or containers, you can add and remove interesting interactive elements to your site without needing to know how to code them yourself.

Figure 5.21 shows what some of the widgets on this demo site look like in place. Again, as I said in Chapter 2, widgets are great and can you can add really neat stuff to your blog using widgets, but you can also go overboard. Too many widgets slows down how fast your blog loads. When in doubt, have a friend check your site on their computer to see if it still loads okay for them. If it takes a minute or two to completely load, you probably have too many widgets!

FIGURE 5.20
Just a few widgets in place as an example.

FIGURE 5.21

Widgets in place. Why don't you Like me on Facebook?

That's about all we need to do to your site at the moment to get you going to the next step—writing. If you're feeling a little lost with WordPress, don't worry—its Help section is great. You can refer to it anytime from the Help menu, and it should clarify something for you if one of the features has changed between my writing this book and your reading it.

With the foundation in place, let's get to writing—or at least creating content.

Focus on the Content— What to Put in a Personal Blog

Because this is a personal blog, what kind of content you post is up to you. You might have posts, videos, podcasts, pictures, or whatever suits you at the moment—whatever tells your story. This is fantastic, really, because it gives you a tremendous depth and breadth of things you can have on your blog. This range of ideas is perfect for when you get hired for your first professional blogging gig or when your boss asks you to write, set up, or own the company's blog.

> **NOTE**
>
> If you are like many people, you might also have a business blog at work where you can't talk about everything freely, so having a personal blog frees you to do that. I do this myself because there are things that I want to write about that just aren't appropriate for my work blog (even if my personal blog is admittedly somewhat of a business blog, too).
>
> If you intend to run both personal and professional blogs, it won't take long to realize it's a bit of a high-wire act. I was fortunate in this regard because my bosses accept that I have both kinds of blogs; because I keep those lines very clear, they don't censor me at work or at home. Okay, sometimes I slip a bit from one side to another, and so will you, but we are all human, after all.

What do you put on a personal blog? Well, the sky's the limit. Throughout this chapter, I'll cover the different ways you can fill your personal blog with content. Let's start with the simplest; the basic blog post.

Writing

Chapter 3, "Creating Content for Your Blog," discusses writing in a general way, but in a personal blog, giving readers a look into your life is what brings people back to read more posts. Some of my favorite blogs have been ones where the posts were about the lighter side of family life, or a person's struggle with cancer, or a recovery from an accident. A very popular blog told the stories of a paramedic in London, UK. He related what life was like for him when saving lives, witnessing tragedy, and even the drudgery of his job. This was a great read.

What pulled it all together was the writing style or voice. Personal blogs are more informal. This isn't where you'd expect a long treatise on the meaning of life; it's where you might find the funniest street signs you see on your way to work. How about the guy you buy your paper from? There can be great stories there.

> **TIP**
>
> It's hard to just sit down and pound stories out on command, so if you're trying to capture these kinds of stories, try to jot them down as they happen.

Don't worry that your writing isn't "good enough," because it is good enough; just write your stories. No matter what your stories are, write them with passion and realism, and people will enjoy them.

Also in Chapter 3, I gave basic instructions on how to write posts on a WordPress-based blog. In this chapter I'll add to those points as needed—primarily in the sections related to images and videos—but for the most part I'll talk about "the other stuff" that makes a great personal blog.

Topics

One of the unfortunate examples of blogger stereotypes is the infamous "cat blog," which refers to personal blogs that are just writing about and having lots of pictures of an owner's cat (or dog). Okay, it's true. Cat owners often do mention them from time to time, some people far too often.

FOCUS ON THE CONTENT—WHAT TO PUT IN A PERSONAL BLOG

You can gather a lot, though, from the way people write about their cats. They love their cats and want to share their cats' lives with the world. The topic is close to them and, most of all, personal. It's something with which other obsessive pet owners can identify. This is the key for your blog. You're not writing for the people who have no interest in your passion, but rather those who share it. It doesn't matter if the topic is cats, crocheting, or reflecting on the nature of humanity; topics for your personal blog are entirely of your own choosing.

With that said, let's take a look at some popular categories of personal blogs.

TIP

Ideas for topics and posts come at the strangest times and places. Keep a small notebook and pen handy to jot them down! You could even email them to yourself, and that's really geeky.

Hobbies

We all have hobbies, even geeks like me. Often it's a hobby that you're really passionate about (such as woodworking, stamp collecting, fishing, wines, cooking, trains, or photography) that are often some of the best and most rewarding topics for personal blogs. Write your blog like you'd talk about it to another enthusiast. Share tips, tricks, pictures of your latest creation, and in-jokes that only a true aficionado would get.

On my personal blog (which does get professional often), I have talked about my passions for cooking and photography. I've shared recipe creations and photography tips/finds.

A FEW OF MY FAVORITE PERSONAL BLOGS

Marshall Kirkpatrick
Technology Journalist

What I Learned from a Night Editing Wikipedia
4 Comments and 0 Reactions 11.27.11

This Friday evening I stayed in, not feeling well, and spent my night doing more editing of Wikipedia than I've ever done before. After reading Danny Sullivan's frustrated blog post about his recent experience being shut down on Wikipedia, I thought it would be good to share a different experience. I think Wikipedia is super important and I love it, but editing it is not easy to do. Not because of the technical requirements, those are pretty simple, but because of the way the community there can articulate its expectations.

(more...)

About Me

I am a senior writer at ReadWriteWeb.com and CEO of PlexusEngine, which you can read about here.

I live in Portland, Oregon. This is my personal blog where I share my own opinions about web tech and the news.

To request information about my consulting services please email me at: Marshall@MarshallK.com

See my major media citations.

Contact me

marshall@marshallk.com, via ☎Twitter, or by phone at +1 503 703 1815

Subscribe

2927 readers

Or see my email subscription page

There are a ton of personal blogs out there that I like and respect, but the following are a few of my favorites:

- ▶ Joey deVilla "The Adventures of Accordion Guy in the 21st Century"—www.joeydevilla.com
- ▶ Marshall Kirkpatrick—marshallk.com
- ▶ Erin Kotecki Vest "Queen of Spain"—queenofspainblog.com

Spend some time reviewing these blogs, because they might give you some ideas for what to do with your own blog.

The comments I get on those posts are something that I truly look forward to. How often do you get to "geek out" on your hobby?

> *Write your blog like you'd talk about it to another enthusiast. Share tips, tricks, pictures of your latest creation, and in-jokes that only a true aficionado would get.*

I know that often the other people in our lives get a wee bit tired of hearing about how you just found a great way to store all your sandpaper so you could find them and keep them sorted by grade, or about the awesome new pattern for knitted laptop covers you found. However, an audience of like-minded hobbyists never gets tired of those things. Whether it's just one facet of your personal blog or the primary focus, talk about your hobbies. Make this your little corner of the world where you can wax poetic on good-fitting lens caps and not feel like it's strange at all. (It isn't strange, by the way. I hate poorly fitting lens caps!)

Life

Yes, "Life" is a broad category, I know, but life is like that, isn't it? Whether you talk about love found or love lost, your partner, or your kids, sharing the stories of your life is something that can be very therapeutic. Savoring the victories and sharing the defeats is something everyone can relate to and enjoy reading. Not in a shallow, schadenfreude kind of way, mind you, but rather in that more positive and constructive way all individuals like to share their lives.

In my personal blog, for example, you can find entries about dealing with divorce and loss,

mourning and marking the anniversaries of my father's passing, and marking the rite of passage of my first "heart scare." These are the real, gritty parts of life, which are the things that connect humans and people. Don't shy away from them; embrace them. Yes, there is a limit to what you should share, and I'll delve into that later in this chapter. There are some things that you might not feel comfortable sharing or that you feel comfortable sharing, but the *other people* in your life don't. Respect that line and try to stay on the "good" side of it. Yes, you will slip now and then, but if your heart is in the right place, it might escape unscathed.

One note that I reiterate later is that when you publish something online, it's there forever. Delete isn't really delete, because the content is cached and stored all over the Internet. As my friend and journalist for the *Vancouver Sun* Gillian Shaw says, "Don't put something online that you don't want to see printed on the front page of the paper."

Just "Stuff"

There is a lot of space between life and hobbies, so I've called that space "stuff." It's not the most eloquent descriptor, but it works. This category includes movies, music, books, and day-to-day issues that are general chit-chat. For like-minded people, it's always good to read about what someone thinks about a movie or book. Where else can you post those silly pictures you find online or those bad jokes that proliferate on the Internet like rabbits?

Privacy

When you choose to blog, you are choosing to live a portion of your life in the public eye.

Sure, most of the things you write are innocuous, but sometimes they aren't. Again, that's fine because you're choosing to reveal those things about yourself. What about the other people in your life? Yes, there's the rub. Although deciding your own level of privacy online, and that "line" will float and change over time, is relatively easy, you have to also consider other people and how they might or might not be included in your writing.

> *"Don't put something online that you don't want to see printed on the front page of the paper." —Gillian Shaw, Vancouver Sun*

Relationships

Because this is a personal blog, delving into the world of relationships seems like a natural topic area. Many of the women I know write about their (mis)adventures in dating, being married, or being a parent. Interestingly, not as many men write about the same things, with the exception of parenting. In any case, my friends who write about their relationships do so either with the full knowledge of their partners or write so their partners (or dates) remain anonymous. For married couples who *both* blog, there is an even more interesting dynamic, but again, there are agreed-upon rules. Don't be surprised that the first question you're asked when you announce, "Honey, I'm starting a blog!" is "What are you going to write about?" which isn't really about your topic per se as much it is asking, "Are you going to be blogging about me/us/the kids?" This is the moment to have the ground rules established.

> *When you write about your partner, show him or her the post before you post it. If your partner wants something gone, make it gone.*

Even if you're going to be blogging about your pets, model trains, or knitting patterns, because blogs become a personal outlet, the other people in your life creep into your writing. Figure out early on how comfortable your partner is with being included in your writing. When you write about your partner, show him or her the post before you post it. If your partner wants something gone, make it gone. Even if you're just referring to him or her as "my dear hubs" or "my darling wife" or "the love of my life," give your snookie-poo a chance to say no. As time goes on, the rules and lines might change. This is a natural evolution, so don't push it at the beginning. Respect the boundaries that have been established, and if later on you want to push them, ask first.

Children

Where kids are concerned, it's a horse of a different color. The world today is not like the world I grew up in—not at all. My personal line is that pictures of my children online are private to friends and family only. I don't use their full names, and I avoid discussion that makes them personally identifiable online. Other friends of mine have pictures of their children online and use their names. The line you draw is up to you and your partner. Where children are concerned, you're not just talking about personal privacy but their personal safety. When your children are old enough,

SHOULD KIDS HAVE THEIR OWN BLOG?

This is a great question both for parents who blog and for those who don't. Pretty soon, your kids might ask about having their own blogs. Before you say no, you should know that there are safe and secure ways for your kids to blog. My favorite, and easiest, is to set up a private blog on WordPress.com. Not only can you shield a WP.com blog from search engines, you can set it so it is visible only to approved members. To everyone else, it isn't there. My daughter has had a blog like this for years. It's nice and safe and secure. When your kids are old enough, you can talk about making the blog public, but in the meantime, think of how much the grandparents, aunts, and uncles would like to read updates online. Yeah, it's pretty cool.

It's important if your children are active online, and especially if they blog in semipublic, that you set some ground rules about how they conduct themselves online, such as the following:

- ▶ Emailing people that you, as a parent, don't know
- ▶ IMing people you don't know
- ▶ Giving out personal information, such as a real name, hometown, address, or phone number
- ▶ Meeting people they've met online in the real world
- ▶ Using webcams and voice chat

One thing that will probably grate on your kids is having the computer in a public part of the house and not in their rooms. Yes, there will come a time when they are old enough for the computer to be in their rooms, but early on (elementary age, especially) kids' computer use should be supervised. In the age of inexpensive laptops and netbooks, this is going to get harder and harder to enforce, but it's important to make sure your child is safe online.

they can participate to a degree in the discussion. My daughter has veto rights on pictures that I put up even for friends and family to see. In the end, you are going to have to make your own decision. Honestly, don't take it lightly.

Comments

Chapter 4, "Building a Community Around Your Blog," explores more about comments in detail, mostly in terms of how they relate to building a community. For a personal blog, commentary is continuing the discussion or the story. As I said in Chapter 4, although individuals might leave comments that are inappropriate or abusive, the best way to engage them is to not engage them at all. Sadly, these sorts of comments are one of the dark sides of the Internet. I've known bloggers who have had serious run-ins with people who crossed the line, but these have been the glaring exceptions and not the rule. I have found comfort, solace, support, congratulations, and good laughs from the comments left on my blogs over the years. Rarely have I ever had a comment that strayed into the realm of troll, and when they did, the comments were so asinine that I let them stand as a testament to their own stupidity.

Although I started this section with the caveat of the bad things that commenters can bring, let me close with the good. I have found that when I have written deeply personal posts, ones that talk about life struggles or successes, the comments have always been the best parts of the posts. They have not only shown me the depth and warmth of the human spirit, but also that as a writer that I moved people. When the story I tell elicits the emotions in my readers that I felt while writing it, then "I done good." People relate to and comment on things like struggles with grief and loss but also successes. I've written about missing my father, but also how he is still my greatest inspiration (this book is dedicated to him). When I've written about topics that everyone can relate to, I get the best and most heart-warming comments. Enjoy your comments. They might very well be the best part of the blog.

Multimedia

In 2009, the World Wide Web turned 20 years old, and the Internet itself turned 40. From the beginning of the Web and the first websites, it was more than just text. Images and sounds played a huge role in bringing it to life. These days, seeing a site barren of pictures seems like an error, and often it is. Although you might not think your personal blog will contain "multimedia," you'd be wrong. Pictures, videos, music, and podcasts are all forms of multimedia that are getting richer and richer by the day—you're likely to find a use for at least some of them on your blog.

This section explores using pictures, video, and audio (podcasts) in your personal blog. In this chapter, I'm not going to delve into the how-to aspects of videos or podcasting—that's saved for Chapter 10, "Creating a Multimedia Blog." This chapter talks about what *most* people want to do—share things they find online (like YouTube videos) in their posts.

Pictures

Putting pictures, whether yours or ones you like by others, on your blog is one of the easiest ways to punch up your blog and add some color and spice. WordPress keeps making it easier and easier to add pictures into your posts, so the hardest thing might be taking the picture in the first place! Before discussing how you get a picture into your post, let's talk about copyright.

Make Sure You Have the Right to Post It

I know this seems like a really strange thing to say, but one of the biggest problems online is people posting and republishing images without the permission of the artist or even giving the artist attribution for the work. Clearly, this doesn't apply to photos you've taken or other works you create yourself, but it applies to pictures other people take and other art online. Often the easiest way to find out whether you can use the image is to look at the information around it. For example, I put this as part of the description of pictures I post online: ©Tris Hussey, 2009.

When you see "Non-commercial use permitted with attribution," it means that if you aren't a company who makes money through your website, you are free to re-post/use my picture as long as you give me credit. If you're a company, you're not allowed to use the image without my permission. Sometimes that permission comes with a price tag; sometimes not. I love to see my works used on my friends' websites. If someone really likes a picture I took of him or her, I can't think of a higher compliment than for that person to want to use it to represent himself or herself online. To do this, my friends ask me before posting the picture, and you should do the same for other artists.

Always remember that just because you found the picture online or in a Google Image search, it doesn't mean that you have the right to use the work of art. It doesn't even matter if your intentions are good (for example, promoting the artist), because in most cases it's illegal. So, look at the picture and determine what the "rights" are. See whether you can use it free and clear (public domain) or have limited rights (noncommercial use only) or all rights reserved (hands off, buddy). If you're not sure, you need to ask.

Posting and Sharing Pictures Online

Putting your pictures into your blog posts is only half the battle. Since the advent of the digital camera, the number of pictures people can take and save has become tremendous. Because the pictures are already digital, moving them from your computer to blog is a pretty straightforward process. What if you want to have whole albums online, or even just a whole bunch of pictures? The answer is right there on your computer.

First, start with iPhoto (Mac), Windows Live Photo Gallery (Windows), or Picasa (Mac and Windows), which are all great solutions for managing your pictures on your machine. iPhoto is pictured in Figure 5.22.

After you start organizing your pictures on your computer, you can then start posting them online as well. Lots of photo-sharing services exist out there, ranging from Picasa and Flickr to SmugMug and SnapFish. Each of them offers its own additional services, but in the end its core service is uploading your pictures to the Internet and sharing them. Most services enable you to mark the pictures public or private, title them, and share them with family and friends through email. Some additional services include grouping pictures into sets, tagging, editing, and requesting physical prints (and other items) of the pictures. When you view a photo-sharing site, look at what you get free versus what you have to pay for. Look at how long the company has been around and how many users it has. For example, Picasa is owned by Google, and Flickr is owned by Yahoo!. Both of these Internet giants aren't going anywhere anytime soon and have tens of thousands of users each. In my opinion, either of them is a safe bet. Personally, I use Flickr and have tens of thousands of pictures stored there.

FIGURE 5.22
A look at iPhoto and my collection of pictures.

> **TIP**
>
> There are a lot of popular online photo-sharing sites: Flickr (my preferred), Picasa, SnapFish, and SmugMug (more for pros).

Today's images from most digital cameras have very large file sizes, like 2–5 megabytes each, and dimensions of more than 4000×2000 pixels. Many blog engines, like WordPress, automatically create smaller versions for you, but the original is still stored on the server, taking up space in your account, and the server has to work pretty hard to resize those images. For my blog posts, I always resize images when I export them from iPhoto or other photo-management tools. I reserve my full-size, high-resolution images for Flickr.com, which is designed to host and manage high-resolution pictures.

Having your pictures online at one of these services does two things for you. The first is obvious—you can point readers easily to your set of pictures about your new project. The second is actually much cooler. You can often post pictures to your blog right from the online photo service. Flickr does a good job of enabling you to post all pictures as you upload them, or posting ad hoc as you need them. You can also get easy to copy and paste code for a given picture that you can use in a blog post (I usually do the latter).

Photo management tools like iPhoto and Picasa have an option to resize the picture when you export a copy to your hard disk. For a standard picture that you'd like to have people be able to click and see a larger version, having the longest edge scaled to 1500 pixels is fine. If you are going to put the image into a post, resize images to about 500 pixels max.

As a personal blogger, this saves you both time in uploading *and* server space because Flickr or Picasa are storing the actual file, not your server or host (this is very important for WordPress.com users). How do you get a picture into a post? That's what I'm going to show you next!

This an example of what this export process looks like in iPhoto.

Getting a Picture into Your Post

The good part is how to get those pictures into your post. Assume for this example that your picture is on your local drive. You've exported it from iPhoto or Live Photo Gallery (optional), and you've already resized it to fit your blog (optional). From there, use the following steps.

1. Click the Add Media button in the post editor (see Figure 5.23).

Add New Post
Enter title here
Upload/Insert
Add Media
Paragraph

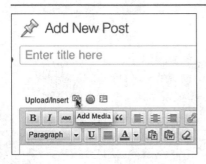

FIGURE 5.23
The Add Media button in the WordPress post editor.

2. Find the image on your hard drive. You should already know where the picture is, but if you're unsure, start your search in the My Pictures (PC) or Pictures (Mac) folders.
3. Drag the image file onto the window, and the image will be uploaded automatically (see Figure 5.24).
4. Adjust how it will appear (size, how the text wraps around it, and so on). This is where wrapping text around the image or having it stand alone comes in. What you're looking for are buttons or option buttons that say, for example, Align Left, Align Right, or No Alignment. Align Left puts the text on the right, and Align Right places text on the left (see Figure 5.25). When you're ready, click Insert into Post.

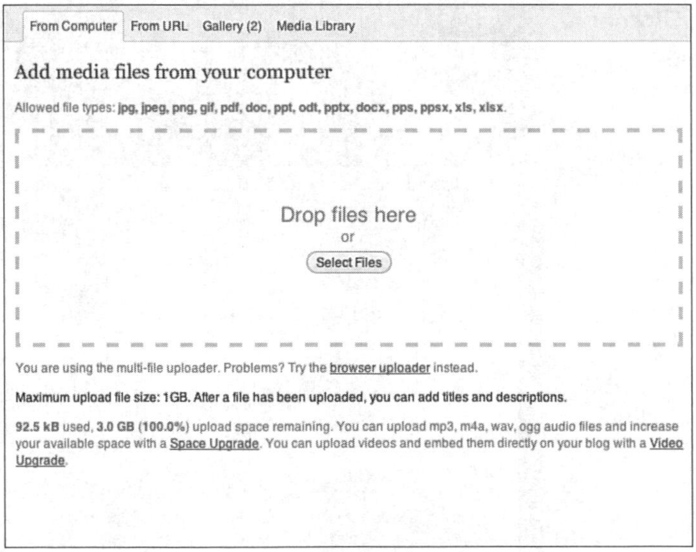

From Computer
From URL
Gallery (2)
Media Library
Add media files from your computer
Allowed file types: jpg, jpeg, png, gif, pdf, doc, ppt, odt, pptx, docx, pps, ppsx, xls, xlsx.
Drop files here
or
Select Files
You are using the multi-file uploader. Problems? Try the browser uploader instead.
Maximum upload file size: 1GB. After a file has been uploaded, you can add titles and descriptions.
92.5 kB used, 3.0 GB (100.0%) upload space remaining. You can upload mp3, m4a, wav, ogg audio files and increase your available space with a Space Upgrade. You can upload videos and embed them directly on your blog with a Video Upgrade.

FIGURE 5.24
Choosing a picture from your hard drive to upload to WordPress.

FIGURE 5.25

Adjusting image settings in WordPress.

The result should look something like Figure 5.26.

> **NOTE**
>
> When you upload an image, WordPress automatically does all the resizing for you. It creates a thumbnail, small, medium, and large versions of your image so it is less of an issue than it was previously, although I still resize images myself. It's just a good habit to be in!

That's pretty much it. It's not exactly rocket science, is it? People often feel that placing images in a post is difficult, but like most things, after you get the hang of it, it really isn't. If you'd like to make it harder on yourself, be my guest (maybe try doing it blindfolded), but I don't think you really need to do that.

As you get more comfortable with putting images in, you'll understand how and where to place images to give you the kind of look you're after in your post. It just takes practice.

FIGURE 5.26
Image in place in a draft post.

Adding Videos to Your Posts

As I said earlier, we'll get into *how* you create video blogs and podcasts in Chapter 10. In this section we're going to talk about how to add videos to your posts.

Even if you *do* wind up creating your own videos, you'll still need to know how to put them into posts. And let's face it, sometimes we want to embed a great video into our posts that *isn't* ours, but is just awesome.

Because putting video clips into posts has become so popular, the folks at WordPress have made it drop-dead simple. Let's go through it step by step:

1. Go to the video on YouTube and copy the URL of the video from the address bar (see Figure 5.27).

2. Start a new post and click in the post where you'd like to put the video. Paste the URL you copied in step one into the post area. You'll need a blank line above and below the URL you've pasted for this to work (see Figure 5.28).

FIGURE 5.27
Video on YouTube to put into a post. We'll copy the URL from the address bar at the top.

FIGURE 5.28
Pasting a YouTube video URL into a post.

3. When you're done, click Publish—and you're done! It's really that simple. You can see the result in Figure 5.29.

That's it. Really. I know lots of steps for basically copying and pasting a link. Regardless, I know lots of people who like to post short videos, just to mix things up a tad. Why not? It's pretty easy. So fire up that web cam and start recording. Movie Maker and iMovie have all the tools you need to get started.

Growing with WordPress.com

Chapter 2, "Installing and Setting Up Your Blog," explored the different ways to host a blog. Looking back at how I managed my blogs over the years, I don't think I would do too much differently. I started on Blogger, and then I bought a domain and used that with my Blogger blog until I moved to Blogware and

FIGURE 5.29

The result. An amazing YouTube video in a clever and witty blog post!

later to WordPress. Each step along the way, my blog grew as my blogging career grew. For most people, I suggest starting off with a WordPress.com blog. Get used to blogging and see whether you enjoy it. Dip your toes into the blogosphere a little at a time. If you think you'd like to be more serious about blogging, buy a domain name for yourself and pay for the domain mapping extra on WordPress.com.

If you grow beyond WordPress.com, shop around for a good web host and move your blog there. Moving a blog and domain is beyond the scope of this book, but trust me, it isn't hard. With each step along the path, you and your blog are growing with each other.

If you want to jump right in with both feet, or have a strong geek network to help you get set up, by all means buy a domain straightaway and sign up for a hosting plan. I caution you that you are putting money on the line for this. A good web host is about $10–12 a

month, plus your $10 a year for a domain. No, not a lot of money, but if you find yourself not blogging much after a month or two, you're paying for a blog to just sit there. However, if you start with WordPress.com, which is free, if you don't blog for a while, you haven't spent any money to keep that blog there.

There is a "middle way" that you might consider, as well, which are some of the paid upgrades through WordPress.com. In the three years since the first edition of this book, Automattic has made WordPress.com a real contender in the hosted blog market. Frankly, if I didn't need to have a hosting account to test new tools and services, I might very well just use WordPress.com with a simple domain upgrade (between $5–$12 a year) for all of my needs. Yeah, it's that good.

Figure 5.30 gives you a look at what some of the upgrade options are on WordPress.com, which you can check out from the Store menu.

FIGURE 5.30

Some of the upgrade options on WordPress.com.

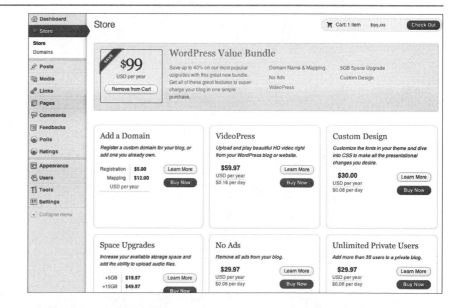

This is just something to think about.

There you have it. Everything you need to start a personal blog. Ready? Set? Blog!

Summary

Your personal blog is your own soapbox on the Internet, and building it is a rewarding experience. After deciding what you want to write about, even if it's just your day-to-day life and experiences, figure out whether you'd like to use a hosted blog service like WordPress.com or do it all yourself. After you have your blog set up, pick a theme that pleases you and get going!

Don't forget about your own levels of personal privacy and the privacy of those around you. It's a good idea to know how much you want to share online and where you're going to draw the line.

After you get going, you might like to start adding video and start podcasting. Remember it's fun and easy, and you might have everything you need to get going already! Most of all, have fun. Never lose sight of the fact that this is your space online and you are doing this to share your passions with the world, whatever they might be. That's how almost all bloggers started: They just wanted to tell their story.

CHAPTER 6

Creating a Business Blog

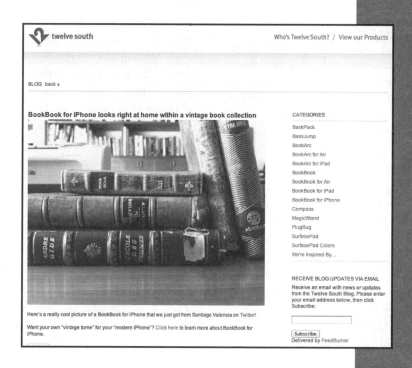

As described in Chapter 3, "Creating Content for Your Blog," in the beginning, all blogs were personal. Anything else just wasn't "blogging." In January 2005, all that changed—January 24–25, 2005 was the first Blog Business Summit. It was a watershed moment when people starting talking about not only the business of blogging (like being a professional blogger, which I already was at the time) but businesses using blogs to reach, connect, and communicate with their customers.

At the time, business blogging was something completely new and not terribly welcome in the blogosphere, but times have changed and businesses that don't have blogs and RSS feeds are getting left behind. However, not every business needs or should even have a blog. Part of the essential ethos of blogging is openness, transparency, and honesty. If your corporate culture cringes at an employee writing, "Yeah, we blew it on that one, but here's how we're going to fix it…" just stop here. If you're getting the dictum from on high that "We shall have a blog, and it shall be good. It shall be the best thing we've ever done," proceed with caution; the winds of corporate change can be fickle.

If you're getting the dictum from on high that "We shall have a blog, and it shall be good. It shall be the best thing we've ever done," proceed with caution; the winds of corporate change can be fickle.

Every company I've worked for since 2004 has had a blog, and I've generally been the primary blogger. Until recently, I've been working either at a tech, blogging, or media company, all of which need a blog to maintain competitive advantage in crowded markets, but when I started working for a retail computer chain, we knew that a blog was *essential* to reach customers. In fact, major retail chains like Best Buy and Future Shop (in Canada) have made blogs *an essential part of their marketing plans*. So, should your company have a blog? I'm going to say yes, even with the previous caveats. Remember, a blog is about writing. It's about expressing your passion for something. If you're really and truly passionate about what you do, you are probably your company's best cheerleader. Tell the world how proud you are. Tell the world when the CEO has been invited to speak somewhere. Just tell the world your thoughts on an industry topic, just to show the world how on the ball you are. Passion! Use your passion to make people take notice and think, "Wow, they've got it going on over there at John's Joinery Junction."

You might be worried that no one wants to know about your business and that you won't generate any traffic. Uh huh. You've got customers, right? Well, they probably want to know about your business. If you're an accountant, you can write about "The top 10 things you can do to make your accountant's life easier." Imagine how much easier your life would be if all your clients did that? Are you a lawyer? Write about the "Things to consider when writing a will" or "Are online will kits legal in my state?" I'm sure you can think of hundreds of questions and topics people ask you every day in your business. All of these questions can become the seeds for great posts—and posts that once written can stand the test of time (aka "evergreen").

Content

A business blog is a somewhat different animal than the personal blog discussed in the preceding chapter. You have a business reputation to uphold, and there is certainly some professional decorum to maintain. So "Pinup Fridays" probably isn't a good topic for you. Before you get too far into the "thou shalls and thou shall nots...," let's talk about writing.

Writing

Regardless of how good or bad a writer you *think* you are, chances are if you're thinking about writing a business blog, you're probably not a slouch in the writing department. Being a fairly decent writer is a core competency of everyone in business. With a personal blog, lapses in spelling, grammar, and structure can be overlooked, but on a business blog it reflects poorly on your business. You don't want a prospective client saying to themselves, "Jeez, they couldn't even spell check their posts. How will they handle my business?"

If you've had a personal blog for a while, it's time to step it up a notch. Time to break out Strunk and White's *Elements of Style* (required reading when I was in graduate school) and bone up on those rules of "affect" and "effect" and "further" and "farther."

You don't want a prospective client saying to themselves, "Jeez, they couldn't even spell check their posts. How will they handle my business?"

CAN A FICTIONAL ENTITY AUTHOR A BLOG?

This was a big question in the early days of blogging. Blogging stalwarts felt that only "real" people should be blogging, especially for a company. There were a couple notable character blogs that were pretty controversial at the time: the Denali Flavors Moose blog and T. Alexander from the Gourmet Station blog.

For a number of months, this was an all-consuming tempest in a teacup, with all sorts of name calling and unpleasantness; however, when it all blew over... Sure, characters can blog. It became clear that whether it was fan fiction or a company mascot assuming the role of "spokesperson," it wasn't who the "author" was purported to be, but rather what and how things were said.

Businesses find it helpful to have one "person" be the voice for the entire company, but have several folks write behind the scenes because there aren't enough people in the company to dedicate one person to blog. The hardest part of having multiple authors blogging is keeping the voice of the writing consistent. One easy fix is to divide up the tasks. Maybe only one person writes longer, more intricate posts, but others do things like a weekly post of interesting links, while still someone else does a photo of the week. Mix up the type of posts and the people writing them, and you'll have a dynamic blog with a lot less effort!

This doesn't mean that you can't write with energy and passion; it just means that you need to write with energy, passion, and correct grammar. Everyone has a story to tell—you just have to find the right voice to tell it. Finding that voice is that much harder when you have the constraint of having to be more formal than a personal blog, but constraints can lead to more creativity. It's going to take time and practice, but you'll get it. Your writing voice will come out and be heard, and when it does, it's an amazing feeling. So let's start breaking down the components of your writing.

Tone and Style

The tone and style of a business blog is always a tough thing to establish. I've been lucky because I've always blogged, even on my business blogs, with a similar tone and style as my personal blogs, but that's because I came in with a tone and style that people wanted. If you're starting out fresh, the best thing to do is pass the post around. This doesn't mean blogging by committee (a sure, slow, and painful death for any blog); it means sitting down with a few people, and probably the boss, and saying, "Okay, here are a few posts that I'd like to put up on the blog over the next week. Do these sound right to people?" Take their feedback seriously. You might be too informal in your posts, and you need to tone it down a little. Maybe the boss really likes your less-formal posts, but wants to keep them for an online "casual Friday" approach.

Many of the businesses I've worked for have been start–up companies with younger businesspeople running them. Sometimes, the posts could be too informal, this is when having older advisors can help you (and give you a smack upside the head, if needed). I can't give you a perfect rule for tone and style, but I can say that if you wouldn't say it out loud to the boss, then don't post it on the blog. Beyond that, you just have to go by what your gut tells you. Your gut is usually right.

Topics

The range of topics you can cover in a business blog are surprisingly broad. Yes, I have seen some posts on business blogs that make me wonder, "What were they thinking?" Very often, those posts magically disappear (funny that). However, by and large writing for a business blog is very much like being at a business networking event. When you meet someone for the first time, you introduce yourself and what you do. You might get into what your business does and what your industry is all about, but it's going to be pretty superficial stuff for sure. If the person is interested in your particular business or industry, he or she might ask you a specific question, which, being the polite person that you are, you will answer as best you can. If later in the evening you run into people who are also in your line of business, you might talk shop a little. What are the latest trends in your industry and what does everyone think about them?

Guess what? You have at least four solid posts right there. The following are some of my favorite business blog post topics:

- Description of your industry or niche
- Industry trends and your thoughts about them
- Answers to common questions about your business
- Current news (think informal press release with a link to the formal press release at the end)

- ▶ Community, charity, and volunteer work (see Figure 6.1)
- ▶ News from conferences

You get the idea. Very often, the stuff that you might otherwise brush off as boring are things people, potential customers in particular, find interesting.

FIGURE 6.1

Molson Coors Canada in the Community from its blog, which shows how large corporations give back to the community.

Online Press Kit

One of the greatest changes that blogging and social media has wrought has been its effect on how news is gathered, reported, and disseminated. Today not only journalists, but bloggers are looking for information on your company online. It is expected that at the very least you have your press releases on a section of your site (and a blog is a great place for them).

There is a lot of hype right now about the "social media press release" and how it is somehow different. My feeling is that you build your press materials (including photos, bios, and additional material) into a section of your blog. This does several things for you right off the bat. First, it makes the material much easier to update than traditional websites. Next, search engines find and index content much more easily (more on that later in the chapter). Finally, blogs are inherently social-media enabled. With simple plug-ins, like Share This (available for most blogging engines), readers can share your content via email, Facebook, Twitter, and many other social networks.

I am often frustrated at how little information businesses post about themselves *on their own websites*! If you want bloggers and mainstream media journalists (who often blog on their media outlets' websites) to write and comment about you, help them by providing the information. If you don't provide the information, bloggers will try to find it elsewhere, and it might not be accurate or up to date.

The virtual newsroom is a *great* way to leverage your blog and social media and can become a repository for all types of media on your company. I highly recommend that you at least give this a try.

Privacy

Although personal bloggers think about privacy in terms of themselves, their family and friends, and so on, for a business blog you have to add a layer of complexity. You want to be open and transparent (key rules for blogging), but at the same time not give away trade secrets. It can be a fine line between sharing information that helps sell your company and disclosing information that could put you at a competitive disadvantage to other companies that offer similar services.

Like a personal blog, other people in the company might not want to be included in the blog by name or at all, and you need to respect their privacy. If you are posting pictures from a company picnic or the like, make sure people are okay with that going up before you post it online.

> *You can't control what people do on their personal blogs per se, but it could be considered a fireable offense if an employee divulges sensitive information to the public.*

It's hard to say if privacy is more or less of an issue on a business blog versus a personal one. On one hand you *should* know better than to blab about company plans and strategies, but on the other hand there might be other people within your company who might not see things the same way and just do it on their own blogs. In a business blog, even if you have only one official blogger, you might have far more unofficial ones blogging on their own. If their own lines of personal privacy don't match yours, it can lead to trouble. An important

thing to do in these cases is for you or your manager to make it clear in your company's blogging policy what is expected of employees who blog, whether it's for the company or for their own personal blog. You can't control what people do on their personal blogs per se, but it could be considered a fireable offense if an employee divulges sensitive information to the public. If you are clear from the beginning, you significantly reduce that risk. As the unofficial blogging policy at Microsoft says, "Don't be stupid."

Comments

Chapter 4, "Building a Community Around Your Blog," explored comments, mostly in terms of how they relate to building a community around your blog. On a personal blog, commentary is continuing the discussion or the story. For a business blog, the people in the community are your customers and colleagues. Many business bloggers have found their greatest product champions through their blogs. If someone cares enough about your company or product to leave you a comment, *listen to it*! Even if it's something that you don't want to hear, like a product didn't meet expectations, listen and read. If you want to do what you do better, can you think of a better way to learn how than by getting comments straight from your customers? Feedback from someone who says, "I think your toasters are great, but the adjustment knob seems to go from untoasted to charcoal too easily. Can you put in finer gradations?" is gold! The person said that the toasters are great but...well, now you know an area to work on!

Encourage comments on your business blog by keeping comments open on posts, even if they have to be moderated (which is fair), and respond to all the comments on your posts within 24 hours (at most). Moderation can be a very important part of a business blog's comment system because you don't want inappropriate comments on your blog, ever. It doesn't matter if those comments reflect badly on the company or just one person. There are two simple and easy solutions to this issue: a comment policy and comment moderation. By default, most blog engines have comment moderation turned on, and the typical setting is that after one or two approved comments, that person's comments are posted without moderation. For a business blog, you might not want to take that risk, so keeping moderation on for everyone, all the time, is a sensible way to handle it. Therefore, you should make sure that in the comment form, you state that all comments are moderated and provide a link to your comment policy.

It's not unusual for commenters to complain that negative comments about a company aren't posted on a business blog. Sometimes fair, respectful criticism is a really good thing that you should allow. It shows that you, as a business, are open to change and criticism. However, comments filled with venom, obscenities, and *ad hominem* attacks aren't welcome on any blog, much less a business one. If valid points are intermixed with the vitriol, you might consider asking the commenter to resubmit the comment (giving guidelines for language, and so on). If the commenter declines, the original comment can be deleted without worry of offending someone.

A comment policy simply is writing out the level of decorum you expect on the blog. Continuing with the business networking

A SAMPLE BUSINESS BLOG COMMENT POLICY

How This Blog Brews

Cheers and welcome to the Molson Blog, a place where you can read some of the latest news about Molson in the Community across Canada. This blog is a place for respectful dialogue with Molson team members, Molson customers and anyone with an interest in our community and our beer.

Our hope is to create interesting conversations around Molson news, however, please remember that Molson works within a highly regulated industry, which means there are certain topics we won't be able to discuss here and comments relating to legal or regulatory matters will not be posted. Also please keep in mind that other community members may claim expertise or status (legal, medical, etc.) that they do not, in fact, possess, and use discretion in following their advice.

Respectful and sociable conversation is how we will approach this blog, and we ask that you respect the following discussion guidelines. All comments will be moderated and any comments falling outside of the discussion guidelines below will not be published.

Discussion Guidelines for Molson Blog Readers

Molson Blog aims to brew honest, friendly and courteous conversation. Please be respectful and civil to bloggers and others members of the community, even if you disagree with them.

Do not post anything that could offend another member of the community. Anything containing profanity, sexually graphic, or offensive language, etc. will be deleted. We do not allow harassing, threatening, racist, abusive, hateful, violent, or obscene language or behavior.

continues

Molson will decide (in its sole discretion) what is inappropriate for this blog. If you have complaints or questions regarding any of the content posted on this blog, please contact us.

Also note that:

1. Participation in, suggesting, or encouraging any illegal activity is cause for immediate deletion, and may be reported to the appropriate authorities.

2. Any articles, news reports, or other copyrighted material included in the posts must be with the permission of the relevant copyright owners.

3. Do not flood or spam, post chain letters, pyramid schemes, junk mail, or URLs for outside sites that violate any of these guidelines.

4. No commercial solicitation or advertising will be allowed.

Molson blog is about Molson's products and the community of Molson's customers. Please keep all comments related to the subject matter of the post as off-topic or spam entries will be immediately deleted. If you have a question or concern not relating to the topic of the post that you need to communicate to Molson, please contact 1-800-MOLSON1 to be directed to the best person to answer your question/comment.

We ask for your email address when you post a comment. Your email will never be published, but will be used to verify your comment and possibly to contact you in relation to your comment. We will not use it for any other purposes without your permission

—From the Molson Coors Canada Blog

function metaphor, there are rules that are followed in such a setting, such as topics that are allowed and not allowed, and what language is acceptable and what is over the line. Just make it clear that people leaving comments are doing so at your party in your living room and certain things will not be tolerated.

Blogging Policies

One of the hottest topics discussed at early business blogging conferences was company blogging policies. In larger companies like Sun Microsystems, Microsoft, and Boeing, employees were often writing personal/business blogs at work with the support and backing of their employer. Support didn't mean that the employees had carte blanche to do anything they pleased; it meant that employees wouldn't be fired out of hand for blogging, and often the company provided the technical resources to have a blog. In general, companies that originally started openly supporting their employees blogging were the ones that realized that the horse was already out of the barn and trying to stifle conversation would be worse than trying to monitor it.

Sun Microsystems had one of the best corporate blog policies going. It was a detailed document that covered the gamut of topics and scenarios that could arise for a blogger, everything from your picture you used on your site to how to criticize Sun products. Microsoft didn't have an official policy, per se, but had a mantra, "Don't be stupid," that covered the bases pretty well. Another piece of advice is if you don't feel comfortable with your boss/VP/manager reading that post, it's probably a good idea not to post it.

NOTE

Sun Microsystems led the business blogging/employee blogging charge for many years. Its blogging and comment policies are still referred to as best practices.

You can also implement an official or unofficial review and approval system where one person reads and approves posts before they go live. This can be frustrating for both the writer and the person approving the post. If time is of the essence, waiting for an approval is maddening. Likewise, if you're busy and you get three or four posts to review and the authors are clamoring to get the posts up right now, that might cause your blood pressure to go up a few points.

A mid point is just asking people to read the post before you post it, but if they are busy you might be told to post it and maybe edit later. That kind of arrangement develops over time as people trust that what you're posting is okay and is not going to get the company in trouble. At my company, bloggers read over each others' posts before they go live to check for typos, clarity, and formatting. I usually harp on adding tags and selecting the right categories for the posts, but that's my role in the company (as the primary blogger).

Like comment policies, the best blogging policies are the simplest ones. The more you try to define, outline, delimit, or constrain, the more questions you're going to have to deal with in the long run. Simple is good. Simple works. Simple is, well, simple. Sun Microsystems' blogging policy is an example of a great blogging policy. It is clear, detailed (but not overwhelmingly so), not written in legalese, and current.

IDEA GALLERY

http://blogs.oracle.com/jimgris/entry/sun_blogging_policy_evolves

SUN MICROSYSTEMS' COMPANY BLOGGING POLICIES

Sun Microsystems was acquired by Oracle in 2010. Although the original document remains as a "masterpiece" of policy, Oracle hasn't maintained a public version. The following is from the original version, and the link refers to a 2008 revision of the policy:

Sun Microsystems led the way with corporate blogging policies for many years, and today, I think it is still one of the best out there. It covers many common scenarios and questions, but without burying you in legalese. This blogging policy is available not only for Sun employees to read, but everyone else as well. The policy puts a clear stake in the ground on how it expects their bloggers to behave.

It's far too long to post in its entirety here, but here are a couple of relevant sections:

BE INTERESTING, BUT BE HONEST

Writing is hard work. There's no point doing it if people don't read it. Fortunately, if you're writing about a product that a lot of people are using, or are waiting for, and you know what you're talking about, you're probably going to be interesting. And because of the magic of linking and the Web, if you're interesting, you're going to be popular, at least among the people who understand your specialty. Another way to be interesting is to expose your personality; almost all of the successful online voices write about themselves, about families or movies or books or games; or they post pictures. People like to know what kind of a person is writing what they're reading. Once again, balance is called for; a community site is a public place and you should avoid embarrassing the company and community members. One of Sun's core values is integrity, so review and follow Sun's Standards of Business Conduct in your online community contributions.

Sun's blogging policy might seem a little intense, but remember that this is a company built on geeks. Geeks like detail and know how to handle lots of different scenarios.

Multimedia

When I say, "business blog," you might not automatically think "multimedia rich," but that's selling the potential of these blogs short. There are hundreds of easy ways to pull in pictures, audio, and video that not only liven up your posts, but also help make your point. I'm going to look at multimedia from the standpoint of busy business people whose job isn't to shoot video, take pictures, or record podcasts all day. I take a simple, pragmatic approach to multimedia, so don't worry about me telling you to turn an office into a recording studio. Adding pictures to illustrate a point or show off a product is obvious, but what about video and podcasts? As you get more and more into blogging, you might feel the desire to record a podcast or video interview. Just roll with it; audio and video are easy to record and post online. Be creative and note what other business blogs in your niche are doing. Imitation is the sincerest form of flattery! Learn from others and you might find yourself doing amazing things on your blog you might not have considered before.

Pictures

Business blogs are not usually associated with having lots of pictures in the posts, but remember, sometimes a picture tells... You get the idea. The most important things to remember when posting a picture online are

- Do you have the rights/permission to post it, and if you do, have you attributed the photo to the artist correctly?

- How big is the file you are uploading? Remember to check the height and width and the number of kilobytes the picture takes up.

- Did you insert the picture into the post correctly so it looks good?

Make Sure You Have the Right to Post It

As a business, you are under the section of "commercial use" under copyright law. For example, nearly all my pictures posted on Flickr are marked as noncommercial use only, a topic covered extensively in Chapter 5, "Creating a Personal Blog with WordPress.com." Essentially that means to you as a business blogger: Hands off, unless you ask and receive permission first.

Posting and Sharing Pictures Online

Depending on your business, you might like to upload pictures to one of the Internet photo-sharing sites like Flickr, SmugMug, Picasa, or SnapFish. The benefit of using a service is that you are, essentially, backing up your pictures to an offsite server, and it makes posting your pictures online a bit easier. Photo-sharing sites give you easy-to-code html codes for embedding individual pictures into posts or your blog. For example, if you were just at a tradeshow and wanted to show off your booth, having the pictures on Flickr is a great way to share them. If you create software, having your screenshots and other visual materials not only makes it easier for you to use the pictures, but

Flickr becomes another touch point for search engines to index your content.

Other than that, however, for most businesses, having photos on a photo-sharing site is a nice to have feature, but not a need to have. There are, of course, exceptions. If your business is involved in the arts, or is involved in tourism, or can otherwise benefit from heavy use of photos, having an account with a capable photo-sharing site can be helpful. As previously mentioned, many of the software companies I know and work with host their screenshots on Flickr. Photo-sharing sites are for more than vacation and baby photos; these are great places to archive images and gain additional search engine traction.

If you'd like to learn more about photo-sharing sites, Chapter 8, "Creating a Visual Artist's Portfolio Blog," has more in-depth information on these services. I recommend Flickr as a photo-sharing site for businesses and personal users. Creating a Flickr account is as simple as creating a Yahoo! account (Vancouver-born Flickr is owned by Yahoo!, Inc.). After creating your Flickr account, I strongly recommend upgrading to a Flickr Pro account for about $25 per year. You receive unlimited uploads per month as well as unlimited sets of photos. The cost is a real bargain and unlocks the power of Flickr for you.

Some businesses might also want to have a Flickr *group* to which the public can contribute. A good example of this is the group I set up for the Vancouver International Airport Authority (YVR) to let plane spotters and other aviation enthusiasts contribute their own pictures (see Figure 6.2). Initially the group was closed and

ABOUT CREATIVE COMMONS

The Creative Commons (CC) system is a universal, iconographic depiction of what the usage license is for a particular work. CC uses symbols to represent things like commercial use permitted or not, attribution required or not, and derivative works permitted or not and on what conditions. For example, my Creative Commons license for my photos looks like this:

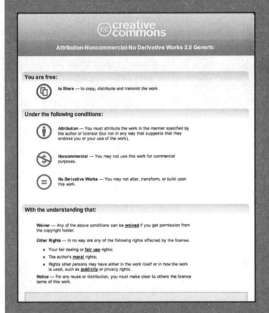

It means Attribution-Noncommercial-No Derivative Works. In English this means that you may use my works as long as you give me credit and it is for noncommercial use only. You may not take my work and use it as a part of another work.

Some people in the intellectual property field feel that CC isn't worth the paper it's printed on, and there are too many loopholes to make it effective. I think it's better than nothing and it makes a clear statement about my intentions.

In the end, as a business blogger, if the work says "noncommercial," it's off limits unless you ask the artist. If you want to use such work for your commercial blog, you are likely to have to pay for a license to use the work.

by invitation only, but as YVR became more comfortable with the group, and *crowdsourcing* in general, the restrictions were opened up.

NEW TERM

Crowdsourcing is tapping into the Internet at large for feedback, content, or help. Crowdsourcing helped YVR find new and diverse images for the airport terminal by just searching and asking the photographer's permission. The additional cost was limited because many people were flattered to have their pictures displayed at Canada's second largest airport!

Inserting Images into Your Posts

One of the best things about using blog engines is that they are so utilitarian. The process for putting an image into a business

blog post is the same as a personal blog. Refer to Chapter 5 when you're ready to put an image in your post.

Logos and Corporate Images for the Media

As a blogger, when reviewing a company's product, I often need pictures of that product to use in my posts. I *could* try to find them elsewhere online, but wouldn't it be better if they provided images for me? The same goes for your company logo, pictures of your executive team, and anything else a blogger or reporter might need to do a story on you. You might not want to put the giant print-ready images on your site, but you can put web-scaled versions (images about 600 pixels wide are perfect) and contact information for higher resolution images, if needed.

FIGURE 6.2

The YVR Connections Flickr group showing just some of the user submitted pictures.

Don't dismiss this out of hand, even if you are a small business. What if the local paper wants to do an article on you and they need a picture? Wouldn't you rather they have a really good picture that you *like* than something they find online or send the photography intern to shoot? That's what I thought. Make this a part of your digital newsroom that I talked about earlier in this chapter, and you are well on your way to using a blog for serious business.

Podcasting

We've all had those moments when we're writing an email and reach the point where we stop and think, "This would be easier if I called…" That's just one of the aspects of podcasting—saying more than you could easily write out. How about a short interview with people at your company? I use podcasts to educate and teach people about WordPress. I record a few short WordPress tips and post them. When people are searching for WordPress information, find it, and listen to it, they might learn something and think "I think this guy might be able to help me."

Certainly, not everyone is comfortable recording his or her voice, but if you have aspects of your business where your employees or customers *could* benefit from an audio tutorial or news break (think of people listening to their iPods on the way to work), you might give it a shot.

As I mentioned in Chapter 5, I'm going to cover all the ins and outs of podcasting—and video blogging—in Chapter 10, "Creating a Multimedia Blog." This chapter whets your appetite for getting into podcasting and Internet radio.

Internet Radio to Build Your Business

You've heard your share of "industry experts" on the radio, TV, and so on, right? Now is your chance to *be one*. Using services like TalkShoe or BlogTalkRadio, you can have your own call-in show online, whenever you want. Like all Internet services, both services take only a couple minutes to set up. Both have free plans (TalkShoe only has free plans) so there is no harm in trying both of them out to see which you like better. Chapter 10 will go over how these services work, but let's see how they work for a business blog. In fact, I'll tell you how *I* used them in *my* business blogging.

I had a weekly show on BlogTalkRadio for almost a year. My business partner Jim Turner (Genuine Dad) talked about the latest news in social media and had a number of high-profile people as guests. We used the show as an industry roundtable. The purpose of the show wasn't for direct selling or pitches; it was to expand our profile and reach. It worked. The show ended up serving two purposes: Clients listened to it during the pitch phase, and it was a service we offered to clients. Jim and I helped clients set up their own shows and even be guests on the shows, so we could help them get established.

Jim and I barely scratched the surface with using Internet radio for business. We could have sold advertising spots on air, and we could have done special "training" episodes to sell, but we didn't. Don't get me wrong—that's fine; we were making the choice to do it how we were doing it. Lots of other businesses are going the extra mile in their shows and being far more commercial, and I think that's great.

Having a show where you get to be the host, have guests call in, and have live text chat is a potential gold mine for advertisers and potential business leads for you. You might be thinking about now that no one would be interested in your show. I think you're wrong. Do you have industry trade shows? Association meetings on a regular basis? When you sit and talk shop with people, don't you wish you could capture all that great discussion for later?

Now imagine firing up the speakerphone, calling in, and having a live show from the convention floor. How about an interview with someone well known in your industry? With a podcast you can do that, no problem, and then edit the show later. With something like BlogTalkRadio or TalkShoe, you can do it right then and there. Live radio at its best.

I encourage you to at least try a couple of shows. If you have cheap or unlimited long-distance calling, I don't think you have anything to lose. You might, in fact, get bitten by the radio bug like I did.

Video

Business and online video aren't two things that many people put together; however, more and more businesses are using simple, easy videos as ways to showcase who they are and what they do. With today's low-cost video cameras, it is easy to shoot a video you can be proud to post online. I recommend that businesses put some time and effort into a video that they are going to post online. A little work in iMovie or Windows Movie Maker goes a long way to separate your video from the waterskiing squirrels. Both programs are very easy to use, and I cover them in more detail in Chapter 10.

Show People How It's Done with a Screencast

One great application of video on a business blog is the use of *screencasts* of your product or service in the form of how-to videos. Suppose you have an online order form and are getting a lot of questions about how to use it; you could record a little video with a voice-over explaining the form and demonstrating how to fill it out properly. An example I often see, and refer to often myself, is when you have a piece of software that you'd like to explain. Nothing explains how to use a piece of software like watching and listening to someone use it.

If your business does anything related to computers (online order forms, software, websites, and so on), a screencast can tremendously reduce the number of questions you have to field. Screencasts even work for employee training or explaining the steps to do something on the computer. I think after you start using screencasts for your blog, you'll find yourself using them for more and more things.

> **NEW TERM**
>
> A screencast is a video recording of a computer screen. It's great for all sorts of uses, whether it's showing off an application or explaining how to use a program or website.

One of the best screencasting applications I know (and use) is called Jing (www.jingproject.com) from Techsmith (the makers of Camtasia and Snagit). Jing is a free screencasting and screenshot program both for PCs and Macs. Jing is dead simple to use and makes recording a screencast easy. There aren't a lot of bells and whistles to it, but as a starting point, you can't beat it. If you find that you need more than what Jing has to offer, its big brother Camtasia is available both for Macs and PCs and is a very powerful and easy screencasting tool (see Figure 6.3).

Posting Online

So you have this great video of your CEO being interviewed by the local paper, and you want to post it online. What do you do? Although there are many alternatives to YouTube (Viddler, Blip.tv, and Flickr), some of which have "professional" or "premium" plans that offer more options and sometimes the capability to upload larger videos, YouTube is *the* destination for people searching for video. You might think that using YouTube isn't "professional" enough, but you'd be wrong. Because you can now customize your YouTube profile and channel your page to your liking, your space on YouTube can look great and reflect

well on you as a business. Like photo-sharing sites, putting your videos on YouTube gives your company another SEO boost. Your company name, link to your website and blog, plus all the other data you include with the videos can only *help* you be indexed by search engines and found by potential customers.

Because everyone wants to post videos into his or her blogs, at least at one time or another, blog engines have all made inserting a video into a post as simple as copying the URL of the video from your browser's address bar and pasting it into a simple tool in the post editor. Chapter 5 has all the steps you need (which just consist of copying and pasting a link) to get your YouTube masterpiece into your posts.

Chapter 10 covers how to record and edit videos, so until then, think of all the ways a short video could help your business and customers. Believe me, there are video applications for almost all businesses.

FIGURE 6.3
Camtasia for Mac in action as I record taking a screenshot to email to a friend.

Building and Hosting Your Business Blog

Chapter 2, "Installing and Setting Up Your First Blog," discussed where to host your blog and a little about choosing a host as well. In Chapter 5, I recommended starting out with WordPress.com because it's free and easy, but for business bloggers, I recommend stepping things up a notch or two.

Choosing to use WordPress.com is still a great option, especially if you don't want to have to bother with web hosts and servers, but you should at the very least purchase a domain name and sign up for the premium domain mapping option. This gives you a blog that has the address of www.yourgreatbusiness-blog.com, but still has the comfort of knowing that you have all of WordPress.com and Automattic's support staff behind you. If you want to podcast, purchase the extra space option as well. Now, if you start to do the math, you might find that it is better to pay about $10–15/month for a web host of your own.

> **TIP**
>
> Remember that WordPress.*com* is the hosted service. WordPress.*org* is where you download WordPress to install yourself on your own web host.

You still need to purchase a domain name (you were going to do that regardless, right?), but with a web host secured you can easily host your own podcast files. Additionally, on WordPress.com, you are limited to the available themes and you can't install additional plug-ins. You have neither of these restrictions when you have your own web host.

Although I know a number of business bloggers that use WordPress.com, personally I think it is well worth the investment to have your own web host. If you already have a website, you might just be able to add a blog onto it for no additional cost per month. You just need to install WordPress yourself (or find someone to help you with it) to have your blog up and running in short order.

Choosing a Template for Your Business Blog

A business blog has to look professional, so choosing the right template is critical. There are thousands of free themes and templates available for WordPress, Movable Type, and Drupal blogs. There are also hundreds of premium themes you can purchase. With either option, look at free themes first. You want to find something that complements your company's image and doesn't look like everyone else's blog. Starting with free options gives you a fantastic range of options that you can quickly review and try out. This way, if you later opt to pay for a custom theme, you have a much better idea of what you like and don't like.

Theme developers are becoming more and more sophisticated in how their themes are built and what additional features they offer. Some themes now have built-in SEO tools, media galleries, and choices of layouts. It is well worth your time looking at the range of blogs out there and what themes they are using (look at the bottom of a blog's page for a link to the theme developer's site). I think you'll be very surprised to see how many "regular websites" are actually built on top of WordPress and Movable Type.

Stats

I discussed blog stats in Chapter 2, and here, I want to add that your boss will want to know what's going on pretty often. Google Analytics has an easy way to keep your boss informed of all the latest info on the blog. Look for the email button located above a report (I usually choose the main dashboard report) and click it. There, you can choose to send out a one-off email or schedule reports to be emailed out periodically (see Figure 6.4).

Business bloggers should also leverage the power of Google Blog search to see who is linking to you and talking about your posts. It's a very simple search to do, and you can add that search to your RSS reader and check it frequently. In Figure 6.5, you can see I entered "link:trishussey.com" into Google Blog Search (http://www.google.com/blogsearch), and it returned a list of all the posts that linked to my personal blog.

FREE VERSUS PREMIUM THEMES

In your search for themes, it's not going to take long before you come across links, banners, and ads for premium themes in which you might wonder if paying money for a theme is worth it. Personally, I use both free and premium themes in my work. Often, premium themes are better designed, better supported, and better coded than their free brethren. However, free themes are, well, free and you can't beat that price. My advice is for your first blog, stick to free when you're starting out. See how you like "this blogging thing" and take it from there. I suggest giving premium themes a serious look though after a short while. The professional and polished look of the premium themes is well worth the price. Of the current crop of theme designers, I really like the themes from Studiopress.com (I have developer licenses for their suite of themes that give me access to all their themes). The developers and designers of StudioPress themes are great. Using themes from StudioPress has saved me hours of development time on projects. As a business blogger, you get the benefit of a professionally designed, technically sophisticated, and *supported* (you can ask questions if something doesn't look or work correctly) theme.

Look at free themes, and then look at premium themes to see whether they both match your budget and the look and feel you want for your blog.

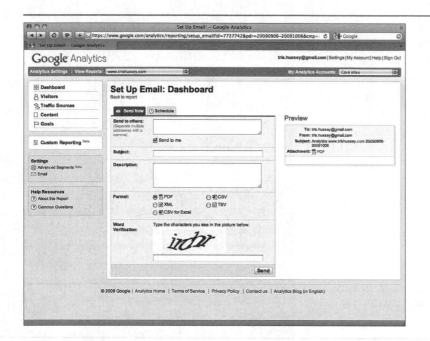

FIGURE 6.4

The scheduled report page at Google Analytics—a great way to keep people informed of how the blog is doing.

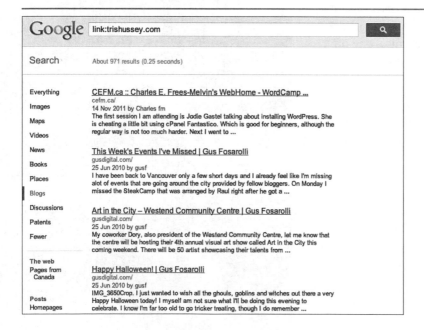

FIGURE 6.5

Google Blog search looking for links to my personal blog.

Think about your blog stats in a larger fashion. Getting tied up in specific numbers will, I promise, drive you crazy. Look at the trends. Are visits and page views increasing or decreasing? Are there certain days that have more traffic than others? Are certain search terms being used to find your blog that you find surprising? (On my personal blog, "yam fries recipe" is often number one, and I posted about that only once!)

These are the stats and metrics that will really matter in the longer term. If you concentrate on writing great content and engaging with your readers, and the rest will work itself out.

Summary

Although a personal blog is all about you, a business blog is all about your business. Choosing to start a business blog is opening a conversation with your customers, colleagues, and the world. This might seem like a scary thing at first, but the rewards can be tremendous. Having a direct line out to the world to talk about your successes, new products, and even let people see the human side of your business is advertising that money can't buy.

Because you already know what you're going to talk about, the next step is setting up the blog. I always recommend that businesses buy a domain name. Even if you use a hosted service like WordPress.com, ensure that your blog is using your domain name. I also recommend running your business blog on a regular web hosting account so you have complete flexibility and control over the look and feel of your blog, and you have the freedom to expand into podcasting or video blogging without very many barriers in front of you.

Don't forget to consider implementing a blogging and comments policy for your company (if one doesn't exist already). Because this is the public face of your company online, you need to make sure you put your best foot forward.

Regardless of all these considerations, this is still your place to show off your business and show the world what you know and think about your field in general. Just get out there and say your piece, show your passion for what you do, and share with the world.

CHAPTER 7

Creating a Website

Isn't This a Blogging Book?

Right now you're probably wondering if you're still reading the same book. I mean, "Creating a Website"? Isn't this a book about creating a *blog*? Well, yes, it is a book about creating blogs, but here's the interesting thing that I learned in the four years since I started to write the first edition of this book—after people start using tools like WordPress to blog, they ask the next logical question: Can I make a "regular" website with this tool, too? This chapter comes as a result of presenting a seminar at WordCamp Whistler (B.C.) in 2009 and teaching one-day workshops for the University of British Columbia on the process of using WordPress to create a website. I decided to include this chapter in this book about creating your own *blog* because I felt that many people—especially freelancers, small-business people, and similar folks—could benefit from seeing how they could combine a personal/business/portfolio blog with a larger website. It's all about consolidating your efforts while making your online presence *more attractive* to search engines.

So, yes, this *is* a blogging book, but it's also a book about building your online presence, and no online presence is really complete without a website to serve as a home base.

Blog Engines to Run Websites

The idea to have a blog engine to run a website isn't new at all. In fact, before there were blogs (per se), large companies were building websites using *content management system (CMS)*. Using CMS allowed companies to train employees how to update the website's content without the need to teach them how to under-

stand and learn HTML (the code behind websites). As you already know, bloggers figured this out as well, and simple CMSes were built to power blogs. Originally, blogs couldn't support content like static pages (the WordPress Page content type), nor could they have static content be the home page of a blog. It wasn't until blog engines grew to include these two features that we could *consider* using a blog engine to make a website.

> **NEW TERM**
>
> A content management system is web software that separates content, which is stored in a database, from its "look and feel", which is drawn from templates. Blog engines are, in fact, just content management systems (originally) geared toward a particular purpose—blogging.

After blogs crossed that chasm into a world where creating a "website" using a "blog engine" wasn't just a pipe dream, blog engines—WordPress especially—started to mature at an amazing rate. It seemed that *bloggers* were getting pretty tired of having to maintain two websites (a blog and a "regular" website) too, just as companies were getting tired of corporate CMS platforms that cost tens of thousands of dollars to buy, run, and maintain. Everyone wanted the easy, convenience, and multimedia savvy of blogging engines in their websites. But there was another factor that *really* tipped the scales in the blogging engine's favor—Google's love of blogs.

Blogs Are the New Websites

I've talked about this in other chapters, so this isn't a new revelation for this book, but Google (and search engines in general) *love* blogs. When consultants, freelancers, writers, and other bloggers realized how much more search engine traffic blogs could generate, their blogs became their websites. There was a time, short lived, thankfully, that tech pundits were saying that the era of the website was over and all you needed was a blog. Truthfully, we all knew that there was still a need for basic, static content on any site. For your personal blog, that is often your About page; for businesses, it could be any number of things (contact us, company info, product pages, and so on), so although having *only* a blog hasn't replaced having a website, using a *blog engine* is slowly replacing other ways to build websites.

If you don't believe me, look carefully at how WordPress.com and WordPress (the DIY version) describe things on setup and settings pages. Whereas in 2008, you were creating a new "blog" and your "blog name" and "blog address," today the term "blog" has for the most part been replaced by "site" throughout the WordPress interface, code, and setup.

Let Technology Help You

If you've been following along with this book and have created a WordPress.com account or have installed WordPress yourself, you've figured out that none of the "techie stuff" is very hard. If you've picked a few different templates to try and switched them around, you've learned how quickly and easily you can change the look and feel of your site. If you've played with posting content, including putting

a movie or image in a post, you know that even creating and posting isn't hard, either. It comes down to this: Using a blog engine to build your website is letting technology do the hard work for you. If you don't like the header image on your site, upload a new one. If you want different widgets on your sidebars (or header or footer or wherever your theme allows them), then change them. Essentially, blog engines have made a lot of the tough technology aspects of running a website easy. This, then, leaves you to worry about one thing—content.

It's About the Content

This is probably the only part of the process of creating a website (or a blog) that I can't really help you with. We've talked about content in Chapter 3, "Creating Content for Your Blog," and creating content for your "website" is no different than creating content for a blog. Sure the *intent* might be a little different, but the goal is the same—to inform and explain to others what you're about. One of the suggestions that I make for people who are starting off creating a website using a blog engine is to worry about the theme last. It's far too easy to get caught up in picking this theme or that, this color or that one, or magazine or traditional style that you forget that you need content to fill out a site. A great theme is empty without content. So, work on creating and figuring out your content *first*; then, when you have a good handle on what sections you'll need, and maybe have some placeholder content written, you can start picking a theme knowing that you have some content to fill it out.

Does a Website Have to Have a Blog, Too?

When I'm showing people how to use WordPress to create a website, I'm always asked if you have to have a blog with your website. The answer is simple: no. In this context, when I'm talking about a "blog," I'm talking about the regularly posted entries about a particular topic. Ironically, I've found that some of the best websites built on blog engines have their "blog" as a separate website entirely. Sometimes, working in the needs of what you want in a *blog*, even how the blog looks and behaves itself, clashes so much with how you want your *website* to look that it's easier to have the blog and website portions of your online presence be separate sites. Yes, this goes against how I introduced the chapter, but you'll see that, in fact, the evolution of having two websites (blog and website), then one website (website and blog merged together), then back to two websites shows how we've come to understand how different content needs to be displayed differently *and* that because it's so easy to maintain a website using a blog engine, it isn't that much additional work to have one website that is more static (your main website) and another that is more dynamic and more frequently updated (your blog).

Getting Started: Technology

As with all of this book, I'm going to use WordPress as the example for building a website. Also, instead of using WordPress.com to build the website, we're going to go with the install WordPress yourself route. Although you can certainly build a website using WordPress.com, I've found that many people feel hampered by the limited number of "website focused" themes on WordPress.com. Remember, too, that you cannot edit the theme itself on WordPress.com. Yes, you can edit some aspects of the look and feel through a paid add-on; however, when customizing a website, you often need to go beyond that level of customization. Finally, many people building websites with WordPress.com find they need a few more features (e-commerce, forums, slide shows, for example) than WordPress.com has to offer, so being able to find and install plugins is essential to making their website what they need.

Domain Name

For this section, we're going to proceed with the premise that you want your own domain for your website. Again, you can use WordPress.com and have yourcompany.wordpress.com and later (or immediately) buy the domain and use it with WordPress.com, but for the reasons given earlier, I think that many people will outgrow WordPress.com when used as their primary website. Buying a domain is also part of having a professional presence and bearing online. Refer to Chapter 2, "Installing and Setting Up Your First Blog," on how to choose the right domain for you.

Host

If we're going to install WordPress, we need a place for the files to go. I've talked with a lot of people who go to WordPress.org, download WordPress from there and then wonder what to do next. Is this how you maintain a blog you have? Do you just have a blog now by down-loading the software? None of those things are the case. As discussed in Chapter 2, you need a host for your WordPress files to live on and run. Chapter 2 also goes over how to pick a good host and offers suggestions of hosts to use. WordPress.org also maintains a list of hosts that they recommend here: http://word-press.org/hosting/.

Platform

Although I chose WordPress for this example because I think it's the easiest for the novice to set up, configure, use, and maintain, WordPress isn't the only game in town. Many people build great websites using CMS similar to WordPress, such as Drupal, Movable Type, and Joomla. If you don't want to use WordPress (or have hired someone to help you who prefers Drupal, for example), don't worry; many of the general concepts discussed here still apply. Drupal works a little differently from WordPress, but as far as building a website using a CMS goes, Drupal (and all other blog engines) follow similar philosophies.

After you've purchased your domain and have found a good host, you're ready to get started. You might think that the next thing I'm going to talk about is installing WordPress—but you'd be wrong. We'll get there (and we're going to take the easy route, too), but first you need to think about what content is going to go into your new website. If you have an exist-ing website, now is a great time to step back and take a fresh look at what you already have published. If you don't have a website, this is an *essential* exercise to go through to get your new website off on the right foot.

Getting Started: Content

Content is king (or queen), so they say about the online world, so if that's true (psst, it really *is* true) the single most important thing you can do is to plan your content for your website before you do anything else. This doesn't need to be a tedious exercise involving offsite meet-ings, trust-building games, or breakout groups. Planning your content is often as simple as taking out a pad of paper (yes, I said paper) and starting to write down the sections that you'll need in your website. Don't get caught up right now in deciding whether the pieces are in the right order or if you have a hierar-chy established—just start jotting things down. By the way, the other great thing about build-ing a website with WordPress (or other CMS) is that nothing is set in stone. If you need more (or fewer) sections later, or if you need to move things around to different "sections," it's not a problem. With a couple of clicks—or, at worst, copy and paste— you're done. In the "Building" portion of the chapter, I'll talk about how to plan for expansion and changes.

Story

As you've been getting all the content sections down on paper, I hope you start (even uncon-sciously) thinking about the *story* you're going to tell through your website. No, I don't mean story as in, "Once upon a time there was a lonely geek who longed for a geek girl…"; I mean the larger message that you want your visitors to get when they go through your website. Is it that you offer the best service or the best widget or products—or what? It's the overarching story that will help guide you through the rest of the process of building the website. Everyone has a story. Now is the time to put your content together so that story comes to life. I know this sounds a little "out there," but when I've been asked to help people "fix" a "broken" website, one of the biggest problems was that there wasn't a story or common thread to the site. I know you have lots to say, and you want your website to say everything you want. The trick is to weave all the things you want to say into something that makes sense. When a website makes "sense," it's easier for people to find what they are looking for and understand what you're all about.

Sections

Now that we have content and you're thinking about what your story is, it is time to start putting some structure into those sections. I'm sure many of you have been doing that automatically, but for a lot of people it's just easier to dump all the ideas on the table (so to speak) first and *then* organize things. Step 1 is to look at what you have put down for content and sections and compare that with your story. Think about the big groups that you'll want to organize your content into. Maybe limit yourself to five big sections at first, and then add more if you feel that one section is getting too large. For example, you might have big sections like these: About Us, Products, Locations, Careers, and Resources. Those are pretty big buckets that should hold *most* of what you have to say. You work through the sections that make sense for you, then start putting the pieces in underneath those big sections. Sometimes a subsection will need a sub-subsection, and that's okay. Just don't try

to split things too finely, or you might wind up with a lot of pages with a sentence or paragraph where some of those pages could have been combined.

Think of this as an iterative process. Take a crack at the organization, put it down, then come back to it. Remember, nothing is set in stone here, and if you find that some pieces fit under two or more big sections, don't worry! You aren't going to have to create the content twice—you'll just link to it from several places. If nothing else, building a website this way is *flexible*. You don't have to worry that you got it right the first time.

At some point you're going to hit a crucial piece of content—Copyright and Privacy, for example—that doesn't fit in any section. That's okay, there are *always* a few pieces of important content that don't fit into the overall site. Those pieces will sit outside the overall structure, and I'll be willing to bet that those pieces of content are the ones that are often stuck in the footer of sites.

Required Content

Before we move on to the "building" process, don't forget the little pieces of content we often forget to include: contact us, privacy policy, terms of use, and so on. Yes, many people don't have to worry about those, but if you're building website for a company, you do. The funny thing about pieces of "required content" is that you often don't realize they are required until the last minute. Ironically, these are often the pieces of content that take the longest to come up with.

Getting Started: Installing WordPress and Other Key Components

Now that the process of getting your content in order is coming along—it's a *process*, it's almost never complete—it's time to create the place for the content to live. It's time to start setting up your website itself. As I said in Chapter 2, although you can install WordPress yourself, I've found in the past few years, there are fewer and fewer reasons for people to do it themselves. In fact, as most of the basic maintenance functions have become automated, it has become less important for *most* users to understand the inner workings of WordPress. Like the rest of this book, I'm going to focus on all the things you can do—and there is *tons* you can do—without knowing the inner workings of WordPress or how to code.

This section of the chapter is very much like the previous chapters that talked about creating different kinds of blogs. Because you have already read how to create a Post, a Page, and how those interfaces work, I'm not going to belabor those points. What I *will* discuss is how to best use the various content types to give you a clear, coherent, and easily maintainable website.

Installing WordPress

Follow the process outlined in Chapter 2 for installing WordPress through a "one click" or "easy" install on your host. As I said in Chapter 2, that's going to be great for most people. Sure, a professional web developers like to upload and install manually, but that's just overkill. Don't forget, unlike WordPress.com-based websites, *you will need to keep WordPress and all the plugins updated yourself*. The update process

is a simple, one-click (or two at most) affair, so don't worry about needing to do it; just remember that you will periodically *need* to do it. I'll cover updates in the "Maintaining" section at the end of this chapter.

After WordPress is installed on your host and you have your site up and running, what's next? You're pretty much ready to get started, right? (If you've read Chapter 2, you know there isn't much additional configuration needed at this point.) Almost. One of the things I glossed over in Chapter 2 was *installing* themes and plugins. I talked a little *about* them, but not really how you *find them and install them*. Because one of the important (maybe essential) parts of building a website with WordPress is being able to tap into the wealth of plugins and themes that are available—many of which are geared toward the "WordPress as website" crowd—I probably should pass that wisdom on to you now.

Installing Plugins

At this point you might be thinking, "Hold on, throughout this book you've been saying how great WordPress.com is. How *most* people don't need more than is offered there." That is true. *Most* people *don't* need much (if anything) more than what is offered at WordPress.com to have a great blog, even a great business blog. However, I've found that although using WordPress.com to build a traditional "website" is doable, and you can get a great result (and this is what I teach in the classroom), many people who want websites also want more flexibility, features, and customizations than WordPress.com allows for (even if you pay for premium extras). This is why hosting WordPress yourself is often the best way to go. You can add the features you want and need as well as pick a theme that is more to your liking *and* that you can edit yourself. Adding those features and themes is done through installing plugins and themes, and like everything you've read thus far, it's a very easy process.

You can install themes or plugins one of three ways:

▶ Use a cool, new, easy way

▶ Take a couple extra steps, but still use an easy way

▶ Use the old-school, manual way

I'll talk mostly about the first two ways in this section and introduce the third way (which isn't used often by nondevelopers). The process for finding and installing plugins or themes (using either of the first two steps) is almost identical—

when you get the hang of one, the other is old hat. Let's start off with plugins.

Within your WordPress admin area, pass your mouse pointer over the Plugins button and a submenu will appear. Choose Add New from this menu (see Figure 7.1).

On the next screen you have a several choices on how to *find* the plugin you want or need (see Figure 7.2). We're going to proceed with the assumption that this is a brand-new site and that you need the basic plugins to get going. Although you could try to search for all the things you need, the easiest way is to click the Featured or Popular menu choices. (I suggest starting with Featured.) These give you lists of plugins that either the developers and maintainers of WordPress feel are of particular note (Featured) or *everyone* installs (Popular). If one of the plugins seems like something you might need or want (don't worry, I'll give my recommendations shortly), click the Details link below the plugin's name, and you'll see something like Figure 7.3.

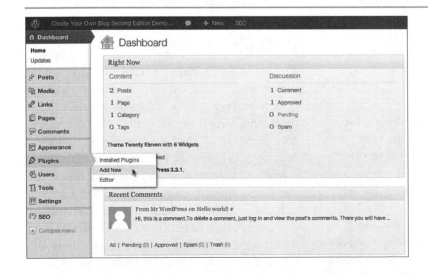

FIGURE 7.1

Getting to the section to add new plugins from the admin dashboard.

FIGURE 7.2

The initial Install Plugins screen.

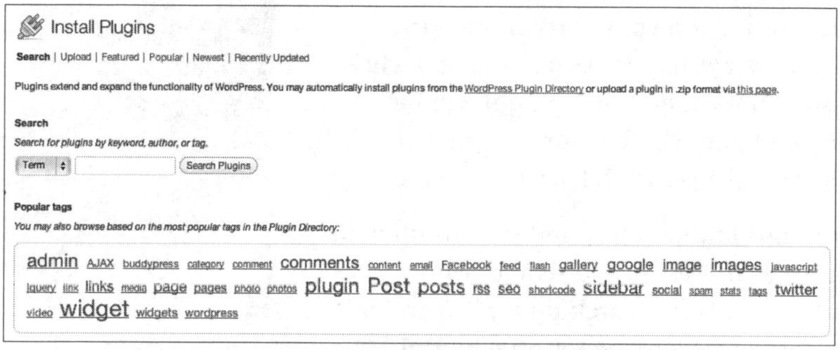

FIGURE 7.3

Plugin details for Contact Form 7.

The plugin I've selected for this example is Contact Form 7, one of my recommended plugins. If everything looks good to you, click the Install Now button, the plugin will be downloaded and installed for you, and you'll get a screen like Figure 7.4 when it's done.

You can also find plugins, and still install with this painless process, using search. Figure 7.5 shows the results for searching for "calendar." In this case I was looking for an editorial calendar to manage post topics across the days, weeks, and months, and it looks like "Editorial Calendar" might be just the ticket. Like the other plugins listings, you click the details link to learn more and install the plugin.

NOTE

Why not just click the Install Now link and skip the whole reading of details? Actually, when I'm setting up new sites for people, I often click Install Now for the plugins that I know I need and want. For this chapter, I'm encouraging you to read the details page so you can gauge if the plugin has the features you want.

Thus far we've been finding and installing plugins the "new, cool, easy way," but what about the "couple of extra steps way"? That's next.

FIGURE 7.4

Contact Form 7 is successfully installed.

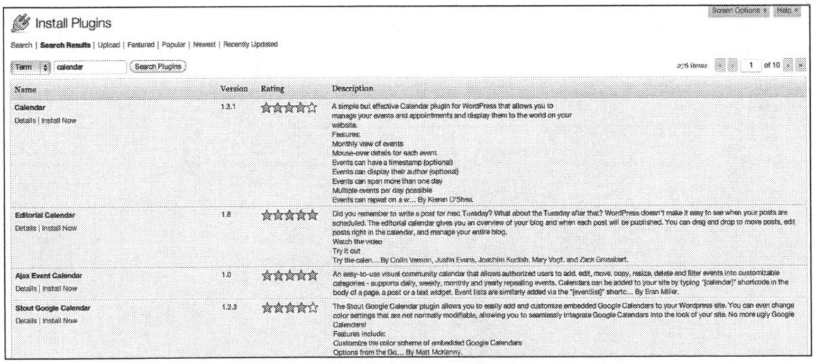

FIGURE 7.5

Searching for plugins using the keyword "calendar."

In your browser, head over to http://word-press.org/extend/plugins/ and you'll see something that looks rather familiar (see Figure 7.6). Yep, those are the Featured plugins you saw before within the admin area of your site. The reason they look the same is that when you are looking for plugins (or themes) from *within* your site, you are actually searching the official WordPress plugins and theme repository at WordPress.org. This is why these two ways to install plugins have essentially the same degree of difficulty, with just a couple of extra steps thrown in.

In this case, if you repeat the search for "calendar" you'll see that you get the same search results. When you click Editorial Calendar on WordPress.org, you get all the information you saw within your site, but a lot more, too (see Figure 7.7).

Now instead of clicking Install on this page (notice there isn't a link that says Install), click Download and a ZIP file will be saved to your computer's hard drive. To actually *install* it on your blog, you need to go back to your site's admin area, get to the Install Plugins screen, and click the link that says Upload. On that screen click the Choose File button and find the ZIP file that was downloaded. Figure 7.8 shows what this looks like on my computer. Click the name of the file and Open; then when the dialog box goes away, click Install Now. Like magic, the file is uploaded and installed.

FIGURE 7.6
The WordPress.org plugins repository.

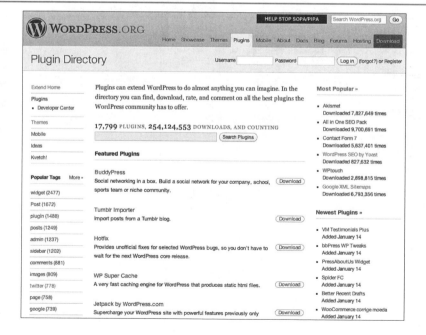

FIGURE 7.7
Editorial Calendar plugin details.

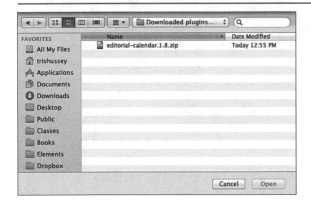

FIGURE 7.8
Getting ready to upload and install the plugin from a downloaded ZIP file.

GETTING STARTED: INSTALLING WORDPRESS AND OTHER KEY COMPONENTS

You might be wondering why you'd bother going to WordPress.org at all to look for plugins. One simple reason: level of detail. When I'm looking for a new plugin or trying to configure a plugin, I often look for the plugin on WordPress.org so I can get a much greater level of detail than I get through the admin interface. The example with the editorial calendar showed that you get (and can watch) a video and see *a lot* more information about the plugin at a glance when you're on WordPress.org versus looking at the condensed version through the admin interface.

The third way to install plugins is to follow the previous steps to find and download the plugin from WordPress.org, but instead of uploading the ZIP file through your admin area in your web browser, you upload the *unzipped* file via FTP to your host. Figure 7.9 shows what this looks like for the demo site using the FTP client Transmit.

To upload a plugins, drag the folder editorial-calendar to wp-content/plugins/ and then activate the plugins on the main plugins screen. Why would you go this route? If you are setting up lots of sites with all the same plugins, it's easier to download, unzip, and then upload via FTP all the plugins (and themes) at once than it is to do one by one. If thinking about FTP and uploading and unzipping scares you, don't worry, nowadays *most* people never have to use FTP on their websites. In-browser administration rules the day.

STAR RATINGS VERSUS DOWNLOADS

You've probably noticed that all plugins and themes have star ratings, and plugins have information on how many times they have been downloaded. Which matters most? Both, but let me explain. Suppose you wrote a plugin and you think it's great. You submit it to WordPress.org for inclusion (and there is an approval/vetting process for all themes and plugins that are in the repository) and it's accepted. Then you get all your friends to go and rate it 5 stars. However, in reality, the plugin is pretty bad, and no one downloads it. So you have a high-star rating, but low downloads. Conversely some of the most popular, most used, and best plugins have only 3.5–4 stars (rarely 5), but have *millions* of downloads. Which is better? Here's another twist: a brand-new plugin hits the scene, and is great, but has very few reviews and very few downloads. What now?

I think you already know the answers, which is why you can't go by downloads or star ratings alone. You need to look at the detailed information about the plugin to decide. In general, you can't go wrong with one of the Featured or Popular plugins, but if you're searching for a plugin (like an editorial calendar plugin, as was the example here), you need to exercise a bit of caution and read a little about the plugin. Don't be shy to ask the WordPress.org forums about plugins or recommended plugins. Sometimes we all just need to double-check if we're on the right path.

FIGURE 7.9
Using the FTP client Transmit to upload a plugins folder to the demo site.

Recommended Plugins

The preceding section covered finding and installing plugins in a nutshell. I did promise my list of recommended plugins (as of early 2012), so here they are:

- **Akismet (installed, but not activated, by default).** The leading anti-spam plugin for blogs.

- **Contact Form 7.** Simple, easy contact forms. As well as other form tools that come in handy.

- **Jetpack by WordPress.com.** Brings many of the extra features of WordPress.com blogs in with one plugin. Essentially replaces a dozen or so plugins in one fell swoop.

- **WordPress SEO by Yoast.** Powerful and easy tools for optimizing and tuning your blog for search engines.

- **WP Super Cache.** Makes cached (or saved) versions of popular Posts and Pages so your site loads faster for visitors.

- **WordTwit.** Automatically updates your Twitter account with your new Posts.

- **WPtouch.** Provides a mobile-friendly (and iPhone optimized) theme for your site. Automatically switches between the two.

- **WP-DBManager.** Automatically backs up, repairs, and optimizes your WordPress database.

- **Polldaddy Polls & Ratings.** Gives you easy polls and ratings on your Posts and Pages

- **Hotfix.** Downloads and updates WordPress with the little fixes between updates.

Installing Themes

Now that we have installing plugins under our belts, let's move on to installing themes. As I said in the beginning, installing themes works *exactly* as installing plugins. The first step is to go to your Themes section in the admin area of your site by selecting Appearance, Themes from the admin sidebar. On the Themes page, click the Install Themes tab at the top (see Figure 7.10).

FIGURE 7.10
The Install area for themes.

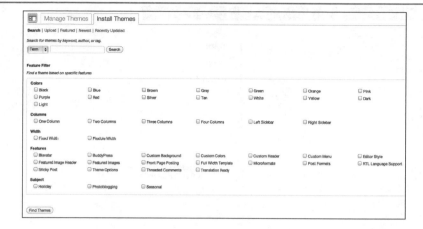

Like plugins, there are Featured themes, and if you click that link you'll get a list of a few hot, interesting themes to check out (see Figure 7.11). You can click the Preview link of any theme you like. If you find one you want to use, you need only to close the Preview and click the Install link to install the theme into the site (see Figure 7.12).

FIGURE 7.11
The Featured themes list.

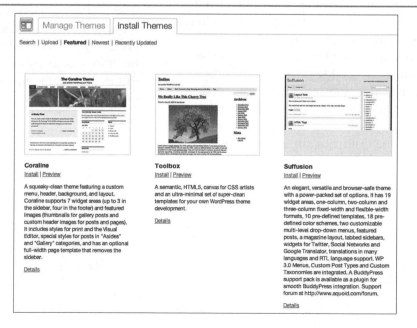

FIGURE 7.12
Installing Suffusion.

Like plugins, themes aren't automatically activated after they are installed. WordPress gives you the chance to activate the theme or plugins when you're ready—not just when it feels like it. As with plugins, you can search for themes using keywords, but I find using the Feature Filter much faster. If you configure the screen as shown in Figure 7.10 to search WordPress.org for blue themes, with three columns, the ability to set custom backgrounds, and that supports custom headers and custom menus, the results will come back looking something like Figure 7.13. Now, instead of installing or previewing the theme

here, let's move over to WordPress.org and see how the download and install through your admin area works (the second way to install plugins and themes).

Head over to http://wordpress.org/extend/themes/ and compare Figure 7.11 and Figure 7.14; you'll see the same featured themes. Nice! I clicked the Check Out Our New Filter and Tag Interface link and set up the same search I did within the admin interface of the site. Lo and behold, in Figure 7.15, you see that I found the same themes!

FIGURE 7.13

Results from the feature filter search.

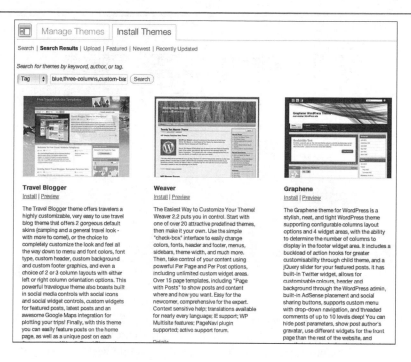

FIGURE 7.14

Featured themes at WordPress.org.

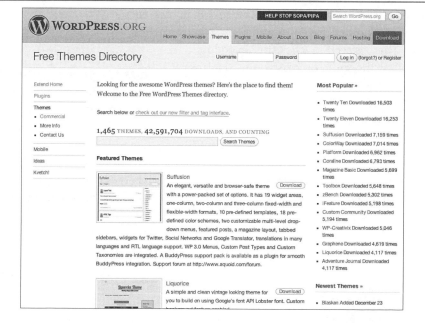

FIGURE 7.15

Results of the feature filter search on WordPress.org.

If you click, for example, the Graphene theme (clicking the picture brings up a preview), you'll come to a details page shown in Figure 7.16. Like downloading a plugin from WordPress.org, clicking the download link downloads a ZIP file to your computer. Switch back to the admin area of the site, and on the Install Themes section, click the Upload link and follow the same process you used to install a plugin. You can see how it looks in Figure 7.17. One click of Install Now and you're ready to try out the theme!

Like plugins, you can upload themes via FTP as well. Instead of putting the folder you get when unzipping the file into wp-content/plugins/, put it in wp-content/themes/.

If you think you're going to start editing the code of your themes, you should get comfortable with this process. Editing themes and uploading them through FTP is the best practice when creating or editing the code of themes.

Later in the chapter, I'll talk about how to choose a good theme for a website, as well as how to configure and customize your theme without needing to know (virtually) any code. What we've been doing up to this point is very *foundational*—we're laying the groundwork for creating our website. So now that we have a site set up and know how to install plugins and themes (which we'll need later), let's start putting this site together.

FIGURE 7.16
Looking at the details for Graphene.

FIGURE 7.17
Installing Graphene from a downloaded ZIP file.

What Will the Home Page Be?

One of the first, and most important, things to decide when building a website is whether your home page will be static or modular. You already know that the term "static" doesn't mean that you can't ever change or update the content, but that you're using the Page content type so you have a home page that will have the same content until you edit it. Modular, in this case, means that your home page is composed of different sections so that different pieces of content are shown without your having to edit the home page itself. For example, in the static scenario, you create a Page with nice graphics and text that welcomes people to your site. You then tell WordPress to use this Page as the home page for the website. WordPress will take care of putting the menus and sidebars in place (depending on your theme), but the content will stay the same until you edit that Page again. In the modular scenario, your home page is more like a blog, but you tell your *theme* what content to display where. Maybe you pick a couple featured posts for the top, and then across the bottom are widgets that pull the latest Post from particular categories and display them. In this case, the home page will change whenever you create a Post in a particular category, but you haven't edited a specific piece of content (or Page or Post) to update the home page.

Essentially it comes down to this: When you're using a static page, you're changing a *WordPress* setting to display the content; when it's modular, you're only changing options connected to the *theme* you're using. If you change your theme, your home page will revert to listing the latest Posts in your site (that is, a regular blog kind of look). I know this is rather confusing right now, but it will make more sense as we move through this section. I'll show examples of how each of these choices look and work, and then it will become clear for you. First, let's talk about why you might want to choose one kind of scheme—static or modular—over another.

Static

When you think about websites, a static home page is what probably first comes to mind. You come to a website and see some nice pictures and text telling you what the site is about and for. You get an idea of what you can expect and what you might find inside. In this case, using WordPress to power our website, picking a static home page option—using a Page as the home page—makes a lot of sense. Create

one Page, put in nice pictures and text, and you're done. Many themes offer Page templates to display the Page without sidebars, which can look great for a home page—showing nice, open space and a good header at the top for navigation. When we first started using WordPress to build websites, this was how most of us did it. We used the built-in settings of WordPress to use a Page as the home page and display all the Post content differently. So why still choose a static page now when there are other options available? The static page is simple, and it works. Create the Page, change the setting in WordPress to display as the home page, and be done. That's it. When you need to update your home page, you edit that Page (or even create a new Page and have WordPress now use *that* new Page as the home page), save it, and you're done. There's not a lot of configuring, tweaking, or even a lot of additional content to create. How do you pull this off? I'm glad you asked, let me show you.

First, let's look at the demo site with the "normal" settings (Figure 7.18):

Nope, not a lot here, only the first default Post and one more created earlier. The only Page is the default sample Page that is created when you install WordPress. So let's create the Page that's going to be the home page for this site.

> **NOTE**
>
> I'm using the Comet theme for these examples. You can find it on WordPress.org at http://word-press.org/extend/themes/comet.

FIGURE 7.18
Yep, a basic blog. Not
much to see here.

I'm going to make this Page about the second edition of this book. I have an image of the cover (the image for the first edition, because I have it handy), some things that have been updated, some things that are new, and the date when people can expect the book to be on the "shelves" (because a lot of books are sold electronically, "shelves" aren't really around,

are they?). You're seeing the end product here in Figure 7.19, but it didn't take me long to put this together. Note that I've chosen the Full Width template for this Page. This gives me the broad and open look I want for the home page (no sidebars). With a quick click of the Publish button, this is what the final result looks like (Figure 7.20).

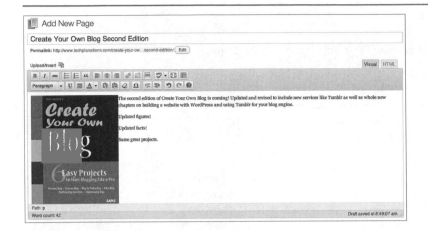

FIGURE 7.19
Creating the Page to be the home page.

FIGURE 7.20
The published Page using a full-width (no sidebars) Page template.

Great, but this isn't our home page just yet. We need to change a setting first—one simple setting and we're done. Back in the admin area of the site choose Settings, Reading. At the top, you see the settings for what the Front Page (a.k.a home page) displays. Click the option button for Static page, and for the Front Page choose the page you created (its title is listed), as in Figure 7.21. Leave the Posts page setting the way it is for right now. Click Save Changes and...that's pretty much it. Figure 7.22 shows the Front Page/home page for this demo.

FIGURE 7.21

Changing the Reading settings to make that Page the home page.

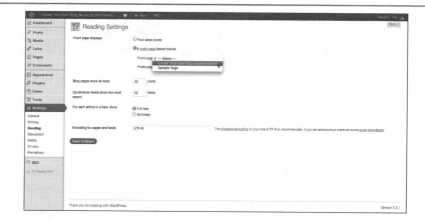

FIGURE 7.22

Ta da! The final product with a Page as the home page.

Sure, there is a lot left to do before this is a fully fleshed out website (there is pretty much no content for people to read), but if you needed to show your boss, "Hey look, I've started on our new website," this is a good start. I think you can see why this is a great way to go for creating a website. Simple, easy, and if your boss were to ask, "Oh, can we say this on the page…?" you can probably answer, "Yes! And …there is the change." As much as you can see how great this is, it is pretty limited. If your boss, for example, said: "Oh, can we have a list of our newest products here on this space here (pointing vaguely to a spot on the page)?" you might feel kind of stuck. Maybe it could fit in the footer if widget spaces are there (for Comet there aren't). You could go with the default Page template to bring the sidebars back and maybe list them there—that might work, but it spoils the look, doesn't it? For this kind of situation, we go for a modular home page.

Modular

Modular home pages are really nothing more than a theme that displays more than just the most recent posts on the home page. You see them all the time online—they have different sections with different content in them. Not just on the sidebars (if there are any on the home page), but the page is wide and has sections. Often, when you're looking for a theme that looks like this, you can find them called Magazine themes, but more and more as WordPress is being used to build "regular" websites, there are more "nonblog" themes. Regardless of what they are called—I'd search

for "magazine" theme first because they are by their nature modular and often work well for websites—all modular themes work pretty much the same way. The home page is divided into sections, and you define what goes into each of the sections. Some themes—for example, the premium themes from StudioPress.com—rely on widgets to allow you to highlight featured posts or place other things (we've talked about widgets before, so you know how flexible they are) on various parts of the home page. Other themes— ToomMorel Lite and ColorWay—use theme options panels where you can enter the titles, words, images, and links that you want in each of the sections. It's this difference that makes *showing* you real examples tough. In the earlier static example, because we're working with WordPress settings—settings that generally work the same regardless of which theme you're using—I could have picked almost *any* theme and created an example that you could follow. With modular home pages, every theme handles things a little differently, so examples aren't easy (or that helpful) to come by.

What's more important in this discussion is *why* you might want to choose a modular home page layout over a static one. I'll give you that very succinctly—more content in a smaller area. Modular home page layouts let you get a lot more content, and different types of content, onto your home page than you can with a static page. Take the demo page for the StudioPress theme Associate (http://www.studiopress.com/themes/associate) (see Figure 7.23).

FIGURE 7.23
StudioPress Associate
child theme for the
Genesis framework.

You see bold images, text, blog posts, and other features at a glance. That's pretty amazing stuff. Although I often suggest a static page for simple sites, for most people I work with who are developing a website on top of WordPress, I recommend using a theme with a modular home page layout. The amount of flexibility gives you so much potential. Want to have a small video playing on your home page? Not a problem. Your Twitter stream? Okay. Content from other sites, your other blogs, images, slideshows, downloadable PDFs, or a form to sign up for your newsletter: You can "cram" all that onto a modular home page and it won't look crowded at all. The one downside I find

with modular layouts is deciding what goes where *and* creating the content to be there. With a static home page, you have something that could even be an elegant Coming Soon page, but with a modular page, for a site to look "finished," you have to have something in all the boxes.

Now that you've been thinking a little about what your home page will look like–or maybe you're more confused than ever, which is okay—let's move on to how to choose a good theme, and then we'll go over the *easy* ways you can customize it to make your site look amazing.

Choosing and Customizing Your Theme

If you were wondering why we went through the exercise to decide if you wanted a static or modular home page *before* talking about choosing a theme, now you know. If you think a modular home page is where it's at for you, then looking at themes that *don't* have a modular home page is rather pointless. By now you should have a good idea of what you'd like your home page and website to look like. You might even have sketches of layouts—I do it all the time when working on websites—things you'd like to see and have. If you need to have a space for a YouTube video to be on your home page, you need a theme that can support it. You might need wide sidebars to have the content you want. Maybe you don't want sidebars at all, but a full-width layout. You now should have a much better idea of what you want than when you started reading this chapter.

So how do you find the right theme? Although you *might* not find the perfect theme there, start with the WordPress.org theme repository. There are *thousands* of themes *and* the themes (and plugins) have at least had a basic check for compatibility, security, and assurance that the theme doesn't link to scams or malware. If you download free WordPress themes from any old site, you're taking a big risk. Even themes you buy—premium themes—should come from the sources recommended on WordPress.org. We've talked about how to search for and install themes already, so that's the first step. Start searching at WordPress.org; maybe start with a color or the number of sidebars or a feature like custom menus. Don't expect to find

the perfect theme right off, and don't eliminate buying a premium theme (often they are $100 or less) that has all the features you need, as well as support and updates. Yes, I generally use premium themes in my work. I find that starting with a solid, elegant, well-designed foundation saves me hours and hours of time—not just time while I'm *building* a site, but afterward as I need to expand, maintain, and update the site.

Headers

One of the *first* things you see when you come to someone's page is the header. Your header can be text, an image, or a combination of both, but whatever it is you need to think about it for a moment. One of the main features in most modern WordPress themes is the capability to set a custom header image. The themes that support Custom Header images give you the dimensions of how big the banner should be. If you upload an image that is *larger* than the indicated size, you'll be able to crop it with WordPress. If the image is exactly the dimensions indicated, it will be used as is. However, if the image is smaller, *it will be stretched to fit the space*. This looks ugly, so avoid doing this. Just a few minutes in a graphics editor can give you a header of the right size that looks great.

Take some time with your header. Decide what you want to convey to your visitors when they first come to your site. Some themes have another trick up their sleeve. For a few themes (like Twenty Ten and Twenty Eleven) if you set a featured image in a Post or Page that is large enough, the featured image *will become the header image.* This is very handy when it comes to making special sections of your site where you want to promote particular things. So, you could have the featured image for a page related to your products have a collage of all your products, or a section on your location, or a panoramic picture of your building. The potential is limited only by your imagination—and your theme, of course.

Backgrounds

Although many people like to set a background image for their websites—not picking a color, but an actual image—I take a very cautious approach to this. The problem with image backgrounds—and I've made this mistake on a number of occasions—is that they are easier to do *wrong* than to do *right.* You've probably visited websites where the background image distracted, or obscured, the content you were there to find. Maybe the text was too light on a light background or too dark on a dark one, or the images were so jarring that you couldn't stand the website. Like Custom Headers, many WordPress sites support uploading your own custom background image or changing the default background color. This is fine, but before you upload that image to tile or place, stop for a moment and ask yourself if you *really* need to change the background the theme came with. Suppose you want a great image to tile horizontality only. To ensure that your pages look good on lots of different devices, you need to not only make your image *extremely wide* (like 3000 or more pixels) but also ensure that if the visitors screens are small (many tablets still use

1024×768 resolution for their screens, compared to 1400×900 for many widescreen laptops) the background doesn't interfere with the content.

No, it's not fun. Yes, it can be a chore. This is why you need to ask yourself, "Do I have the time for this right now?" Maybe it's better to work on getting your website up, running with all the content in it, and then see if a custom background is in the cards for you.

Menus

In previous chapters, I glossed over using custom menus in WordPress, because, in truth, working out your menus on a personal blog—even a business blog—can be secondary to other concerns (like posting content). When you're building a *website,* however, setting up your navigation menus is *essential* to how well your website works. Lucky for you, working with menus under WordPress is a snap. It's so easy, in fact, that many people I teach think there is some other trick to it. (I suggest they can try it blindfolded if they want.) This section comes in two parts. Part one talks about what should go into your menus. Part two is how to put that together with WordPress. Let's start off, then, talking about what should be on your menus.

When you come to a website, and you're looking for something, what's one of the *first* things that you do? You look at the navigation menus. You see if there is a Products or Locations or Careers or whatever section. If you find what you're looking for right off the bat—either in a primary or secondary menu—then the site designers did their job. If you have to resort to search (searching through help sections excluded), they didn't do their job. Simple as that, your navigation menus need to direct people toward what they will be most interested in *and* where you want them to go. Here are some examples of menus from different sites (see Figure 7.24).

The top one is from my personal site/blog, and the next two are different versions of a navigation menu for a computer retailer. These might not be the best examples in the world, but I'm sure you get the idea. The important thing is how I made those menus in WordPress, and that is where we're going next.

From the admin area of your site, Menus are found under the Appearance section of the sidebar. WordPress Menus are simple, but they do have a few parts and tricks to them. First, you have to *create* the menu; click the tab with the "+" on it to make an empty menu and give it a name (the name doesn't matter, really; it's just for you to know what it is), and then click Save Menu. Assuming that your theme supports WordPress Menus (if it doesn't, save yourself a lot of grief and find one that does—most new ones do), to the left you'll see a box called Theme Locations, and it has a place to choose which of the menus that you've created should appear on the theme. Some themes support more than one navigation menu (a rather handy feature, I think), but let's assume that your theme supports only one. From the pull-down menu in the Theme Locations box, select the name of the menu you just created and click Save. At this point your theme is using a blank, empty navigation menu. That's okay; we'll be adding things to it shortly (see Figure 7.25).

FIGURE 7.24
Three different takes on menus.

FIGURE 7.25

Our empty menu— named, saved, and selected.

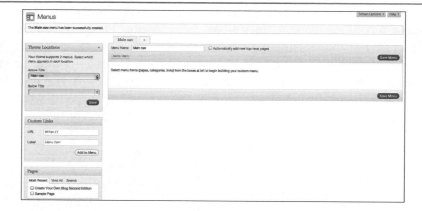

Below the Theme Locations box (as you've probably noticed) are the boxes where you can add things to your Menu. The Custom Links section lets you create a menu item for anything you can link to, even if it isn't on your website. The Pages section enables you to add any static Page to a menu—as well as a quick check box for creating a link to Home— and below that, you can add Post Categories to your menu. A couple of important notes are that Categories don't appear in this section until there is *at least one post* in that category. So, if you're planning things out for your site structure and menus, plan to create place-holder Posts under all your categories with dummy content so you can lay out the Menus. Adding items to menus is as easy as click and click. Click the check box for a Page or Category and then click Add to Menu. The item will appear at the bottom of the menu area to the right. Don't worry if items aren't in the right order or even if you want them to be submenus of each other, because all you need to do is drag the items into the order you want. As you are dragging around, you'll soon notice

that you can make any item a primary or submenu item of another. You can even *repeat* menu items if you want visitors to find the same section under different menus. (I do this often when a particular section could be classified under different parts of a menu.) Before you go check out your menu in progress, be sure to click Save Menu. That's it! Really! You can always edit the names of items (which is another handy feature) and change your mind at any time. Play around with the menus to get the feel of them *and* to see what looks best where.

Widgets

It terms of creating a website, using widgets for your website is no different from what I talked about in Chapter 2 for other blogs. I will repeat my advice to not go crazy adding widgets to your sidebars, headers, or footers. Too many widgets looks cluttered and can make your site load more slowly than it needs to. From the standpoint of creating a website, and right on the heels of the previous section, one of the very hand things about WordPress Menus is that *any menu can also be a widget*. So you can create a special menu to use the sidebar of your site to help visitors find more sections of your website without having to clutter up or complicate your main navigation. This is a handy way to create quick access to careers sections, details on product sections, or any section that is deep with content that you'll like to give visitors a hand finding.

You might remember that earlier, when I was talking about modular home pages, I mentioned that a lot of themes use widgets to pull off the modularity. This is the other great use of widgets, and although it might be confusing at first to be adding *content* to your home page through a widget, after you get the hang of it (and if your themes like the StudioPress ones are well documented and come with nice widget extras), you'll find that a widgetized, modular home page can save you a lot of time and energy in laying out and planning a very interesting and dynamic home page.

Choosing Content for Your Website

I purposefully left this section until almost last. Up to now, we haven't talked about content much, and that's because after years of creating websites and blogs—especially now in the era of WordPress and other CMS-powered websites—I've found that if you get tied up in creating your content before you have some of these core parts done, you will wind up with a mess of a website. Sure, you might need to create a placeholder Page or Post to see if your ideas will work, but worrying about the *actual* content should be left until you have your

plans in place. This section isn't going to talk about the mechanics of creating content with WordPress—you already know it from having read the other chapters in this book. This section focuses on a much more important, and tricky, point: which content types are right for your website.

Post or Page

If you've been reading this book thus far, you *might* be thinking that if you're creating a website with WordPress that most—maybe all—of your website will be composed of Pages. You might very well be wrong about that, and here's why. Pages in WordPress are intended to be pieces of content that stand by themselves. They don't need to be connected to other pieces of content by time, taxonomy (Categories or Tags), or any other relationship. Content such as your About Me page or Contact Us page stand alone. Other sections, like privacy, terms of service, and even history of the company, can be static content. They stand alone. On the other hand, you have Posts, which are *all* connected to each other in some way, shape, or form. Don't think of a Post as a blog post. Think of a Post as a piece of content that is related to other pieces of content. For example, think about a product section. Your product section is composed of, well, products, so each product item you create would be placed in a Products category first. Then you might have subcategories of your products (price, type, color, size, and so on). Because WordPress knows how all these pieces of content are related to each other, it can *automatically* have a page (note the lowercase "p") that lists all the items in that category (an Archive or Category Page). You might have gotten a feeling about this looking at the earlier menu examples. Listing everything under a category is an easy-peasy thing for WordPress to do.

My general rule is to create Pages for items that don't need to be connected or related to other things and Posts for content than needs to connect or have a context to other pieces of content to fully make sense (like looking at one class in the scheme of all the classes you might offer or one store location related to all other locations). Don't worry if you guess wrong—I've done it hundreds of times—and create Pages for content that turns out should have been Posts; you can always copy and paste the content from a Page into a Post. It's a little tedious, but it isn't the end of the world.

Categories and Tags

If you're using Posts in your site, you'll be using Categories; that's a given. All Posts need to be assigned to at least one Category, and if you're organizing your content this way you're likely going to need more than one Category to organize things. Tags, on the other hand, are a different story. You don't *have* to use Tags when you use Posts; they are optional. However, I would argue that you *should* Tag all your Posts for one reason and one reason only—search engines. Tags are a source of metadata—keywords—that search engines use to help place your content into context with not only the rest of the content on your site, but all the content on all the other websites on the Internet. Remember, Categories are the big buckets that you organize content into, and Tags are the keywords that specifically relate to that piece of content. The terms and words people would use to search for that specific Post in addition to the general Categories.

Don't worry if you don't think you have a handle on this right now. Sometimes, it takes some practice and seeing how other sites use tags. Really good websites built on WordPress often don't display the Tags that are defined for the content, but they are hidden and defined in the code for search engines to find. Just remember, use Categories to organize your Post content into big groups and Tags to define the keywords for that piece of content.

Images

Clothes make the man, and images make the website. I don't need to rehash the *how* of images for your website, but I do want to spend a little time on the *why*. Images, pictures that illustrate your point, are tremendously powerful. Consider this book. There are figures throughout. Why? Because the images I include here help explain and make my point, and make these techie things easier to grasp. For your website you need to be in the same mindset. Think about the imagery, the icons, and the photos that make your point.

If you're using a static home page, you need to consider what visitors will see when they first visit your site. Is it a giant blob of text? Or is there a powerful image—and text—there to catch their eye, grab their attention, and draw them into your website. You have just a few seconds to "win over" visitors before they click the Back button or close that browser tab, so make the most of those moments. If you're using a modular home page, you have *more* weapons at your disposal. All the modular home pages that I've worked with—including all the examples in this chapter—have a "featured image" or "featured post with featured image" function. Many of these featured image tools allow you to overlay (or at least include close by) some explanatory text, as well as link to the content you're highlighting. Many of the featured post/image tools let you define *several* featured posts/images and have them slide by in a slide show (they are called "sliders"—I know, not very creative). Think of the impact those bring: the interactivity, the potential connection with your visitors, all with very little work on your part. You create the content, pick the image, tell the theme what to use, and—ta da!—you have a site with a very nice touch of cool.

Multimedia

Videos. Everyone loves videos in their sites and home pages. Hey, don't get me wrong, I love them, too, and frequently have videos as modules on my home pages. Again, you know how to do this stuff. What you need is the *why*. The why is interestingness and the certain pull that only a video can bring. The only caution I have with putting videos on your home page is to make sure they are *not* set to autostart/autoplay. It's a pet peeve of mine when websites just start playing a video when I get to the page. I know, it's a bit silly, but you're reading this for some of my opinions as well as my knowledge/tips, so there you have it.

As for the rest of your site, go for it! If you think a little video will demonstrate your point, include it. Remember, part and parcel with having videos on your site is having a video channel on YouTube or similar site (I rather like YouTube myself). Make sure you take a little time to customize your YouTube Channel to match your branding and include links to your website, blog, and so on. Like all social media channels, your presence on YouTube can

be a really powerful way to get more visitors to your website—if they can find it from YouTube. On your site, think about have a special Post category for Video Reviews or Video Messages or Interviews, so your visitors can quickly find all your video masterpieces in one place.

Documents

Many websites have downloadable documents—whitepapers, forms, media kits—and your website can have these, too. Just upload your documents through the Media section (or while you're creating a Post or Page, no matter) and you're on your way to have a document library as part of your website. WordPress manages documents through the same interface and section as images, music, or videos—it's all just different forms of media to present to visitors. But remember that offering scads of documents is not an alternative to writing Posts or Pages. Documents that you include in your site should augment or complement your content, not replace it.

At this point in the chapter, you're essentially ready to go. You have a plan, you have a site, a theme, a content strategy—you've probably even been creating things as you've been reading this chapter. I could wrap this chapter up right now and you'd be pretty well set. There are, however, a few last details and tricks of the trade that I want to pass on.

Final Touches

Although your website is almost ready to go, there are a few final touches to keep in mind: measuring success, getting the most from search engines, and maintaining your new website. None of these things are hard, and what I'm covering are more "don't forget to…" points than anything else. Let's start off with how to measure your success.

Measuring Your Success

In Chapter 2, I talked about Google Analytics, so that's what this section is about. From Chapter 2, you should have enough information to get going, but I want to flesh things out a little for you. First, make sure you have your Google Analytics account and profile all set and ready *long, long* before launch. Set it up when you're just starting off. It's really easy to forget to set up Google Analytics when you're in the midst of getting a site ready to launch, so do it now.

The key part of using Google Analytics is the tracking code that's embedded into all the pages of your website. Many themes give you the option to put your Google Analytics code into the header or footer of your theme, but I'm going to advise *against* that approach and recommend that you use a plugin like Google Analyticator instead. The main reasons is that the plugin approach ensures that even if you switch themes, your Google Analytics code is still being put into your website. I've made the mistake in the past of putting the code just in the theme, then changing themes, forgetting to add the code, and suddenly missing *months* of data. Don't follow my lead on that boo-boo, use the plugin instead.

The next thing is to use the WordPress stats that are rolled into JetPack by WordPress. These aren't the best stats for analysis, but they do

give you reliable *live* data on how your site is doing. I refer to both datasets with my sites so that I not only have live data—yes, Google is starting to offer live data, but it's a feature that's only in the testing phase right now—but I have comparative datasets. If the numbers look about the same, all is good; if they differ, I have some investigating to do. Also, I have *backup* datasets; if either of the services goes down for a short period of time, I'm still covered with at least one good set of data.

Now, let's talk about success. I want your website to be successful. You want your website to be successful. The first tip I'm going to give you is to not get tied up in specific numbers of page views or visitors right now. When your site launches, and I know you'll be obsessively checking your stats, watch the *patterns* that will start to emerge. What pieces of content are most popular? How many pages are people going to each visit? How long are they staying? Are people going to the home page and nowhere else? It's the *patterns* that are going to be important for your first few months. This is the time to see if visitors can understand your navigation. This is when you start to gain more insight into what people are looking for—finding and not finding—on your website. Yes, of course, if part of your website's goals is to drive people to an online store, you need to see how that is working. Still, early on you're going to look for patterns, not numbers.

Recap: Use a plugin to add your Google Analytics code, use Jetpack by WordPress to get an extra layer of stats, look at the *patterns* in your stats for the first few months and not the numbers.

Search Engines

Here's the good news. Because your website is running on WordPress, about 90% of your search engine work is done already. Yes, really. The rest is going to come down to this:

- ▶ Good writing
- ▶ Categories and tags
- ▶ Using a plugin like WordPress SEO by Yoast or All in One SEO Pack (one or the other, not both at the same time)

These three things help put a polish on your SEO. When you write well, with good, descriptive titles, search engines can (and will) index the content better. Put your major point in the first few sentences of the page. Have the title reflect what the Post or Page is about (detail isn't important, just not "A post") and when combined with the keyword tools like WordPress SEO, search engines will find you. Now if you're not sure your website is being indexed by Google and others, make sure your Privacy settings aren't blocking search engines (when you're setting up your site, allowing indexing is the default). It's also worth a visit to Google Webmaster Tools (https://www.google.com/webmasters/tools/home) to verify your site and see if Google is reporting issues with it.

This is one of the best parts of using WordPress to power your website. You really don't have to worry about SEO much, you just write good content and the rest will fall together.

Maintaining

The final bit before you're all set is to keep an eye on the Updates indicator on your admin Dashboard. Because you're hosting this site yourself, you need to keep WordPress, your plugins, and even your themes updated. These updates aren't just to add more features or fix bugs, but also to patch potential security holes in the software. It's essential at least once a week to give a quick check to see if any updates are required, and if so, to update. Updates take only a couple of clicks and are handled automatically; you just have to click to start them. Most of the sites that are compromised by hackers are compromised because of out-of-date software—don't let your site become one of them. Stay up to date.

Summary

This chapter has been a significant departure from the rest of this book, but it is about leveraging a powerful tool to do something that lots of people need—build a website. Most people don't want to learn how to code, and those of us who do know how to code don't like to do it all the time. Everyone appreciates tools that help them get the job done quickly and easily. Building a "regular" website with WordPress is a natural outcome of starting a blog with WordPress. After you see how powerful—and easy—the tool is, you begin to wonder if you can use it for other things. And we're not talking about carving a turkey with a chainsaw, we're talking about using a simple Content Management System to build simple websites. Eventually you might find you've outgrown WordPress's capabilities. That's fine—WordPress wasn't built to be the ultimate website tool. There are plenty of tools you can move up to, and the best thing is that many of them work and act like WordPress.

Happy building.

CHAPTER 8

Creating a Visual Artist's Portfolio Blog

When I was first working on the outline for this book, I put the various chapters in place to (somewhat) build upon each other. As a photographer and occasional poet (don't ask, I'm not telling where that stuff is hidden online), using the Internet to showcase my work is fulfilling. It's like being able to have a whole section of a gallery, or a whole gallery, to myself. Not only that, I get to design every inch of the gallery to suit me and my art.

You can have that feeling, too. This chapter is written with a bias toward showcasing the visual arts (photography, sculpture, paintings, jewelry, and so on), but it could very easily be applied to speaking, acting, or music. Run with your creativity! The whole idea and philosophy is to design a site/blog that showcases you. You know you're worth it, so let's do a good job of it. If you're a graphic designer or write code or programs or design websites, I'm not leaving you out here. I consider all those to be creative arts. If you go to WordPress.org, you'll see at the bottom of every page is "Code Is Poetry," so I'm not the only one who feels this way about coding.

Roll out a canvas, because you're going to paint your work, writ large, across the Internet.

What Makes for Good Content on a Portfolio Blog

Very much like the personal blog of Chapter 5, "Creating a Personal Blog with WordPress.com," a portfolio blog is all about you. Your art and creative works might be taking center stage, but if you're like me, your creativity and art is as much a part of you as your hair or skin. The goal of a portfolio blog is not only to showcase your works in the best light possible, but also to have it reflect you and the art itself.

Let's take photography, for example. Having a blog with a black background, a scrolling slideshow of your pictures, and shadow boxes to look at a particular picture makes each image stand out. The colors and contrasts can easily be seen and appreciated. For an actor, having a selection of video clips or audio segments that when clicked zoom to focus on that example and blur out the rest of the site makes that performance stand out.

Now, imagine being a writer, and the contrast between the background and text is poor, and there is no way to find out how to contact you—not very effective. How about a graphic designer who has made such an elaborate site that it takes forever to load, and after it does, you can't figure out how to navigate the site? My philosophy is pretty simple: If you want to show off your works, visitors should be able to immediately see how to get to them. Maybe (I think this is cool myself) front and center on your home page is a slide show of your latest works. As each slide comes in and out of view, information about it appears near it. Perhaps there's a link to buy it online, something like "Love this picture? You can buy a print of it online right now!"

The important thing to keep in mind is to treat a portfolio blog like any other portfolio. What do you want to show, and how do you want to show it to cast your work in the best light possible? Start there and work outward. That's the foundation of everything we're going to talk about in this chapter, which is written from one artist to another; written to help you create an online showcase and portfolio.

Because you already know how to create your works, let's look at how to best showcase them online.

Picking the Right Tool for the Job

Showcasing your work online is just like how you set about creating it in the first place—you pick the right tools for the job. If your work is written, you have it fairly easy, because the Internet is made for text…unless you illuminate manuscripts. Then you need to take pictures of your work. When I showcase my work, or the work of friends and colleagues, I look at what the art form is and decide what would best express what they do. Sometimes—sadly, all too often—artists get stuck with a "typical" website for their works. Frankly, "typical websites" are terrible for artists. Sure the Web might be made for multimedia, but a lot of web designers aren't familiar with it. Even more problematic is that many web designers don't really *get* artists. Let's put an end to that right now. You, maker of creative works, need to make the site yourself.

Okay, but what *is* the right tool for the job? If a website isn't right, then what is? The answer should be obvious by now that blogs are by their nature multimedia aware. This makes showcasing your works *a lot* easier than it was even a short while ago.

For the photographer, you are going to want the capability to have sets and slideshows that allow people to browse through your pictures. For a singer, you need samples of your work as MP3s and pictures of you in performance. A craftsperson needs to photograph her work, and then set up a site that, like a photographer, allows people to browse what she's made. Writers, videographers, everyone…all forms of media are welcome within a blog. I hope that by this point you've discovered that setting up a blog isn't rocket science. You don't have to be

IDEA GALLERY

http://www.studiopress.com/themes/landscape

SIMPLE OR COMPLEX, A PORTFOLIO BLOG IS ALWAYS COOL

Later, this chapter shows you examples of portfolio sites that should inspire you, the sort of sites that would challenge all but the most talented of web geeks to design. This is why, to start things off, I'm showing you sites that we mere mortals could pull off.

The blog shown here isn't really a blog at all; rather, it's a demo of the StudioPress (www.studiopress.com) theme Landscape, which Brian Gardner designed for portfolio blogs. This theme is simple, clean, and extremely easy to set up. The only thing fancy about it is how it looks (and how Brian built it).

This simple black-and-white theme isn't boring in the least. I'd be willing to bet that when you looked at this theme you knew exactly what to do. Remember, often the people you want to look at your portfolio aren't other artists as much as potential clients. You don't want them thinking that all you want to do is something that pushes the boundaries of design. Those are great, too—don't get me wrong—but you also want visitors to be able to see and appreciate your works without frustration.

a computer geek, or have a bevy of them on standby, to put a great looking blog together. Dispel the notion right now that you *can't* do it, because you can and will.

WordPress.com

If you're not a geek (or a wannabe geek), using WordPress.com to set up your portfolio is the *easiest* way to go about things. You won't have to worry about updating WordPress or plug-ins. It's all handled for you, behind the scenes. For many artists, starting out with the basic, free WordPress.com blog (which would end in .wordpress.com) is going to be just fine. Keep on your radar, however, buying that domain name. Review Chapter 2, "Installing and Setting Up Your First Blog," to refresh your memory on this topic.

If you have a blog on WordPress.com, you are given two GB to store pictures and other files— but *not* audio files (for example, MP3s). In the scheme of things, two GB of web space is actually *a lot* of space to have at your disposal, but you might use it up quickly if you're storing high-quality images. To solve this problem, store your high-resolution pictures on sites like Flickr, SmugMug, and other media-sharing sites. Doing this not only reduces the space you need at WordPress.com (or any other host, for that matter), but you'll also get a nice boost in search engine rankings as well.

At the risk of sounding like a broken record, I want to emphasize the importance of buying a domain name for yourself and using it on WordPress.com. As discussed in Chapter 2, using your own domain makes you look more serious and professional about what you're doing, compared to someone who hasn't taken the time to do this. I think many people, especially those who don't think of themselves as

particularly techie, are under the misconception that buying a domain and connecting to a host is a difficult task. Honestly, it isn't. Even the least techie Internet user can search for a good domain, buy it, and follow the directions to be able to use it on WordPress.com or any other host for that matter.

Not to mention how cool it will sound when you can say at a cocktail party, "Oh yes, I bought another domain today and mapped it to my portfolio blog with a CNAME." Yeah, see?

DIY or Self-Hosted Blogs

The step up from WordPress.com, as you know from Chapter 2, is the self-hosted blog. The benefit to you, as a portfolio blogger, is more flexibility with using themes and you'll be able to add plugins to your blog. The drawback is that you also have something to maintain and keep track of. This isn't hard, nor is it time consuming, but there is a bit of a learning curve (I stress the *bit* part). Which is right for you? Let's tackle that next.

How Do I Choose Between WordPress.com and DIY?

Your decision is going to come down to two factors: your time and your money. WordPress.com saves you time and money because for many people free is just fine. If you buy a domain through WordPress.com, mapping it to your blog is a paltry $17/year (that includes registering the domain), and if you already have a domain, it's only $12/year. DIY costs you money for a domain (about $10 a year) and a hosting fee (about $10–15 a month), and you have to invest a little more time getting things going. The trade-off is control. On WordPress.com, or any hosted service for that matter, you are limited to which theme you can use, and you can't use additional plugins. You don't have these restrictions with DIY. For my time and money, I choose DIY most of the time. I do set up blogs on WordPress.com to use as examples, but I don't actively use one. I have many friends, though, who are happy using WordPress.com and other hosted services. WordPress.com makes using a domain so affordable that, frankly, *not* trying that option is pretty silly. If you later decide to switch to a self-hosted blog, the folks at WordPress.com will help you make the transition.

Making a Site a Site

You saw what a default WordPress blog looked like already. You don't want that, do you? Of course not. You want something with style, panache, and edge. You want a cool theme. Lucky for you, there are thousands, maybe even hundreds of thousands of free themes to preview and try. A theme is just the first step because the cool stuff is in the add-ons that give your blog some flair. Maybe you'd like a nice photo gallery that runs itself and has nice shadowbox features? Maybe include some widgets to let people *buy* your works? These are all within the realm of the possible, so let's start making some decisions.

Picking a Good Theme for a Portfolio Blog

Themes (or templates) give a blog its look. They are very much like paper dolls, or thin bits that you put on and around your content to give it a "look." Sporty, cool, hip, edgy, elegant looks are available, no matter what

blog engine you use. Personally, I prefer WordPress's theme-template system, but that is also because I am knee deep in it almost every day.

All themes are set up as a group of files, images, and a style sheet that the blog engine uses to render the blog for people to use. In the case of WordPress, the themes call the content from within the theme files. Some themes have special features and layouts that might need a little configuring. Themes for portfolio blogs generally need simple things like defining how big you want the images to be onscreen and where the high-res versions are located. Portfolio themes, like most themes you run into either on hosted services like WordPress.com or DIY, are pretty simple and easy to configure. Remember, this *isn't* rocket science!

> **TIP**
>
> Don't be too cool for school. Although having a cutting-edge, innovative theme is cool, it can also hinder people from actually enjoying your content.

When you're picking a theme, keep in mind a couple of things. First is how flexible the theme is for making changes. If you wanted to edit the theme itself, could you do it easily? Second, and most important, is how *readable* the theme is in a range of web browsers. If you want people to visit your site and look at your portfolio, you *must* make it a pleasant experience. Don't make people guess how to navigate through the site or make them squint to read your text. Figure 8.1 offers a good example of a site that is both elegant and easy on the eye.

When you're looking for great theme ideas and inspiration, visit *Smashing Magazine* (smashing-magazine.com). The roundups of great themes and sites you'll see there are nothing short of brilliant. If you aren't inspired by their examples, I don't know what will inspire you. For the geekier set, their examples for coding and editing themes are fantastic. I bookmark them all the time for reference. Figure 8.2 shows the first two of many free portfolio themes for WordPress. (See the whole post at http://wp.smashingmagazine.com/ 2011/07/05/free-wordpress-themes-2011-edition/. Scroll nearly to the end for the portfolio themes.)

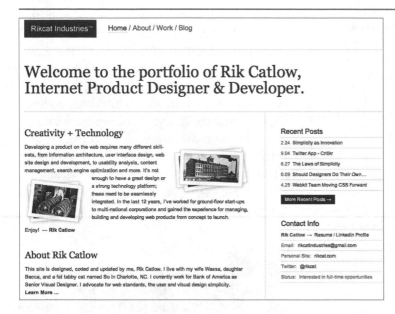

FIGURE 8.1
A simple black-and-white theme can be effective.

FIGURE 8.2
Part of *Smashing Magazine*'s "Free WordPress Themes: 2011 Edition" post from July, 2011.

Whether it's a photography portfolio, video portfolio, or something a little more edgy, there is a template out there for you. The key is looking, previewing, and testing any theme before you decide.

Plugins for Portfolio Blogs

Out of the box, WordPress is a great tool for publishing any kind of content, but you're not publishing just any kind of content, are you? Like having a sunroof or new stereo put into your car, a WordPress plugin adds a little refinement, tweak, or enhancement to your site or blog. For the portfolio blog, beyond the core plugins covered in Chapter 2, you will be looking for and adding plugins that enhance the already impressive multimedia capabilities of WordPress. I'll also get into some additional plugins that can help you make a private client-only area and help sell your works online through your blog. Let's get started with slideshow plugins.

Slideshows

Players and plug-ins for slideshows are common. The leader in the WordPress world is NextGen Gallery (and related sibling plugins), but I have also used one called Featured Content Gallery with great success. The upside to these plugins is that they aren't too hard to implement, but the downside is that it can be time consuming to configure one to test, and then configure another to test. Look at portfolio sites you like and try to determine what plugins they are using. An alternative to using a plugin for your portfolio of images is to use the code from the slideshow on Flickr or SmugMug. If you use either of these services, you can create sets and collections of works

GAINING INSPIRATION FROM THE OUTSTANDING AND OUTLANDISH

I love, and eagerly anticipate, when *Smashing Magazine* does their "…for your inspiration" posts. It doesn't matter if it's fonts, logos, websites, themes, even *buttons*—those posts charge my imagination, but maybe not for the reasons you think.

Lot of themes and site designs inspire me, not to mention trying to discern if the "new" design was derived from another template (you can pick up clues pretty easily after looking at as many themes as I have). What really inspires me are the "Wow, that's, umm, well, interesting…." These are the sites that are so on the bleeding edge that you're not quite sure what you're supposed to do if you found yourself at the page.

I look at the range of sites (ones that I just look at and think, "Cool!" and others where I think, "Huh?") and use them to try something new. I've applied magazine themes to corporate blogs to give them a range of post options from featured posts to small excerpts in a column, and I've used photo blog themes for stores. The key is seeking out the places where you can get lots of inspiration. If you read *Smashing Magazine* online on a regular basis, you'll get that jolt. I promise.

and have slideshows for just those images. Putting the slideshow code in is as easy as copying and pasting into a new page or post. As you add more images to the set or collection, they will be added automatically to the slideshow. The downside is that you don't have a lot of control over the look of the slideshow.

Shopping Carts

If you want to sell your works online, you will be looking at a shopping cart system to use. The kind of plugin you should look for, and the kind I look for, is one that makes it easier to connect to PayPal, Etsy (for handicrafts), eBay, or Shopify.

When it comes to shopping carts, the most important thing is security. You have probably heard of using a "secure transaction" when you do online banking or buy something online. If you run an online store, you need to *provide* that to your customers as well.

Here's the rub. There are good plugins for shopping carts for all blog engines, but Movable Type or WordPress plugins take configuration. Configuring a plugin isn't hard; it's just time consuming. Unless you have a lot of things to sell, skip shopping cart plugins and use services like PayPal, Etsy, or Shopify. Yes, I'm cheating a bit here, but being the pragmatic sort, I know that many of you don't have the time or patience to get it working. (Shopping Cart setup tries both my time and patience.)

You will be happy to know that PayPal, Etsy, and other storefronts make it very easy for you to integrate their systems into your blog. Why? Because then you'll use their service to sell your things (and they take a small cut of that

sale). It's in their best interest to make the whole process painless for you.

> **NOTE**
>
> Do you need to have mobile support? One of my core plug-ins is WPtouch for instant iPhone and mobile support. Why? Is mobile browsing that important? Because it only takes one free plugin, one that you don't even have to configure to be effective, why take the chance? To plan for the broadest possible audience, make sure that people can check out your portfolio while on the go.

Members Only and Private Files

Making a private site or making parts of your site private isn't hard. Built in to WordPress and Movable Type are ways to password protect a post or hide it as private. Going to the next level are plugns that block off the entire site to prying eyes. I combine Registered Users Only and Private Files plugins on my WordPress blogs to make things extra specially locked down. Using both of these plugins makes sure that only people to whom you have given access to the site will see it. Even search engines are blocked! I think photographers especially should take advantage of this to give clients a private place to review photo shoots and pick the pictures they want. Although there might be other uses (maybe a private auction), I think the clients-only portfolio site is one of the best.

Pulling It All Together

I bet you're feeling like you just dumped a jigsaw puzzle on the floor and you're looking at the box top thinking, "Okay, I know I have all the pieces and I know what it's going to look like, but where do I start?"

Nearly all the preceding chapters contain the tools you need to put this all together, from writing to posting to YouTube and even iPhoto. For a portfolio blog, the key is to pull all your material together. I don't mean the blog or picking a theme; I mean choosing what you're going to show and how it will exist online.

When showcasing *anything* visual (graphic designs, photography, and photographs of your works), you want to have at least two versions of each image: a full high-resolution glory (suitable for printing and the media) and a scaled-down version or versions that is better suited to posting online.

For other kinds of works going into your portfolio, make sure you have an online version and possibly an offline version. If you're a writer, think virtual newsroom. Have current works online (and searchable), but have at the ready PDF versions that can be distributed.

> *When showcasing* anything *visual (graphic designs, photography, and photographs of your works), you want to have at least two versions of each image: a full high-resolution glory (suitable for printing and the media) and a scaled-down version or versions that is better suited to posting online.*

The same goes for your contact information and other biographical information. Have good headshots, bios, and other materials available either on your site or by request. Your portfolio is your calling card. It's your business card. It's how you get to show off.

This chapter discusses managing images and documents. I know there are a tremendous number of other art forms (again, I consider coding and website building to be a creative work), but I think from these two examples you can get a good sense of the options and possibilities.

Gathering, Exporting, and Presenting Pictures

How many digital pictures do you have on your computer (or on backup drives close by)? Hundreds? Thousands? Tens of thousands? More? If you're not one of those latter groups right now, odds are you will be eventually. Regardless, the question here is really twofold: first, how to gather all these pictures together and organize them into some semblance of order, and second, how to export them so they are web ready.

Chapter 5 talked a little about iPhoto and Windows Live Photo Gallery and how you use them to save and export files. Here, you explore a completely different scale. There are lots of professional photo-management apps, but Apple's Aperture for OS X and Adobe's Lightroom for PCs and Macs are among the

SHOULD YOU WATERMARK YOUR IMAGES?

As a photographer, I don't really want people to use my pictures without asking, but it happens. So, I watermark my pictures. A watermark is a slightly visible mark that is pretty much impossible to remove without damaging the picture. For my watermark, I use my name and URL with the copyright date. No, it's not perfect, and it can be circumvented, but by making the effort you're making it clear that the images are yours. My watermarks are added automatically when I export from Lightroom; you can do the same with many other tools available online or to download. Other programs can add a watermark for you after you export, and some online services will add one for you.

There is a balance, as well, with watermarks between obscuring the image that you want to present and making it hard to remove the watermark.

My watermarks tend to be more in the smaller type that doesn't obscure the picture. It's clear, however, from all the data around and even embedded into the picture's metadata that the image is mine, and I retain copyright ownership of it.

This might not be perfect, but for me, it's the right balance.

leaders in this area. A view of my current catalogue (just a few of my pictures) is shown in Figure 8.3.

These pictures are all organized by date, but I could just as easily look at them by keyword (when I import a batch of pictures, I add keywords to them) or flag (good, discard, or none), or other parameters. When you're pulling a portfolio together, you could use keywords (or tags if you like) to pull out portraits, head shots, or events, and then have those as a set for people to view. The next step is to take those groups and export them to be uploaded.

Exporting images is an interesting topic. There are two schools of thought. One is to export as high-res as possible so when they are uploaded to Flickr, you have a backup of a "master" picture. The other is to reduce the resolution so that people are *less* likely to try to use your works without your permission. I'm in the middle of those two points. I reduce the size to about 2500 pixels on the longest side, use 80% compression quality as a JPEG, make the resolution 72 DPI (screen resolution), and put a watermark on the picture. For a portfolio blog, you're likely to use an image that is 800, maybe 1000, pixels wide and maybe 600 pixels high. A picture about 800×600 (ish) pixels fits nicely on most screens and themes.

After you export the pictures, and these are going to be close to a megabyte each (maybe larger, depending on how you export them), what's next? The answer *isn't* to upload them to your blog; it's to upload them to a professional photo-sharing site like Flickr or SmugMug (see Figure 8.4).

FIGURE 8.3

A view of just a few of the thousands of pictures I've taken.

FIGURE 8.4

My Flickr page with some of my pictures that I share online.

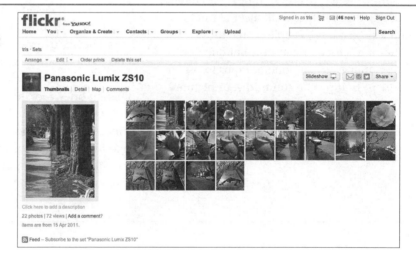

Why do you want to do this? First, both these sites, and Flickr especially, make it easier for people to find you and your work through search engines. If you're an artist, and you want your works to be seen by a wider audience, having a blog is great, and having a blog *and* your pictures on a photo site is better.

Flickr is owned by Yahoo! (it was born in Vancouver, though). Although there is a free account, I recommend paying for Flickr Pro, which right now is $25/year. Flickr Pro gives you unlimited storage and uploads, not to mention the capability to upload HD videos up to 90 seconds long! SmugMug doesn't have a free option, and its plans run from about $40–$150/year. SmugMug is oriented more toward the professional photographer and offers a tremendous number of services for professionals (like being able to offer prints for sale through them), whereas Flickr is for hobbyists and pros who don't need all the features that SmugMug has to offer.

If you have a ton of pictures (like I do), SmugMug has an arrangement with Amazon's S3 storage service to allow you to back up your full-resolution originals (RAW, DMG, and so on). If you need some additional backup and storage for your works for peace of mind, this is a good option to consider.

You might be wondering about the whole "finding pictures through search engine thing," which is good, because it doesn't seem like it would make sense. However, it does make sense because Google indexes millions and millions of images constantly. People search those images for a variety of reasons, but one of the most common is to find photographs to use in projects. So that people can find your pictures more easily, tag your pictures with good, detailed information. Just like tagging a blog post, you can tag a picture. Figure 8.5 shows an example of one of my pictures with a *few* tags.

With all these great pictures online, they also now need to be posted onto your blog. All you need to do is copy the URL of the picture on Flickr and then paste the URL into the Post or Page editor. Yes, the magic embedding that works for YouTube videos works here, too!

For portfolio templates, you will probably wind up uploading many of your images to your own blog for slideshows and then linking to Flickr for more examples. As you develop and enhance your portfolio blog, you will likely come across several ways to do a slideshow. Usually, slideshows require a plugin or two to work, or sometimes you can use Flickr's own Flash-based slideshow to paste into a post. (I do this to highlight a particular set of pictures.) I can't begin to cover the range of different tools to build online slideshows for your pictures, but when you're looking at trying different ones, look for something that says that it works with the blog engine you are using. It is a royal pain to have set up a slideshow only to learn that you can't use it on your blog for one reason or another (speaking from experience here).

FIGURE 8.5

A picture with tags entered to describe it more for search engines.

Final Word on Content

I've covered all sorts of components and content for your portfolio blog, but before I wrap up this chapter, I want to remind you to make sure you flesh out your blog with other types of content. Include pages about shows and awards. Write blog posts about how you make your art and what inspires you. Although your art is going to take center stage, you also want visitors to learn about you, the artist, as well.

You'll probably find it easier to just put up your pictures or videos or what have you, but the additional background about you is just as important. If I'm visiting your portfolio blog, I am certainly going to want to learn about you as an artist and person. So take this time to tell me! For tips on writing and building a community around your blog, review Chapter 3, "Creating Content for your Blog," and Chapter 4, "Building a Community Around Your Blog."

Summary

A portfolio blog is an expression of your art, yourself, and your work. It is more personal than a personal blog. When you're setting up a portfolio blog, the primary consideration is how it is going to look. Although choosing a blog platform, hosted or DIY, is important, all these choices pale in comparison to presenting your work in the best light possible. To that end, look for themes that are designed to present your type of work specifically. Like all the chapters in this book, my recommendation is to buy a domain, get a web host, and set up a WordPress blog. WordPress, unlike many other blog platforms, remains flexible, easy to use, and fully capable of hosting a range of media. Make your portfolio blog something that you are not only proud of, but something that will grow with you as well.

As you build out your blog, remember to include the range of content that visitors will be interested in. Biography, résumé, and influences and insight into your creative process are all things visitors and readers will be very interested to learn and know.

Throughout all this, remember that this is supposed to be a fun exercise, not dreary drudgery that seems endless. Have fun and express yourself—just do it online!

CHAPTER 9

Blogging with Tumblr

Thus far in this book, we've been focused on more traditional applications of blogs—yes, even building a website with WordPress isn't so new anymore. This chapter is a bit of a departure from those chapters (and the ones that follow). In the first edition of *Create Your Own Blog*, there was a chapter on "Lifestreaming," which, at the time (2008–2009), seemed like it would be "the next big thing." The idea was simple: have a single place (something like a blog, but not quite), where you could pull together all your blog posts, tweets from Twitter, videos from YouTube, Flickr images—all of it—for people to enjoy. Turns out, as much as it might have been a good idea (I still think it has merit), Lifestreaming didn't catch on well. The funny thing, though, was that although people didn't want to gather all their content into one place, there was a desire for easier ways to share the things you're interested in, and to do so in a sort-of-blog-sort-of-not kind of way. This is where the services Tumblr have come in—filling a space where people want to share things, but maybe not say a ton about it.

Why Tumblr and Not Others?

You're reading this chapter and wondering: "Why did Tris pick this service when he could have picked …?" It's a fair question, and it's one that I wrestled with both when planning the second edition and when it came to sitting down to write this chapter (in early 2012). Here's what I came up with: Of the growing number of services like Tumblr, and a few *extremely interesting newcomers* like Pinterest, I felt that Tumblr was the best example of what I call "Blogs 2.0." Although Blogger is still alive and kicking—how eludes me, given the sheer indifference Google shows it—Movable Type/Typepad are quickly becoming also-rans, and WordPress is all but crowned the king of all blogging engines, Tumblr has started to try something new: blogging, but with a twist. Tumblr focuses on *sharing* things you are interested in, and they make sharing a quote, a link, a picture, or a video all very easy—easier than WordPress, in fact.

Getting Started with Tumblr

Starting a Tumblr blog might be the *easiest* process of any blogging engine I've ever experienced. When setting up the demo blog for this chapter, I started on tumblr.com. (I logged out of my *real* Tumblr blog, which is trishussey. tumblr.com.) I looked at the home page for a moment, which you can see in Figure 9.1, and wondered, is this all I have to do? Provide an email address, a password, and what I want the URL to be? Actually, yes.

After you enter this information, the next step is to upload a photo, pick a design and name, follow some people, and change your avatar (see Figure 9.2). When those are complete, you'll receive an email asking you to verify your email address. For all intents and purposes, it shouldn't take much more than a minute before you're ready to blog. I'll continue with the setup process in a moment, but first I want to talk about the ethos of Tumblr—simplicity and sharing.

FIGURE 9.1
Tumblr.com—signing up
for a Tumblr blog.

FIGURE 9.2
Welcome to Tumblr,
ready to blog.

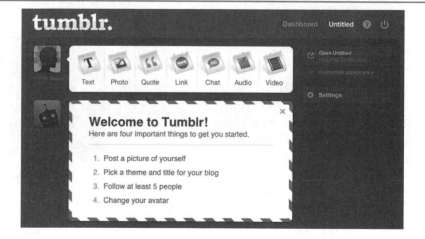

You will notice a few very interesting, and very different, things about Tumblr, when comparing it to WordPress. First, Tumblr is a social network on its own, in many ways like MySpace was. You Follow other Tumblr blogs, and then you can like and reblog posts you like on your own Tumblr blog (or Tumblog). Next, when it comes to posting, not only do you have recommended kinds of content to share and post, you'll find the editor is drop-dead simple. There aren't a lot of formatting options (not like WordPress at all), so a short bit of text is all they are going for here.

Finally, Tumblr *doesn't have comments*. Yes, you read that correctly. There are no comments like on WordPress blogs, YouTube, or Facebook. The founder and CEO of Tumblr felt that comments often got in the way or took away from what people shared. Yes, negative (and hateful) comments on YouTube are certainly sad to see, but no comments at all? I think the way to look at it is sometimes you just want to share something and don't want commentary on it. Something like, "This is a beautiful image, I enjoyed it," can stand on its own. So, let's get to the meat of creating a blog with Tumblr.

Creating a Blog

As I said a moment ago, setting up a Tumblr blog must be one of the easiest processes I've seen in years. If Tumblr is going for simplicity, it certainly hit the mark with the sign-up process. After creating your account, the next steps are easy, but let's just hash through them regardless.

Setting Up an Account

As you saw in Figure 9.1, when you go to Tumblr.com, you are greeted by a very simple form to get started. Yes, it's very much like WordPress.com's process, but much, much more streamlined and elegant I think. Clicking the Start Posting button leads you to a page to enter a CAPTCHA (a necessary evil these days), but on the subsequent page...

You're, in fact, ready to start posting! But let's not be too hasty, Tumblr recommends that you do the following when starting your Tumblog:

1. Post a picture of yourself.
2. Pick a theme and title for your blog.
3. Follow at least 5 people.
4. Change your avatar (from the default picture).

Sure, you could skip the four recommended steps, but let's go ahead and do them. Why? Okay, the picture might be optional, but following people helps you find more interesting content on Tumblr (Tumblr is a social network of its own, remember), and setting a theme makes your new blog look good. The avatar thing I leave up to you. You can see what brand-new Tumblog looks like after I've finished the four steps in Figure 9.3. Sure it's one post, but I kind of like the theme.

FIGURE 9.3

One post, a cool theme, and we're ready to rock!

Tumblr is focused on *simplicity*. From the Dashboard, pictured in Figure 9.4, you see a row of buttons with the different kinds of items you can post: Text, Picture, Quote, Link, Chat (which isn't like an IM chat, but more like a conversation written out), Audio file (maximum of one file a day, up to 10MB), or Video file (via YouTube, or post your own up to 5 minutes long and smaller than 100MB in size).

FIGURE 9.4
The Tumblr Dashboard, access to your blog(s), settings, and the people you follow on Tumblr.

All the posting screens are easy to understand, but you will notice after seeing all the screenshots of the WordPress editor, Tumblr looks *simplistic*. There aren't many formatting options—and that's on purpose. After you accept that Tumblr is about quick, fast, and easy posting and sharing, you will start to feel more comfortable with it.

Writing, Posting, Liking, and Reblogging

I've mentioned already how simple and easy the Tumblr post editor is. Figure 9.5 shows an example for uploading a picture. All the other editor screens are that simple. However, there are some quirks I found confusing at first. One is if you want to have a post appear in the future instead of having it go up immediately upon completion. Instead of a more traditional calendar approach, Tumblr takes the "next Wednesday at 2 PM" approach (see Figure 9.6).

FIGURE 9.5
The editor in Tumblr: simple and easy posting.

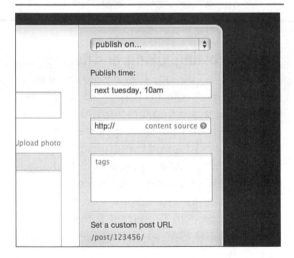

FIGURE 9.6

A close up of the post editor on the date section.

Yes, it's more natural human language, but I also think a tad more prone to mistakes. Beyond that, hey, Tumblr is about as simple as it gets! The basic content types are the following:

▶ Text—Blog posts.

▶ Quotes—Any and all of the great things we hear all the time.

▶ Photo—Upload, pull from a site like Flickr, or take a picture through your webcam.

▶ Chat—Again, not IM; more like relating a dialog or conversation between people.

▶ Audio—Upload your own MP3 (once a day, up to 10MB maximum size) or link to an MP3 elsewhere or on Soundcloud (one of my favorite places to host podcasts).

▶ Video—Upload your own (5 minutes up to 100MB maximum size) or link to a YouTube or Vimeo video.

Most of the content types are pretty easy to understand and imagine how they might look, but Quotes and Chat are different. Honestly, I haven't run across any other blog platform that has those content types *built in* (there are plugins for WordPress that can get you to the same place, but not really in the same way).

Here is an example of a "Chat" (see Figure 9.7):

FIGURE 9.7

How a Chat looks on a Tumblr blog.

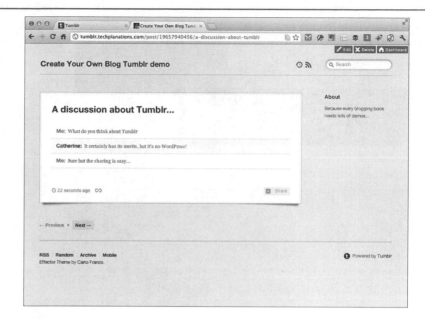

Of course, what might be *more* interesting is how it looks in the editor (see Figure 9.8).

Each line of the chat is on its own line, so you can see how the conversation might flow. You could even imagine writing out a bit of dialog from a TV show or movie this way. Yes, the simplicity of it threw me at first too. Which brings me to Figure 9.9 and the Quote:

FIGURE 9.8

How a Chat looks in the editor window on Tumblr.

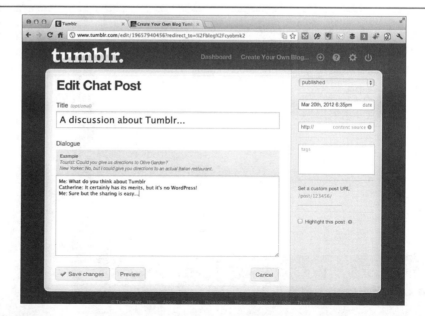

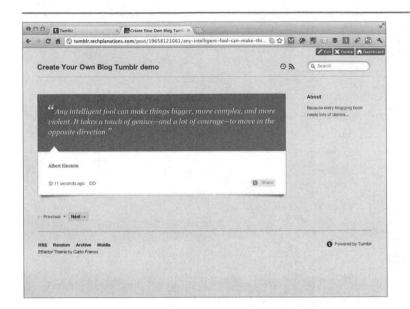

FIGURE 9.9
A suitable quote from one of the greatest minds of the 20th century.

I really like how this particular theme formats quotes. And how does writing a quote look in Tumblr? Glad you asked…(see Figure 9.10).

Again, a very simple and easy editor window. I think it's interesting that the quote portion has no formatting options whereas the *source* section has more options (including the ability to link to where you found a quote online or add other elements).

FIGURE 9.10
How a quote looks on a Tumblr blog.

I think these two examples truly highlight what the founders of Tumblr are going for—simplicity. And as Einstein said...

"Any intelligent fool can make things bigger, more complex, and more violent. It takes a touch of genius—and a lot of courage—to move in the opposite direction."

After you *post* something, several things can happen with that post (or you can do these things to other people's posts). Other people can like the post (users see a little heart symbol if they are logged in to Tumblr) or *reblog* it (again, readers have to be logged in to Tumblr with their own Tumblr blog). Liking and reblogging are two essential aspects of Tumblr's own social network dynamic. The next two are Followers and Following, but we'll get there in a moment.

Reblogging is a *very* interesting part of the Tumblr experience. Essentially, reblogging is seeing a post you like on someone else's Tumblr blog and posting it on yours along with some additional commentary. For example, I saw this apropos post on minimalmac (one of my favorite sites, in fact), pictured in Figure 9.11, and reblogged it on the demo blog for this book (see Figure 9.12).

On the *original* post, this will show up in the Notes section below the post (as do the likes). However, you can't like or reblog a post if you're not logged in to Tumblr, and if you come upon a Tumblr-powered blog, you might just tweet, post to Facebook, or link and post to your blog on another platform. So why is liking and reblogging such a big deal? Well, as Tumblr grows, so does the ability of posts, ideas, photos, and videos to spread to more and more people. It's the social amplification effect that *all* social networks have. That effect, then, starts with following people (and being followed back).

POST BY EMAIL?

Tumblr has tried to make posting so easy that they started, from day one, encouraging people to post by emailing to a special (secret for each site) email address. It's a great idea if you have something to say on the go or a quick thought to zap while you're doing something else. However, if I'm on the go, I'd much rather post using one of their smartphone apps. I've also found posting via email to be *very* hit and miss in terms of formatting and such. For my time, I just stick with the good old web browser.

FIGURE 9.11

minimalmac's Tumblr
blog and a great post.

FIGURE 9.12

The minimalmac post
reblogged on my Tumblr
blog.

Themes

One of Tumblr's revenue sources is selling premium themes (much like WordPress.com has started to do), so as you're browsing through themes, you'll notice some of them have little orange price tags on them. Only you can decide if they're worth the money. Comparing a $49 theme and a free theme, I can see the benefits of paying for a theme that has been coded with more features. However, some free themes (like Effector, which is pictured in Figure 9.13) have a slew of additional features, like customizable headers, backgrounds, and buttons for social networks.

One very interesting aspect of Tumblr is that you can freely edit both the CSS and HTML of your chosen theme to tweak it to your liking. This is more than the settings provided by Tumblr to adjust the theme colors and such. Tumblr allows you—for better or worse—to edit the underlying code for the theme. Looking at the code for a couple themes, I can tell you that editing them isn't for the faint of heart (see Figure 9.14). There is also the potential for the truly *ugly* layouts that became pervasive on MySpace and Blogger when people started editing code (there is a reason we're not all designers), so my advice is to stick to what you know and leave coding to someone else.

FIGURE 9.13
The Effector theme. Pretty spiffy, I think! On the left, you can see the Tumblr theme picker.

FIGURE 9.14
Tumblr theme editor and code for Effector. Eeek!

Followers and Following

Remember those four steps to create your Tumblr blog? The "Follow at least five people" thing? Right, that's because Tumblr wants (rather, *encourages*) you to make Tumblr a destination where you go to find interesting things. When you follow people, their posts appear on your Dashboard when you log in to Tumblr. The more diverse the people you follow, the more diverse the content you see. The more focused...well, you get the idea.

Although WordPress.com *does* have a similar function, they don't push and promote it to the extent that Tumblr does. Of course, you can certainly enjoy Tumblr *without* following people, but truthfully, as I was researching and testing for this chapter, I found that Tumblr

does become more interesting when you follow people there. Also, being logged in to Tumblr allows you to like and reblog content that you read, which again amplifies the network effect of that author's post (and eventually yours).

Is the "goal" of Tumblr to amass a large number of followers or follow hundreds of Tumblogs? No, I don't think so. First and foremost, Tumblr is a publishing and sharing platform—and that should be *your* goal, as well. Sure, having lots of followers increases the chance that what you post will spread far and wide on the Internet, and following lots of interesting people will help you discover interesting things, but I believe those to be ancillary goals. If you don't share, why have the site in the first place? Figure 9.15 shows a few interesting Tumblr blogs you could follow.

Extras and Add-ons

Like all services, Tumblr offers some ways to customize your Tumblr blog beyond what comes in the box (so to speak). I've already talked about editing the code of your template (custom code), which works equally well for free and premium themes. The other option is to add your own domain to your Tumblr blog. For example, I could make this demo blog techplanations.com (as you've seen, I've used as the domain for the DIY WordPress installs) or any other domain (or subdomain!) that I have.

Unlike WordPress.com, Tumblr allows you to do this for *free*. Under the settings for the demo blog on Tumblr, and as you can see in Figure 9.16, I set the blog to be tumblr.techplanations.com using the directions from Tumblr (http://www.tumblr.com/docs/en/custom_domains).

FIGURE 9.15

A few Tumblr blogs from the technology category you could follow.

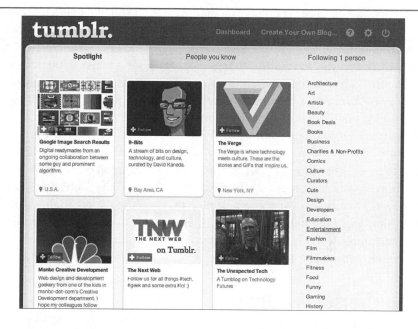

FIGURE 9.16

Additional settings for my Tumblr blog.

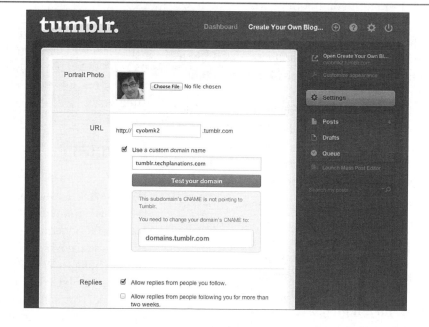

As I've mentioned in other chapters, domain changes take between a few minutes to a few hours to take effect, so as you're looking at the figure, I was still waiting for the changes to "propagate" through the Internet. If you're going to use Tumblr for more than a lark to share things now and then, and use Tumblr as your primary blog, I suggest investing in a domain name and using it here. If Tumblr is going to be another facet of your online presence (maybe you already have a well-established website and now want a simple blog to share), doing as I did here and using a *subdomain* for Tumblr is a good idea (such as tumblr.techplanations.com).

Tumblr Versus WordPress

Because WordPress (both .com and DIY flavors) has been front and center throughout this book, I thought you might be wondering how the two stack up against each other. First, it's not fair or accurate to compare Tumblr blogs to self-installed or DIY WordPress sites. Tumblr is a hosted service, so all the limitations that Tumblr has are better compared to WordPress.com blogs. If you've already decided that a website or blog built on WordPress installed on your own host is what you need, then Tumblr fits in as an additional part of, not a replacement for, what you're doing.

If you compare Tumblr to WordPress.com, the first things that should come to mind are: simple, basic, limited, fast, and focused. None of those adjectives should be taken as slights to Tumblr; on the contrary, Tumblr has done an amazing job of simplifying and focusing posting and sharing. No, you can't easily build your entire website (with a static home page and such) using Tumblr. It's not intended for that purpose.

If you're looking for a way to be able to rapidly and simply share a quick idea, link, picture, or the like, Tumblr is hard to beat. If you're looking for a larger solution with lots of different layout options, different content types (Tumblr is now offering the capability to create static pages in a limited way), and room to grow and expand your site, WordPress.com is the way to go. Although I have many (too many) blogs running on WordPress, I see the potential and place for Tumblr. In fact, if I had more time to curate more than one website (I have a hard enough time keeping trishussey.com updated), I would certainly look at Tumblr as a serious contender for a sharing blog.

Tumblr has made sharing easy and offers almost all its services for free, albeit in a limited way. For example, you can't buy extra storage space on Tumblr as you can WordPress.com, which makes WordPress.com a strong contender for anyone thinking about starting a blog. Tumblr is certainly well supported and growing quickly with a large network of people using it. If you're looking for simple, free, and easy—take a serious look at Tumblr.

Summary

Tumblr is about simplicity and discovery. WordPress, the leading blogging engine, has put focus on making it a solid blogging and content management system. You can have everything from a simple blog to a fairly large website built on WordPress (either .com or DIY), whereas Tumblr is trying to go back to blogging's roots and offer a simple way to share things you find online. Both approaches have their place, and I think that Tumblr could very well be ushering in a new world of blogging.

CHAPTER 10

Creating a Multimedia Blog

This chapter is going to be less about *blogging* than it is about *technologies* for creating content. Podcasts and video blogs remain popular year after year because audio and video are so engaging to users. From your perspective, that of the content creator, podcasts and video blogs are great because they don't require a lot of special gear or software. Almost every laptop and many PCs (and tablets and smartphones!) have all the hardware and software you need to get started.

Just a few minutes in front of your webcam or recording your voice with a built-in microphone, and you're going along the path to being a podcaster or video blogger—or both!

All About Audio and Video Content

I first started podcasting in 2005 with my "Walkabout Podcast." The idea was that I would take a walk (usually to town when I lived on Salt Spring Island, BC) while recording my thoughts on a small digital recorder. It was *very* rough stuff. There was a lot of background noise (cars, gravel crunching under my feet, and so on), and usually I would convert the files to MP3s and upload them without editing. This should have been a recipe for a disastrous listening experience, but people loved them. The amateur, off-the-cuff feel became my shtick and I've kept it ever since.

> *The question for you is, "What do you have to say?" You can do a solo recording or team up with some friends. You can talk politics, tech, or sports—music or no music. You can even decide if you want to host your own show live on the Internet.*

Today I have much better equipment, like a professional microphone, and I do add music, but I avoid doing a lot of other editing. My topics have generally been focused on social media, blogging, and technology area. Because I generally would record what was on my mind, my topics became quite varied. I even did a podcast of a (poor) imitation of Yoda (which strangely enough became very popular) talking about business blogging.

The question for you is, "What do you have to say?" You can do a solo recording or team up with some friends. You can talk politics, tech, or sports—music or no music. You can even decide if you want to host your own show live on the Internet. Like writing, podcasting is open to what you want to give it.

> **NOTE**
> The term *podcast* is often attributed to Dannie Gregoire when it started to enter tech "audioblogging" parlance in September 2004.

At the first Northern Voice conference in February 2005, there was a great session on podcasting and video blogging. I sat in the audience and thought that I could do a podcast without too much trouble, but a video blog—no way. In 2005, nothing about doing a video blog was easy. Video editing software, bandwidth, and storage space weren't cheap (or free). The consensus was that video blogging was only for the really geeky among us who also had access to their own servers (or friends who had their own servers).

Just a few years later, it's a different story. Video blogging is as simple as buying a $150 handheld video camera—or using the video function on your point-n-shoot camera, recording, connecting it to a computer, editing it a little (maybe), and uploading. Done. There are at least a half a dozen free services where you can upload your video and have them host it. Creating your video blog is a two-part process because you'll have your "real" blog but also the "home page" on whichever video-hosting service you choose. Both are going to be crucial to your success as a video blogger. So, lights, camera, action!

Right now, most video blog posts are 10 minutes or less in length (the "sweet spot" is around 4 minutes). Why? Because YouTube and other free video hosts cap video uploads to 10–20 minutes. It's a fair thing, I think, to cap the size and length of videos, and it matches people's attention spans pretty well. Frankly, shorter videos are better; the exception is if you are going to do paid tutorials or seminars. Even then, however, I'd divide the sessions into 5- to 10-minute segments. Why only 4–5 minutes when you can go for 10–20? Experience has shown that many audiences tune out of videos longer than 4–5 minutes. The video has to be *really* compelling to get people to pay attention for longer. Think about movie trailers, how long are they? Exactly.

Right now, most vlog posts are 10 minutes or less in length. Why? Because YouTube and other free video hosts cap video uploads to 10–20 minutes.

Don't worry too much about your style or whether you're going to do interviews or a "talking head" kind of video. That will come later; right now you need to get comfortable recording audio and video. So, enough about content, let's get to recording some podcasts and videos.

Unlike "traditional" blogging, the end result of your podcast or video blog has a lot to do with the quality of the equipment on which it is recorded. Don't worry about needing professional gear; instead, think about your basic nightly news show on TV. Think of the difference between all the ways correspondents call in their stories. The differences among studio to studio communications, regular phone, cell phone, and satellite are all pretty evident. So, a podcast recorded with your laptop's built-in microphone wouldn't sound as good as one recorded with an external headset, but it will sound *much* better than something recorded over the phone. A smartphone or point-n-shoot camera might not look as good as a hand-held camcorder, but it will probably look more composed than the webcam on your laptop. So, although writing is writing and no difference exists in the quality of your posts whether you write them in Word or a text editor or

WHAT MAKES A GOOD MICROPHONE?

If you're looking in the aisle with all the headsets and microphones at your local computer store, you're going to ask yourself, "Okay, seriously, is $40 for a USB headset worth it?" Yes, it is. Having gone through lots of headsets over the years, there is one thing that I learned: Cheap is still just cheap.

For headsets and microphones, there are two places where cheap lets you down: the connectors and the microphone. The cheaper the headset, the flimsier the connectors. Because the wires are thinner, and the connection to the plug and wire isn't as good. At first this won't be a problem, but after a couple months it will be. It won't take long for those wires to start to weaken. I've had my worst wear problems right at the plug and at the microphone-headset junction (where it moves a lot). When you start hearing audio clips go in and out or the microphone levels wander up and down, you should start looking for a replacement headset.

The next big jump in quality was going to a USB headset. Not only could I hear music and audio better, but my recordings were clearer, and when I was using Internet voice chat, people noticed *immediately*.

What makes a headset good is how well the connectors are constructed and how well the headphone-microphone junction is built. I've found the headphone part to come along for the ride if the rest of the headset is good.

If you are really going to set up and get a professional USB mic, shop around. Go to a music store and see what they offer, and read online reviews. I have a strong suspicion that you're going to find microphones made by Blue Microphones to come up in your search. The Blue Snowball is nothing short of *amazing*. It isn't cheap, but it's a mic to look at if you get serious about podcasting.

online, podcasts and video blogs are input dependent. The great thing, however, is that recording an awesome podcast or video blog isn't an expensive undertaking. Before you invest in new gear, use the resources you have on hand. Frankly, there are a lot of very popular podcasts and video blogs recorded on the most basic of gear. What sets them apart? The content.

Podcast Gear

Recording a podcast is one of the simplest and easiest things you can do online. I already mentioned that if you have a laptop, you are already halfway there because chances are that your laptop has a microphone built in. No, it might not be the best mic in the world, but it's a start. If you don't have a laptop, or if your laptop doesn't have a mic built in, you can buy a basic computer headset and microphone at your local computer store. Don't feel like you need a very expensive one to start out with. First, you're just starting out, and second, when you publish the podcast, you're going to compress it, which *generally* eliminates a lot of the benefits of a more expensive mic.

Yes, if you invest in higher-end, professional gear, you will notice the difference, but let's start out simple. Look for a nice headset with stereo headphones. I like having a mute switch on my mic, but that isn't a deal breaker for most people. (I do a lot of audio conferencing, so I like to be able to mute myself during the conversation.) Most good mics are going to be on a stick (or boom) coming from the headphones. You should be able to adjust the mic up and down at least. If you can adjust it closer or farther away from your mouth, that's even better.

You will see two kinds of connections: analog (plug-in jacks) and USB. I used to be a proponent of audio jacks, but now that computers and audio cards are so much faster, I prefer USB. Another reason to opt for a USB-based microphone is that not all laptop or desktop machines have both a headset and microphone jack, and for those that do, they're not always close to each other. Conversely, you're guaranteed to find a USB port on any computer. Buying a USB headset lets you go to most any computer and start recording. As far as sound quality goes, I can't hear a difference, and my professional-grade microphone is also USB, so going with a USB headset is going to be just fine.

Recording Your First Podcast

It's a good idea to have a couple episodes of your show "in the can" (complete) before you launch your site to the world. Giving yourself the target to have three episodes done before launch also gives you plenty of impetus to get things done quickly. If you already have a blog with plenty of written content and you want to add podcasts to the mix, feel free to post your podcast as soon as you feel your recording is ready to post.

When I started podcasting, the hardest part was starting the show. The "well, what do I say" feeling hit me and I would be stuck. After I got the first few words out of my mouth, I was fine, and by the end, I had to remember to shut up and stop recording. Sometimes the best openings are the simple ones. Something like, "Hi, this is Tris. Welcome to This Week in Social Media. (pause for 2–3 seconds) This week we're talking all about Facebook…"

It's a very basic and simple opening that tells listeners exactly what they need to know. The pause after the introduction gives you a nice, clean break to insert theme music. When the music fades out, you get the second half of the introduction. Unlike live radio, you don't have to hit start and stop to bring music into the recording, you can splice a music track in after you're finished recording. Sure, you could play and record the music all at once, but that is more difficult than you might think. If you're doing a show with a guest or more than one person, make sure they know how you do the intro so they don't inadvertently interrupt it or remain quiet when it comes time for them to say something.

When I started podcasting, the hardest part was starting the show. The "well, what do I say" feeling hit me and I would be stuck. After I got the first few words out of my mouth, I was fine, and by the end, I had to remember to shut up and stop recording.

There is no magic to good recordings. Getting a good podcast recorded takes practice. Just do it over and over until you are comfortable when you click Record. If you are more comfortable with it, use a script and talking points for your recording. If you're working with a friend or two at the same location, make sure everyone knows the plan *and* what hand signals to use for nonverbal communication.

I often do a quick run-through, and even record it, to warm up my voice (this isn't nonsense—you need to warm up your voice a bit). I don't do vocal exercises, but the run-through gives my vocal cords time to wake up and be ready for work.

- Relax.
- Take a sip of water (or something) before you start.
- Don't try to have a "radio voice"; just speak naturally.
- Slow down. You're probably speaking too quickly even though you don't realize it.
- Choose a quiet location.
- Turn off your cell phone ringer, computer speakers, and so on.
- Relax (I know I said this already, but this is important).

When preparing for a podcast, there's also the question of whether to go in with some kind of prepared script or just wing it. Although I don't usually work off a script or show notes, I don't recommend the "flying by the seat of your pants" route. Reading from a script is sure to make you sound robotic and unnatural, but working without any notes at all makes it difficult to stay on topic and avoid rambling. If you do ramble a bit at first, don't worry. It takes practice to get your flow right. Heck, I still ramble on the first few takes.

One good trick worth trying is to rehearse what you're going to talk about in your head, so it's not like you're doing it cold. I can tell you that the fact that I usually don't work from notes has driven several co-hosts nuts, but it still works for me.

TIP

If you use show notes, print them in a large font, like 18-point or larger, so you can read and skim them quickly.

Next, you need to think about length. The question of how long your show should be is a tough one. Right now, I'm doing a 5–10-minute show and a 1-minute show. I've also done a 1-hour live show streamed over the Internet (complete with call-in guests and listener comments), and there are plenty of successful podcasts out there that run even longer. Consider the following questions on show length:

- How long do you need to say what you want to say?
- How long do you think people will be willing to listen?

▶ Where do you expect your audience to be listening to your show?

▶ What format(s) will you use to distribute your show?

If you're doing something like an online class, you might be able to have a longer show (especially if people are paying for it), but an hour-long podcast might not work for the commuter listening to you on the bus. I'm leaning toward shorter podcasts now because it seems that all media are getting shorter. Yes, I could be accused of pandering to shorter attention spans, but I'm one of those people with shorter attention spans. I often haven't listened to podcasts because they were too long. I like to multitask, and I can't multitask to a podcast (because I need to pay attention to them).

> **TIP**
>
> Asking your audience or trying different show lengths and gauging the traffic patterns might be the best ways to decide on a show length. Then again, if you have the desire to record a 2-hour podcast, more power to you; just don't expect a lot of people to listen in regularly.

Laying Down the Main Track

For recording podcasts two of the leading applications to do it are Audacity (free, Mac/PC) and GarageBand (part of iLife on Macs). Both apps have lots of power available, and are easy to get started using. Regardless of whether you're using Audacity or GarageBand, the process of recording is essentially the same. You open a new project/episode file, create a base vocal track, and record. In GarageBand when you create a new podcast episode, you get default male and female tracks, a music/jingle track, and a track for images (a podcast can have an image associated with it for branding). Audacity is a blank canvas, but when you click the Record button, a default track is created that becomes the base for the project (see Figure 10.1).

If you're wondering about recording or microphone technique (how to speak into a mic for the best results), I'm not going to go into a lot of detail. Mic technique is something that you will master over time, and it takes a certain amount of practice. Although every mic is a little different, especially built-in mics, the general rules are the same: Speak clearly, speak normally, and be about 4–6 inches from the mic.

FIGURE 10.1
Audacity with a main track, and Record and Stop buttons highlighted.

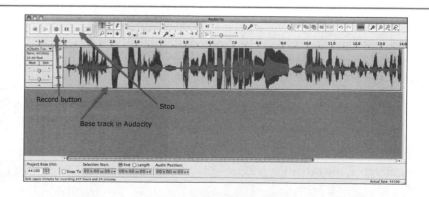

No matter how many podcasts I've recorded, I always do a mic check. In fact, no matter how many times I record voiceovers in the studio, I do a mic and level check first. I've done whole interviews not realizing that the mic was turned off or the battery was dead and have been pretty mortified (and angry) when I figured it out. So a word to the wise—do a mic check. Mic and level checks are easy. I get my mic set up, plugged in, and positioned, and then hit Record. An easy standard to adopt is to say, "Mic check, mic check, one two," and then stop and play back what you recorded. Sometimes the mic is "too hot" (loud) or too soft, and in those cases, you need to adjust the recording levels or your positioning relative to the mic.

> **NOTE**
>
> Ever wonder why people do mic checks by saying, "check one two"? It's simple. Like "the quick brown fox jumps over the lazy dog" uses all the letters of the (English) alphabet, "check one two" covers a good part of the range of normal speaking frequencies. Now you know.

Ready to record? Okay, take a sip of water, swallow, take a breath, hit record, and pause for about two seconds. Even though you're not using physical tape, it still takes the computer a second or two to record the audio, so if you don't wait you might get an intro that starts off a little clipped. If the opening gap is too long, you can always trim the excess when you're done.

When you're recording, make sure all other programs that make noise are closed, your cell phone is off, and that you won't be interrupted. Background noise happens, but the more you can eliminate it, the better the podcast will

sound. You don't need a professional sound booth, just a quiet room. Personally, I find it strange to record in a sound booth; it's too quiet in there. Just to be sure, often I mute my speakers, so if I missed an app that beeps, it won't interfere. Just remember to *unmute* the speakers before playback; it's rather hard to hear what you've recorded when the speakers are turned off.

> *Just remember to **unmute** the speakers before playback; it's rather hard to hear what you've recorded when the speakers are turned off.*

As you record your podcast, be ready to make mistakes. We all do, even professional voiceover people flub up (and it's always funny) and have to start over. When I started out and shied away from editing, I just kept going. Now I might stop and start over, or just pause and keep going. Sometimes you can edit out the flub "in post"; it just depends on how you flub. The first few times you record, you'll probably need some time to warm up before you can relax. I generally do a first take that I discard, and then record a second (or third or fourth) for real. In the first take, I often haven't quite got my point condensed or solidified in my mind. Because I fly without a net, sometimes I need a little practice first.

> **TIP**
>
> In the studio, I just keep recording when someone flubs; it's easier than getting things going again. If you're going to keep recording when you flub, pause for a few seconds, and then restate what you flubbed. When you edit the recording, you'll have a nice, clean place to cut and seamlessly edit the flub out.

Podcast Editing Basics

After you have your show recorded, you might want to do a little editing. This is where GarageBand and Audacity come into their own—they let you take the vocal track you just laid down, mix it with some music, normalize the volume, and otherwise make it sound really cool.

There are several basic edits that you should do. First, trim off the extra dead air at the beginning and the end. If you needed to take a breath to gather your thoughts in the middle of the show, target those areas, too. It's easy to identify longer bits of silence because the track line goes flat in places where no sound is recorded. I find that trimming a bit at a time and listening is the safest way to go. Even if you don't use music, you still want a bit of silence at the beginning of the recording before you start talking. Try it both ways and you'll see that it just sounds better to have a bit of a pause there.

If you made mistakes and want to edit those out, go ahead. As for pauses that came naturally, leave those in. Listen to the way DJs and other people do voice-over narratives, and you'll notice that they let the natural pauses give their words more strength and drama than if they just had several minutes of talking. Not to mention that it would sound very strange to have someone talk without pause for 5 minutes, or even 1 minute, for that matter. It goes without saying that you should save often and play back your edits to see whether they sound right. After you have the vocal track done, let's add some music.

If you are lucky enough to have a Mac that came with iLife, then GarageBand is the obvious choice for you. On Windows (or Mac if you don't have GarageBand), the choice is Audacity (see Figure 10.2).

FIGURE 10.2

Audacity with sample recordings.

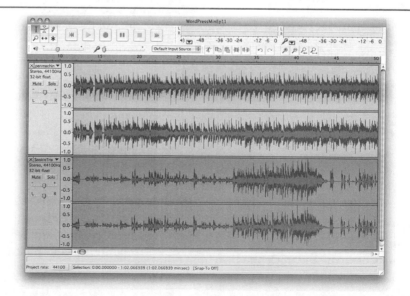

Yes, the Sound Recorder application comes with Windows, but it's ill-equipped for the job. Even Microsoft's own support site says that Sound Recorder is not for podcasting and to use Audacity instead. Audacity is a free, open-source application for recording and mixing audio tracks. You can download it from audacity.sourceforge.net along with extra plug-ins and tutorials. To export your masterwork as an MP3 file, you need to download the *LAME* encoder for MP3s. It is also free, and the Audacity website gives you step-by-step directions to assist with the download. Hardware, check. Software, check. Topic, check. So, next must be recording.

> ### NEW TERM
> LAME stands for—wait for it—"LAME Ain't an MP3 Encoder" because originally the open-source project wasn't an encoder to make MP3s. Now it is, but it is still called LAME. It is the free library that lets you turn a sound file into an MP3.

> ### TIP
> Good editing takes time. The trick is to listen, rewind, listen, edit, listen, and save—often. Then save even more.

Adding Audio Tracks

Both GarageBand and Audacity are multitrack editing programs, which means that to add music to the podcast, you create another track alongside your recorded audio track and put the music there. The mechanics of how to do this are simple; you either import the song into a new track or create the track and then import it.

However, after you dump some music into a new track, you're not nearly finished. If you play the podcast like it is right now, chances are it will be hard to hear your recording over the music, or vice versa. Not to mention that if you wanted an intro track to fit into a pause, like "Welcome to the knitting podcast. I'm your host Darning Needle. [pause] Today we're talking about angora…," it might not fit exactly right. This is the fun part of editing podcasts—getting the music in the right place, fading in and out and in the right places. It's fun because when you get it just right, it sounds awesome.

In most editing programs, you can cut and splice the music into sections, move it to different parts of the timeline, and adjust the volume of a section of the audio track. GarageBand makes this process a little easier by using automatic "ducking" of the Jingle or Music track. Ducking is keeping the volume of the music lower than the other tracks above it (in this case, your voice track). Although ducking helps with making sure that you can hear your words over the music, it isn't 100% perfect. My process is to place the audio track in and listen to the ducked version without adjustments. Then, still listening to the playback, I turn down the track volume of the music to a point where I can hear the music, but still hear my voice clearly. There is a subtle point where you can hear and make out the music and still hear your voice. If you set the music too low, people will strain to listen to the music, which will be distracting to them.

Fades

Deciding how and when to fade music in or out during your podcast depends a lot on the nature of your particular podcast. For example, if I start the voice and music tracks at the same point, I adjust the volume so that when I stop talking for the pause after the intro, the music is louder (see Figure 10.3). Often, I have picked music of a certain length for the part after "Welcome to Social Media this week..." and before the main content of the show. I fade in the music at the end of the intro and fade out as I begin to start the show. If this doesn't entirely make sense to you, don't worry; listen to radio, and you'll hear exactly what I'm talking about.

Ducking, fade ins, and fade outs are nice touches that are easy to include but also give your podcast a nice polished sound. At the end of the podcast, I might fade in some outro music, but just let it run for a bit and then fade it out.

Where do you get awesome music for your podcast? If you answered, "my CD/MP3 collec-

tion," *Bzzzttt!* Wrong answer—thanks for playing. You can't just use any old music in your podcast; you need the *rights and license* to use it as well. What kind of music is that? Podsafe music.

Podsafe Music

Just because you can find a song online, doesn't mean you should or have the rights to use it in your podcast. Music, like pictures, are copyrighted. Artistic works are protected by copyright laws. This can be frustrating, but remember that you, by creating a podcast (or a written work), are also a copyright-protected artist. There's healthy debate about what you should or shouldn't be able to do with someone else's work, but I think we can all agree it's important for creative works to have some protection.

FIGURE 10.3
Audio fade in and out in GarageBand.

Fading in & out music track

WHAT DOES "FAIR USE" MEAN?

Fair use is, essentially, an exception made in copyright law to allow people to use portions of a copyrighted work for the purpose of review, criticism, parody, and other artistic or journalistic reasons. Fair use was first brought into Common Law in 1740 as part of "fair abridgement" from a 1709 British law. Fair use wasn't officially on the books as part of copyright law in the U.S. until 1976.

There are lots of misconceptions about fair use. Wikipedia has a thorough discussion (meaning get a cup of coffee to read) of fair use—http://en.wikipedia.org/wiki/Fair_use—that is worth a read.

One of the key parts of fair use is that it is a legal *defense*, not *a right*. You don't have the *right* to infringe (use without authorization) on copyrighted works, but if you're sued, you can call upon fair use as your defense. It is the *defendant's* burden to prove fair use; the assumption is that there has been a violation of copyright.

Where does this leave you? After all, it's perfectly acceptable for a book reviewer to quote passages of a book in his or her review. Would it then be acceptable to play a portion of a song for a review? What if you really wanted to play a whole song as part of a review of a larger album?

These are important questions that are still being worked out for the online world. I will say that part of proving copyright infringement is both how much of the material was copied *and* the intent. So, perhaps playing one song to talk about the whole album might be okay (especially if you wax poetic about the album, exhorting people to buy it from iTunes).

I don't know all the answers, and the jury is still out (pun intended) on this issue. My advice is to be cautious.

Music is a very interesting, not to mention touchy, subject online. People love music and love to share the music they love with others. This isn't necessarily bad; it's just how it's all done that gets sticky. In the case of podcasts, the issue is payment to the artists for the exhibition of their works. When a radio station plays a song, a royalty is paid to both the performing artist and the composer(s). Radio stations keep detailed logs of what songs are played and how many times. These numbers are then reported back to the recording companies, along with the royalties due to the artists. So when you use your favorite song in your podcast, you are technically broadcasting that song and, therefore, should pay royalties.

When podcasting first started, this became a huge issue. If you use an excerpt of a song for a review, is it covered under fair use? If you do a parody, is it fair use? Can you play a song, giving credit to the artist, and be okay if you were actually promoting the artist? All these questions have been and continue to be discussed, but regardless of how you personally feel about it, there is a great solution that won't step on anyone's toes: "podsafe" music.

Podsafe music is music that is released online for use in podcasts. The creators of the works are not relinquishing their ownership or copyright, but giving you the right or license to be able to use the work, under certain conditions. Generally the conditions were that your podcast was noncommercial and that you gave credit back to the artist (usually a link back to the artist's site). It was a simple and effective way to handle the problem. In fact, many popular musicians released some of their works under Creative Commons podsafe licenses to get additional play and attention.

Finding podsafe music is as easy as doing a Google search for podsafe music. To save you a step, visit my late friend Derek Miller's website, penmachine.com, and check out his podsafe music. I'm rather fond of it, especially because he wrote one in particular for me ("Mighty Mullane"). You can use commercial music in your podcast, if you ask permission and are granted a license. I did this for my early podcasting efforts. I really wanted to use the beginning of one of my favorite songs ("Basement Apartment" by Sarah Harmer) as my intro music, so I asked her label and received permission. It was that simple. As daunting as it might seem to ask for permission from some big record label, you never know until you ask.

Exporting to MP3

Regardless of the tool you use to edit your podcast, it isn't ready for distribution until you export it as an MP3 file. Audacity, GarageBand, and other audio-editing tools save your work in their own file formats so you can edit them, add tracks, and generally tweak your recording. Also, until your recording is exported, it is

uncompressed. The audio is just as you recorded it, but that file would be useless if you tried to share it with people online. When you export your podcast as an MP3, you are combining the tracks together *and* compressing the file to make it smaller. You're probably very familiar with MP3s already; a lot of the music you already listen to is saved in this format. The trick with MP3s is finding the right amount of compression for the audio track.

The MP3 codec is a "lossy" compression scheme, meaning data are removed from the file to make it smaller, but done in such a way that you won't notice a loss of quality—to a certain point. Any audiophile will tell you that any time you compress something, there is a loss of fidelity. The trick is to get the right balance between not enough compression (large file sizes) and too much (small file size, but sounds terrible). For podcasts that are mostly spoken word, I suggest 64kbps (kilobits per second) stereo (which also happens to be GarageBand's settings for "Good" quality). If you have more music in your podcast, try exporting at 96 or 128kbps, but before you upload, listen to all three files. You might not be able to tell the difference between 96 and 128 (much less 192kbps) and if you can't discern a difference, go with the smaller file size. Smaller file sizes not only take up less space on the server, but also take less time to download (therefore, people don't have to wait as long before they start hearing the podcast).

In case you're wondering, the uncompressed songs on an audio CD are 1411.2kbps. This is why when you copy songs to your computer from a CD or download them, they are compressed to 128, 192, or even 320kbps (for very high quality) because the uncompressed files are huge. A CD holds only 700MB of data with maybe 13 songs on a disc. If the songs

SUZANNE VEGA "MOTHER OF THE MP3"

When Karlheinz Bradenburg was working on the new MP3 codec to compress music, he needed a song to test the compression against to ensure he wasn't losing audio quality. According to Internet lore, he was walking down the hall and heard someone playing "Tom's Diner" by Suzanne Vega. He felt that the complexities of that song (a cappella singing and harmonics) would be the perfect test for his new file format. And thus, Suzanne Vega became the unofficial Mother of the MP3.

weren't compressed when you copied them over, you'd fill up your hard drive pretty fast! Both GarageBand and Audacity have presets for exporting the audio you've created into MP3s, so don't worry about remembering specific kbps settings (I certainly don't). There's one last thing before you post your master-work—setting the ID3 tags.

When you buy a song online or copy it to your hard drive, your computer "knows" a lot about the song already, such as artist, album, composer, genre, year, and so on. This data is stored with the MP3 file as additional informa-tion collectively called the ID3 tag. The ID3 tag gives software, and therefore listeners, that additional information about what they are listening to, like who the heck the person is or what the silly song is. When you export files with Audacity, as shown in Figure 10.4, you're presented with a dialog box to fill in this infor-mation (some might be prefilled for you). GarageBand doesn't do this as well (shame on Apple), but you can use ID3 tag editors to tweak any MP3s you created in GarageBand.

FIGURE 10.4
Audacity ID3 tag dialog box.

For the sake of ease and clarity, don't worry about ID3v1; instead, select v2. For the genre, I pick spoken word or other, unless podcast is offered. If I edit the ID3 tags later and can change the genre to podcast, I do. In most cases, however, it doesn't make much difference for podcasts if the genre is specifically on the money. It's important to provide your name, the podcast title, and year as bare minimums because these are used by podcast servers and software to give the listener information about what they are listening to (see Figure 10.5).

Video Gear

I'm going to venture that if you're interested in creating a video blog, you're probably interested in video already. You might already have a video camera and have been doing home movies or have played around with your webcam. If you've been experimenting with video, you know that it all comes down to the camera. Cheap cameras result in cheap-looking video.

Recording video with your cell phone sounds like a simple idea, but the quality of those videos can be hit or miss. That's okay for some things, and there is nothing wrong with using different cameras in your video blog, not to mention videos posted from cell phones that capture spur-of-the-moment action. Most point-n-shoot cameras record video now (many in HD), so you have *another* option for spur-of-the-moment videos. However, unless you're going to use that gritty, bouncy, poor audio quality as your shtick, you're going to need a dedicated video camera. Yes, smartphone cameras *are* getting much better. Yes, the latest iPhone and other smartphones record in HD video, but remember they are light, small, and often the sound recorded is full of background noise. However, camcorders have *also* gotten much better over the years (and more affordable), so if you start to get serious about video, you'll want to get serious about your gear.

FIGURE 10.5

Editing ID3 tags.

Pocket-sized, HD-quality cameras are afford-able for almost everyone, and they are the logical choice for a budding video blogger. These devices do have their limitations, of course. Often they can't record more than a couple hours of video, the microphones are not the best, and they usually don't have a ton of additional settings for capturing video. Shortcomings aside, the sub-$150 price tag makes these pocket-sized recorders something to consider for the casual or novice video blogger.

Stepping up into the world of "real" camcorders brings up the price considerably, but that added cost does bring benefits. Larger camcorders usually offer better quality video, more complexity, more features, and more settings. These devices are for people who are going to shoot a lot of video and want to shoot video that looks a bit more professional.

NOTE

One of the big differentiators between expensive and cheaper digital video cameras is the lenses they use. The quality of a camera's lens has a huge impact on the quality of the video it's able to capture.

Think of these as the step up after you get going. A newcomer to the video world is the DSLR camera. *DSLR* still cameras have been around for years and are known for their capa-bility to capture professional quality shots. Nikon, Sony, Canon, and others have come out with DSLR cameras that also shoot HD video. This goes way beyond the standard movie setting on a point-and-shoot camera (which is often a great option for fast video), because

you can use the high-quality lenses you take still pictures with for video, which brings the quality and versatility to a new, exciting level. Having tested a few of these cameras, I can say that DSLR-based recording has brought a whole new level of quality to video. Certainly, they're not the first choice for a new video blogger, but if you're a photographer who is upgrading your camera body and want to get into video, these are worth serious considera-tion.

NEW TERM

DSLR stands for Digital Single Lens Reflex, which is the fancy way of saying cameras that work like the classic 35mm film cameras with detachable lenses. A DSLR shooting HD video means that you nearly have the power and flexibility of profes-sional video cameras because you can not only control all aspects of the recording, but also change lenses from a wide-angle to a zoom lens. It's nearly versatility personified.

All decent video cameras (and still cameras) have a tripod mount on the bottom of the device. Although you might not think you'll want to mount the camera on a tripod, even if you are just shooting yourself, having the camera steady on a tripod adds a lot to the end result.

TIP

Did you know that the threads on the top of a lampshade holder are the same size as a tripod mount? So if you need a tripod in a pinch, grab a lamp that has a shade on it, take the shade off, and screw on your camera! But don't forget to turn the light off.

All camcorders, or any devices that record video, have a built-in microphone to record audio. The quality of these mics varies widely, but seldom are they capable of delivering more than rudimentary quality. If you're buying a camera and plan to use its built-in mic, it's worth doing a few in-store tests first. With the exception of a few lower-end devices, most video cameras have a line-in or external microphone port. If you're buying your first camera, think of this as a "nice to have" not a "need to have" feature.

> **NOTE**
>
> There are two main types of microphones you're likely to use: omnidirectional and unidirectional. An omnidirectional mic records audio in all directions around it, and sometimes behind (depending on the mic), whereas a unidirectional mic records audio only in *one* direction, usually straight in front of it. Where an omnidirectional mic can make for a noisy recording, a unidirectional mic reduces the background noise. Therefore, tailor the mic you use to the task at hand. There are plenty of situations where you want the background noise an omnidirectional mic picks up.

All set? Have that camera all ready? Cool, let's start recording.

Recording Your First Video Blog

When you're sitting down (or standing up) to record your video, you need to have a good idea of what you want it to look like in the end. Yes, you're a director now (put the beret down), so figuring out how it will all look is important. If you're filming yourself with a webcam (like the iSight built in to my MacBook Pro), you'll be able to see yourself as you film. For something where you are going to use a standalone camera, either a friend is going to have to frame it for you, or you'll need a video camera where the view screen can be turned toward you. I've done a number of the "just turn the camera on myself" videos, and without being able to see the framing on the screen, I just had to guess that I was actually on camera. Sometimes the effect was pretty funny, too.

Recording a video blog post is very much like recording a podcast. The main difference is that people can *see* you in the vlog post and not in the podcast (hand away from your nose, thank you). This is no small thing. It's much easier to control your voice for the purposes of a podcast than it is to control both your delivery and your mannerisms. Many people have no idea what they look like when they talk and are often surprised at the result when they see themselves in a video monologue for the first time.

Like podcasting, it's a good idea to have several episodes of your show "in the can" (complete) before you launch your site to the

Shooting a video is easy; shooting a good video is a different matter. Like photography, there are do's and don'ts to keep in mind when shooting.

▶ **Frame the subject correctly.** Refer to the "The Rule of Thirds" sidebar this chapter. Watch the backgrounds. People don't *usually* have trees sprouting from their heads, so make sure that what's *behind* the subject is okay.

▶ **Use good lighting.** Let's face it, fluorescent lighting makes even a supermodel look like the undead, so try to avoid it if at all possible. Natural light is best, but when you can't use it, use other lamps to light the subject *evenly*. Watch for shadows that make the subject look off. Get daylight bulbs at any hardware store and you can turn just about any light fixture into studio lighting.

▶ **Do test shoots.** If you're using a new system or not shooting where you usually do, it never hurts to do a few test recordings to see how things come out.

▶ **Use a tripod.** Handheld video is great when on the go, but when you want to shoot something that looks professional, put the camera on a tripod.

▶ **Use an external microphone, if possible.** If your camera doesn't have an input for an external mic, you can record the audio portion like a podcaster would and then match up the two.

▶ **Use the Internet for hints and tricks.** I know that there are a ton more tricks to learn—I don't even pretend to know them all, which is why you have the Internet. Search for the questions you have, even "shooting better videos," and I'll bet you'll find some great tips.

world. Set a target of 3–5 completed videos before you launch to the whole world (and iTunes). If you already have a blog and want to add video to the mix, you have other content there already. After recording an episode, post it, but put off your big announcement (and submissions to iTunes) until you have completed a few more.

Part of the recording process, and developing your style, is figuring out if you want to have titles, graphics, or music in your posts. Personally, I don't. I do more "talking head" style. Adding music and titles gives your video all the more punch when it's done. Just like with podcasting, if you're doing a show with a guest or more than one person, make sure they know how you are doing the intro so they don't think something is wrong or they are supposed to say something. While it might be just awkward silence on a podcast, it *looks* like an awkward silence on video (read: makes the person look like a doofus).

Like podcasting, I don't usually have show notes for video, because it doesn't serves me well. Off-the-cuff might work for audio, but when I *look* like I'm grasping for the next thought, well, it isn't so cool. There is nothing wrong with having show notes to help you to keep on track. (Note to self: Use show notes.)

How long should your video be? YouTube has bumped the top length from 10 minutes to 15 minutes (if you are a member in good standing with a solid track record), but in all honestly, 15 (or 20) minutes for a video is a long, long time. Shoot for your videos being about 3–5 minutes long. That's about right for most people's attention spans these days. Yes, you can create longer videos, but I'd say 10 minutes is about the max (even if you can upload longer videos), if you have lots to say, make several segments.

Because you're just recording video right now, let's skip file size and compression until later and focus on time. Although you might record more video than you need, the final product should be 10 minutes or less. Hold the phone. If I don't want to host my videos on YouTube or wherever, can't my videos be longer and of higher quality? Yes, they certainly can, and you can certainly host the videos yourself, but here's why this isn't always the best idea. Bandwidth and server storage space cost money. Google is willing to give it to you free— let them. Unless you are going to be selling your videos as part of a class, having YouTube host the videos gives you not only storage space and bandwidth, but also another place and touchpoint for promotion. Be concise, or at least know you're going to edit the video down to 10 minutes or less. Got it. What's next? Audio—you can't forget the audio portion of the video.

I'm going to repeat myself here—always do a mic check. Always. Maybe the batteries are dead (I've had to *run* out and grab batteries before a shoot) or the audio settings were left over from a shoot outside where there was a lot of background noise to overcome, or the mic isn't on or plugged in. You just don't know, so check. Trust me...recording a great interview only to find there is no audio (and no backup audio recording) leads to fits of uncontrollable swearing.

Getting the mic positioned for the best recording isn't an easy task. A built-in mic can't be positioned. You can be only so close to the mic and be framed correctly for video. This is the point where you do the best you can and try to

THE RULE OF THIRDS

There is a photographic rule called "The Rule of Thirds" that dictates how to frame a subject in a camera shot. It means taking your view finder and dividing it into thirds horizontally and vertically, which is sort of like a big tic-tac-toe box (see sidebar figure).

Where the lines cross are the places the eye tends to look. Putting the focus of your subject (for instance, the eyes) at the top left or right intersection of the grid instead of at the center makes the video look better. It's an odd thing because you know when a video or picture follows the rule of thirds; it just looks right.

improve the audio in editing. You can use an external mic to record the audio separately and then match it back up to the video in editing. Although this might be a little tricky at first, detaching the recorded audio from the video and adding another piece is a lot easier with tools like Windows Live Movie Maker or Apple's iMovie.

Ready to record? Okay, take a sip of water, swallow, take a breath, hit Record, and pause for about 2 seconds. Whether you're using tape or some digital recording media, it takes a couple seconds for the recording to start. If you go right into your intro, you'll most likely be clipped off at the beginning. The wee bit of extra silence can be trimmed in editing, or left if the timing works out right.

Ready, set, … oh wait, I wasn't ready. Can I start over? Be ready to flub. We all do. Professionals flub up all the time (and it's always funny) and you know from watching blooper reels on DVDs that actors do it all the time, which makes it even more amazing that movies actually get finished!

The first few times you record, you'll probably need some time to warm up before you can relax. I generally do a first take that I discard, and then record a second (or third or fourth) for real. In the first take, I often haven't quite got my point condensed or solidified in my mind. Because I fly without a net, sometimes I need a little practice first. When I'm podcasting, a little flub isn't a big deal, but with video it seems that the flubs are always worse. Chances are, and this is absolutely okay, that you're going to either have to reshoot or edit out the flub—unless you're going for the unscripted feel, in which case, make as many mistakes as you want. Now that you have an

episode recorded (may I suggest doing several test videos to experiment on), let's get to editing.

Video Editing Basics

One of the good things about video blogging is that you have free options when it comes to having access to basic video-editing software. On Windows the program is called Movie Maker (see Figure 10.6), and on Macs it's iMovie (see Figure 10.7), which is part of iLife. Both of these applications are designed to be drag-and-drop editing tools where a lot of the work is done automatically for you.

> **NOTE**
>
> There are a few versions of Movie Maker out there. Outdated versions of the software are included with Windows XP and Windows Vista, but you should make a point to download the most up-to-date, and best, version: Windows Live Movie Maker.

As with audio editing, with video editing you're still dealing with timelines, but now you see frames of the video instead of a waveform of audio. It should be easier for you to find the right spots in the video to cut, jump, or add titles because you can see where it should go.

Every video editor has its own tricks up its sleeve, but don't worry about that too much. Programs like iMovie and Movie Maker are relatively simple to use, and there's a lot of help available online. For iMovie, you might also check out Que Publishing's ebook, *Using iMovie '11* (ISBN: 0-7897-4930-0).

FIGURE 10.6

iMovie with events below and the active project above.

FIGURE 10.7

Windows Live Movie Maker with a sample movie loaded.

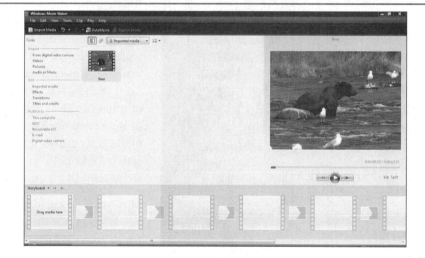

After you get your video imported into the application, your next step is cutting out the parts you don't want. Generally, this means splitting the video at certain points and deleting what is in between. Simple, right? Sure, mostly. It will take practice, for sure. Just like editing audio, editing video takes time. After you get going, you'll probably see why I don't like to edit video and would rather keep the mistakes.

After you complete the edits, you could jump to the export process, or you can gussy up the video with some music, titles, and effects. It's your choice. I've seen a lot of popular video

BASIC VIDEO EDITING

Like editing audio for podcasts, video editing is pretty straightforward, in theory, but in practice it is something that takes, well, practice to get right. The following are some basic video edits:

▶ Opening and closing titles—The trick is to keep titles onscreen long enough to be read, but not so long that people wonder if the video will ever start. It's good to go from a title to the video with a fade. If you just switch (a hard cut), I think it looks jarring.

▶ Fades—Both iMovie and Movie Maker have lots of fade styles to choose from, but the style of the fade isn't as important as the duration. Play and replay the fades so it doesn't look like the screen just blinks or the screen flows like molasses.

▶ Music—If you want to have a soundtrack playing under your vocal track, great, but make sure that you can hear the voices and music at the right level.

▶ Audio track—Listen to your audio track. Listen carefully. Even close your eyes so the video doesn't interfere with what you're hearing. There might be parts where you need to increase or decrease the audio level. Often you can use a built-in audio leveling or normalizing tool to clean up the audio. Just remember to listen, edit, listen. Only save when you're sure the edit is right.

blogs with very little to no editing, no titles, and no music. Then there are some that I wonder how they keep a day job because of their amazing production value. Striking the right balance is up to you.

TIP

It might seem overly geeky, but it's worth your time to mess around with the video (and audio) editors when you're not actually producing an episode. Taking time to experiment and goof around can lead to amazing discoveries, which is highly recommended.

If you are going to do a regular show, I think it's well worth the time spent on learning how to put in titles and transitions. For example, if you're talking about sites or products, using a standard "lower third" title (text in the lower third of the screen) for the URL, product name, or other details is very helpful to viewers. Also, using transitions between places where you made edits makes the edits seem less drastic (be sure it looks right; cutting in the middle of a scene might look strange).

Music can add just the right touch to a video. You see and feel this in movies. The question isn't, "How do I insert a music track?" because that would be the easy part; the question is, "Do I have the rights to include the music in my video?"

In both Movie Maker and iMovie, adding music is just a drag and drop away. After you have the podsafe music in (virtual) hand, you can import it into your video. Like working with a podcast, you can drag the music into the spot where you want it to be and adjust it from there. Where the music starts and ends, how it fades in and out, and its relative volume is all up to you. Each program handles it a little differently. Because all the software makers say that a child can do it, I think it's safe to say that you're pretty likely to be able to figure it out. (Don't forget the help files—I use them, too!) Adding titles and screen credits are easy, too, with the current crop of video editors (you don't want to know how hard it was not that long ago). Again, this is a click, drag, type, and adjust process (see Figure 10.8).

You might be wondering how much I do when I edit videos. Not a lot. Like my podcasts, I keep video posts off-the-cuff and rough. I try not to do a lot with them. I've found that if I get too caught up in getting the right title or the music in the right place, I lose sight of what I was trying to do in the first place. This, however, is just my own thing. So although I do add music to my podcasts (because I like radio as a genre), I keep my videos more

talking-head type. I do the same things in interviews. So editing and tweaking is up to you.

Exporting, Compression, and Video Formats

The easy part is done. Now it's time to get that video out there and online. Wait, how can this be the hard part? I thought editing was going to be the hardest? Sorry, no. You can record a video and skip the whole editing part, but what about exporting and compression? Nope, you have to do that and unlike audio where MP3 is the file format of choice, for video there are several potential formats to choose from, each with its own special pluses and minuses. Remember when I brought up the whole question about where you wanted people to see your video? Yeah, this is where these decisions come in. Let's get to it then.

FIGURE 10.8

Additional audio and title tracks in iMovie.

Do you ever wish that the world of computers and the Internet *wasn't* awash in an alphabet soup of acronyms and terms? Me, too. But it is, and video is no different. There are lots of video formats you might run into or export files to, but the following are some common ones:

▶ MOV (QuickTime)—QuickTime was first developed by Apple Computer in 1991 and served as the basis for the MPEG-4 video standard. MOVs can be very high-quality files (and therefore very large).

▶ WMV (Windows Media Video)—The (current) default Windows video format and the format for HD discs (HD DVD and Blu-ray). Developed by Microsoft, it has wide appeal for its capability to have digital rights (DRM) assigned to it for copy protection.

▶ AVI (Audio Video Interleave)—Once the default video format for Windows, it is often still used for sharing movies online.

▶ FLV (Flash video) Flash video using Adobe's Flash encoders. FLVs can be very high quality and large size. They need a player to be played within a blog post or on a page.

▶ MPEG-4/M4V: This is the current standard for high-quality audio/video with the best balance of compression to quality. QuickTime and H.264 are all part of the MPEG-4 family of video codecs.

▶ H.264: Part of the MPEG-4 video format and how the standard for video compression. If a video looks good on YouTube, it was probably encoded using H.264.

Because Google-owned YouTube is the 300-pound gorilla of the video world, looking at what they recommend for export settings is a great place to start. If you think I'm just cheating, you're missing the point. When Pure Digital first introduced the Flip camera, they made sure that their export settings for YouTube would make anyone's videos look great (and Pure Digital did a fantastic job of this). If you're going to make a drop-dead easy video product and you want to make exporting painless, YouTube's recommendations are a good place to start.

Resolutions

YouTube uses 16:9 aspect ratio players (like wide-screen movies, TV is 4:9). If you are uploading a non-16:9 file, it will be processed and displayed correctly as well, with pillar boxes or letter boxes provided by the player. If you want to fit the player perfectly, encode at these resolutions:

▶ 1080p: 1920×1080

▶ 720p: 1280×720

▶ 480p: 854×480

▶ 360p: 640×360

▶ 240p: 426×240

No, these recommendations don't make much sense on their own. It means scale the video to either high definition (HD) or standard definition (SD) size, use the H.264 compression scheme (this gives the best balance of quality and file size), and keep the audio stereo with standard settings.

What if you want to make the video smaller? What if you produce a great video, export it like that, and it's 3 or 4GB? That's when you need a little help from software.

When you export from iMovie, you're presented with choices from Tiny to HD, each with dots showing what platforms the size/format is best for (see Figure 10.9). To illustrate how size and compression work hand in hand, I shot a 2-minute, 40-second video with my iSight (so for exporting, I couldn't go to full HD) and added a title to the entire length of the video, a fade in and out, plus about 30 seconds of music at the beginning. This is what I got:

▶ Tiny (176×144, iPod format, mono) 1.6 MB

▶ Mobile (480×360, mpeg-4, stereo) 19.3 MB

▶ Medium (640×480, mpeg-4, stereo) 31.9 MB

▶ Larger (720×540, mpeg-4, stereo) 56.5 MB

Wow, huh? That was for less than 3 minutes of video! Using iMovie, the largest size took about 6–10 minutes to render and export. The bigger the dimensions, the longer it will take. In the end, you're looking at 15MB (ish) per minute of video at these settings. Can you do better? Can you use different codecs? Certainly, and experimenting is an important part of getting the right look, but there is the gotcha. If you're trying to reach the widest possible audience, keeping the videos in standard sizes (as per YouTube recommendations) enables you to take advantage of rerendering that hosts will do for you. My best advice, and what I do myself, is to keep up on what video hosts suggest for file formats, follow those recommendations, and be patient. Or you could forget video and just do audio, and life is easy (insert sarcasm here).

FIGURE 10.9
The Export dialog in iMovie showing the options for size and compression.

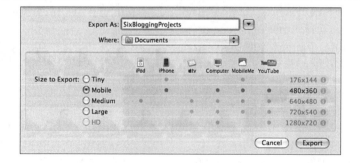

Where and How to Host Your Podcast or Video Blog

The hosting world has changed a great deal since I first wrote about podcasting and video blogging in 2008–9. Back then, *most* hosting accounts came with limits to the amount of storage space and bandwidth you were allocated (total storage space and bandwidth used per month). Today, most of the big hosts offer unlimited storage and unlimited bandwidth. So, you're thinking, you should just host all your videos and podcasts on your own site, right?

Close.

If you're a podcaster, hosting all your files *is* the right decision. The free options for hosting your podcast are few and far between. PodBean (podbean.com), Libsyn (libsyn.com), Blubrry (blubrry.com), and SoundCloud (soundcloud.com) are reliable hosts in the podcasting world, and PodBean and SoundCloud are the only free ones (compared to at least six for video). These services give you storage space and either generous or unlimited amounts of bandwidth for your podcast. They also let you embed a player, like you might for YouTube, into your posts for each podcast.

For my own podcasting, however, I upload my file to my own server space and use a WordPress plugin to insert a player into the post. I suggest that you follow the same path. If you're going to be serious about podcasting (more than an episode or three), get server space and set up hosting. The cost you will pay for hosting is essentially the same as paying for hosting at a podcasting host service, without the benefit of being able to host and control your own site(s). Follow the self-hosted/DIY route discussed in Chapter 2, "Installing and Setting Up Your First Blog."

The video blogger, on the other hand, has a much simpler decision—just post your videos to YouTube. Not only is Google providing the extra space and bandwidth for free, you're posting your video *where everyone is already looking for videos in the first place*. There just isn't the equivalent for podcasting. If you're a podcaster, you're better off hosting your own podcasts and submitting to iTunes to get the word out. With videos, you host on YouTube, submit to iTunes, and post your videos on your blog for a triple-threat promotion strategy. It's times like this I wish I liked doing videos more.

When you post a new episode, make sure you give as much information as you can on YouTube (or wherever you're hosting). This shouldn't be all, though—you need to tie a blog post to the episode that gives more detail than you can include on the video page.

Posting Podcasts and Video to Your Blog

As for your blog itself, you've already seen that posting a YouTube video is a piece of cake (copy and paste and done!), so to present an episode on your blog with additional links, commentary, and all the tags and categories needed is nothing new. For a podcast, you need to take a couple other steps.

First is downloading and installing a podcast plugin to be able to easily embed your podcasts into your posts (and also have a nice interface for iTunes). The plugin that stands out today, just like it did in 2008, is the PowerPress plugin from Blubrry (http://www.blubrry.com/powerpress/). It's the best featurewise (you even get free listener stats with your optional Blubrry account), and it's also actively *supported*, which means that as WordPress is updated, if something breaks, they will fix it.

How do you get your podcast into your post, and how do you get that awesome player? It is all part of using the right WordPress plugins. With PowerPress, adding a podcast episode is just a few clicks away. You just need the URL of the episode that you've uploaded to your host and then you're off to the races. The easiest way to get this URL is to use the media uploader built in to WordPress (see Figure 10.10).

FIGURE 10.10
Copying the URL of an uploaded media file.

WHAT MAKES A GREAT VIDEO BLOG OR PODCAST

Great video blogs and podcasts have several things in common. Here are some tips from the best:

- ▸ The posts around the audio or video are descriptive and even offer more information than is in the segment. Offers links to relevant sites and whatever you think would add more value to the viewer.

- ▸ The posts are tagged and categorized well so that you can find related videos easily.

- ▸ It is easy to share the posts with others.

- ▸ When you visit your YouTube page, there is consistent branding between it and the main site. You know that you are looking at the videos from the same person.

- ▸ Give a clear understanding about what you are going to talk about or show early in the episode.

- ▸ Sum up your podcasts at the end with the key points. Although this applies to more educational podcasts, having a summary of what you talked about is great even for more informational or news podcasts.

If you want to start video blogging, you probably have seen enough videos and posts to know what you like and what you don't. Follow the examples of others. If you like one style versus another, go for it! There is a huge diversity out there; just dip in and pull out something cool.

WordPress has come a long way since 2008, so you can now use the built-in media uploader to upload your podcasts much more easily than in the past, when you needed FTP to upload your files. Depending on your host and its settings, you can upload something between 7–10MB (or more). After the file is uploaded, you can copy the URL from the media page for the next step.

Create a new post, and below the posting area look for the PowerPress box. Next, paste the URL into the space provided, write your post, and publish. The player, download links, even informing iTunes is all done for you. Snazzy, eh?

Submitting Your Show to iTunes

Just like in the online music world, iTunes is the 300-pound gorilla for distributing your video blog or podcast. At first the idea of subscribing to a video blog through iTunes seemed ironic, at best, especially when video blogs existed in a strange sort of nether world between "true blogs" and podcasts. Then iTunes tuned into

podcasting, and the distinction between audio and video podcasts was eliminated. With iTunes on the scene, regardless of whether your video is hosted with YouTube or Vimeo, the best thing to do is to submit it to iTunes.

Although your videos can be found on YouTube, there is a lot of chatter on there because it is a catchall for online video. Video blogs stand out a little better on the other video hosts, but still, iTunes is the connector to iPods, iPhones, laptops, Apple TV...well, you get the idea. The process for submitting a podcast or video blog to iTunes is simple: Make sure you have iTunes downloaded and installed on your computer. Launch iTunes, click iTunes Store, and click the Podcasts link on the top of the store window. (I know you're not producing a podcast, but iTunes doesn't care if it's audio or video—it's a podcast). After clicking the link, you should see something like Figure 10.11.

Click the Submit a Podcast button to see a screen like Figure 10.11

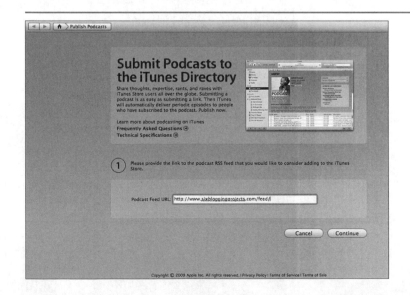

FIGURE 10.11

Submit a podcast screen within iTunes where you paste your blog's RSS feed.

Insert your URL and include the "http" portion, which is either the URL of your blog where you are posting the videos or your video host. Both have feeds, but choose your host as the primary one. You can update the feed address if you need to later. Paste this into the submission box.

The next screen gives you the option to set the topics areas, but you'll get an error if you haven't created at least one episode (two or three is better). The number of topics that you can set is limited. I hope Apple updates at some point to give more choices, or even a better tagging system. Until then, you have to make the best of it. That's all you need to get the process started for your video to be available through iTunes. Note the word "started" here, because someone from Apple reviews each submission to iTunes to determine whether it is worthy of inclusion. Yes, most submissions are accepted, and the process generally takes only a week or two, but you can see that Apple can (and does) decide what is allowed on iTunes. If you are involved in

several podcast projects, the process can be accelerated. When you have one approved podcast in iTunes, getting a second one is much easier.

NOTE

Unlike audio podcasts, you can't sell video podcasts on iTunes. If you want to sell videos, you can list only free videos on iTunes. Those will have to be the lure for your paid content.

After you receive approval for your podcast, you can add categories and keywords. Apple, unfortunately, doesn't give you a lot of options for primary and secondary categories. I, personally, set the genres and such within my WordPress plugin because I have much more control and the ability to define keywords better. The Blubrry's PowerPress plugin example shown in Figure 10.12 shows you how detailed you can be when adding keywords and other data to your iTunes listing.

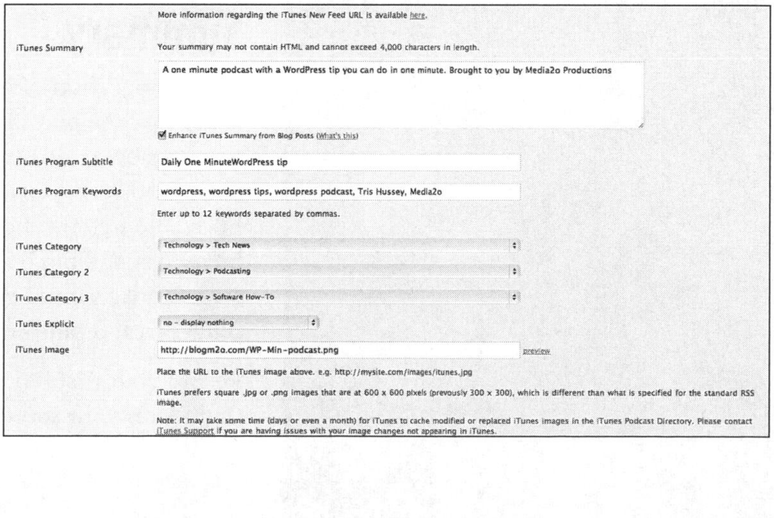

FIGURE 10.12

Additional iTunes settings through advanced options in the PowerPress plug-in.

PROMOTING YOUR PODCAST ON ITUNES

To get more listeners, use buttons provided by iTunes on the sidebar of your blog to direct people to subscribe to your podcast. By pushing them through iTunes, you make it easier for them to download and carry it on their MP3 players, plus increasing your ranking within iTunes. The more listeners you have, the closer to the top of the list you are within your genre.

When you write the post for the episode, make sure there is a link to subscribe in iTunes, and remind people to subscribe in iTunes as well.

Finally, ask listeners to rate your podcast in iTunes. Apple selects highly rated podcasts from each genre to promote on the main page. If you get on there, you will get a sudden increase in listeners.

You can even go a step further and *charge* for episodes of your podcast. While not promoting *per se,* having a $2.00 an episode show does add a bit of exclusivity to your show. It's interesting to note that you can sell episodes of *audio* podcasts on iTunes, but not *videos*. Only studios and networks can sell video on iTunes.

You can update or augment your iTunes keywords from the link Apple sent you. Making your updates through the plugin is faster, easier, and takes effect as soon as you publish your next episode.

Like most things related to the technology of blogging, after you have the initial setup done, it runs itself. I don't worry about my iTunes feed or RSS feed or if my shows will keep playing. I know that if I set it up right, it should just keep working.

After you receive approval for your video blog, you can add categories and keywords. Apple, unfortunately, doesn't give you a lot of options for primary and secondary categories. If you want to update or augment your iTunes keywords, you can do it here or from the link that Apple sent you. For audio podcasts, you have more granular control because most people host their own podcasts now. For video, you're just going to have to manage with what Apple provides. Your best bets will be to keep your iTunes keywords updated and make sure your tags/keywords on both your video host and blog are descriptive.

Summary

Podcasting, short of writing and photography, is my favorite part of publishing online. It is easy to start podcasting with the microphone built in to your laptop or with an inexpensive microphone from the computer store. You don't have to spend big bucks to get going. Don't forget that I started off using a cheap MP3 player with a built-in voice recorder!

Record your first bits of audio, start editing them with your sound/audio editor of choice (which will be Audacity or GarageBand), and then publish as an MP3 file.

Finding a home for your new podcast is as easy as signing up for WordPress.com or buying a domain name and setting up hosting on your own. In the end, I think you'll be happier with the DIY option because you'll have a lot more flexibility to grow your podcast.

After you have completed some shows and then look at your blog, think of how cool you'll feel! Finally, don't forget to submit your podcast to iTunes when you have some episodes done, and you're off to the races!

Being admittedly camera shy, video blogging hasn't been something that I've really enjoyed doing, but you might want to be a TV star with your own channel. If you have a webcam built in to your laptop, you can start right away! YouTube and many other hosts enable you to record straight from your webcam to video. Sure, you get only one take, but if you want easy video posting, it doesn't get much easier. If you don't think you can create video in one take (I know that I can't), both PCs and Macs come with video-editing software that will let you record the clip straight from your webcam, insert some music and titles, and export to be uploaded.

On the subject of exporting, file size is going to be your biggest challenge. Start at 640×480 using the H.264 codec in stereo (two channels). If that is larger than the 2GB limit, try reducing the audio to mono before making the video smaller. After that, it's just a matter of trial and error. Video isn't like audio, where the compression tools are dead simple. There is an art and science to it that has a lot of trial and even more error.

Unlike the podcasting set, video bloggers have it pretty easy, otherwise. There are an easy half-dozen sites that will host your videos free (including YouTube, of course), so all you need to do is put together a small site to promote yourself with a little more flair than a YouTube profile page. For video bloggers, WordPress.com is a great start, but don't forget to buy that cool domain name, just to be safe. Like the podcasting set you can submit your show to iTunes, go ahead…you could become Internet famous overnight!

Hey, is this thing still on?

CHAPTER 11

Making Money Through Your Blog

As a professional blogger, I'm often asked how I make money through my blogs. The answer, truthfully, has always been very simple: People pay me to write for them. This doesn't mean that I don't know about banner ads, Google AdSense, affiliate links, or optimizing my pages for them; it's just that I've usually chosen not to use them too often. As the bonus chapter for this book, this is intended to be the capper; the final piece that you might want or need to give your blog an extra something. Okay, fine—it also helps to pay the bills.

Where do you go from here? It's pretty simple. Money made through your blog comes from one of two places: Either selling space on your blog or selling your words to other people or blogs. As simplistic or crass as it might sound, that's what it all boils down to. Myself, I've chosen the latter. Lots of my friends have chosen the former. Some of my friends have chosen the former and have been very successful at it (*very* successful).

The easiest way to think of earning money from your blog is to break the ways into two areas: direct and indirect. The direct approach encompasses things like getting sponsorships, various writing gigs, syndication, and selling goods or services through your blog. Direct ways focus on you leveraging your talents to generate additional income. Indirect is selling or placing ads on your site. Indirect includes ads, affiliate links, and the sorts of things where you are supplying space on your site for someone else's ad, and taking a cut. This binary (and maybe arbitrary) way of organizing puts the focus on who is doing most of the work: you or someone else.

Nuts and Bolts of Making Money from Blogs

Whether you opt for the direct or indirect route, in general, attempting to make money from your blog isn't a terribly geeky exercise. However, there might be a little code pasting, plug-in installing, and maybe some theme tweaking to get it all together.

Now, if you're going to be a professional blogger and get paid to write posts, the biggest thing to learn is how to write great content and deal with other blogging engines (other than the one you are partial to). Although the idea of making money online is nothing new, the idea of making money through or by *blogging* is rather new. The reason isn't that blogs are some kind of magic website through which it takes a special set of skills to make money. It's because the ethos of blogging was supposed to be above the pettiness of "making money." Long-time blogger and social media maven, B. L. Ochman, (www.whatsnextblog.com) told me once, "Purists are rarely realists." Her advice then was in regard to character blogs, but it rings just as true for making money online. The bottom line is if you want to spend your time writing online all day, you either have to be independently wealthy, have a job where this is tolerated, have no job, or earn some kind of money from it. I chose the last option.

Making Money Directly

Because you know already that this route has been my bias for making money through my blog, I'm not going to pretend that I'm not biased in favor of this mode of income generation. However, it isn't the most lucrative way to make money through your blog. These are active income streams, meaning you have to do something to get something. No do, no get. There are four basic ways to make money directly from your blog:

- ▸ Getting sponsors for your blog
- ▸ Syndicating your posts to other blogs
- ▸ Writing posts on other blogs
- ▸ Selling things directly on your blog

Each of these, of course, has its own pluses and minuses, but they each have one thing in common: You're in control. Let's start off with getting sponsorships.

Blog Sponsors

Sponsorships for blogs generally take a few forms. Often, a hosting company gives a blogger free hosting in exchange for having a banner or mention like, "Server space and bandwidth graciously provided by…." This is a passive sponsorship in that the hosting company isn't paying the blogger; rather the blogger isn't paying for the hosting account either. Another example of this kind of passive sponsorship is a company covering a blogger's travel expenses to attend a conference. What I'd call "active" sponsorships are much less common because bloggers don't often receive money like a grant. If bloggers receive money from a company, it has been in exchange for advertising space on their blog or to write for the company's blog. Neither of these are really "sponsorships" then, are they?

Getting people to sponsor you or your blog often isn't as much something that directly brings money into your blog as it is a means to not have to pay for something you otherwise would. For example, soon after I started blog-

ging, I started using the (now defunct) blogging platform Blogware, which was offered through resellers by Tucows.

Blogware was a great system, but it had a couple interesting quirks. One was the amount of disk space you were allocated (which wasn't much even for the time) and the other was that you had tightly controlled amounts of bandwidth allotted to your blog per month. This was how Tucows/Blogware allowed their resellers to make more money: selling their customers more disk space and bandwidth on demand. Hitting your disk space cap wasn't too big a problem. Sure, it was inconvenient when it happened, but it generally wasn't a showstopper. Now running out of bandwidth? Yeah, that was a much bigger deal. When you ran out of bandwidth, your blog was turned off. Yes, rather inconvenient when you just wrote a killer post and it got some serious link love.

As I started to get more than a little attention on my blog, my friend who was a Tucows reseller had been kindly giving me disk space and bandwidth as I needed it. However, this was costing him real money at the same time. I had an idea—why not ask Blogware/Tucows to sponsor my blog?

So I asked.

And they said yes.

This was the first big thing I "earned" as a blogger. I received access to software and such before, but this was something that I *needed*, something that was going to start costing me serious bucks in the near future. So I got unlimited bandwidth and disk space in exchange for mentioning Blogware and Tucows in the footer of my blog and talking

FTC RULES AND SPONSORSHIPS

Because of the rising popularity of blogging *and* bloggers often receiving things for free (either for review, or as gifts, or whatever), the U.S. Federal Trade Commission (FTC) updated its disclosure rules at the end of 2009 to include social media. This means that if you receive something to review, you have to disclose that you received the item for review and what you will do with it. So, if you receive a free iPhone case for review from the manufacturer, you have to let your readers know where the case came from. It makes sense; although we all try to be unbiased, if you *bought* that case with your own money and you didn't like it, you *might* give a harsher review than if you *were given* the case to review and didn't like it.

For more information on this you can read the release from the FTC—http://www.ftc.gov/opa/2009/10/endortest.shtm—or this good round up from PC World—http://www.pcworld.com/article/173169/ftcs_new_rules_for_bloggers_a_quick_guide.html.

about Blogware on my blog. It wasn't difficult to talk about Blogware because I was a big proponent of it back then (it was ahead of its time in many ways). There are two things to take away from this example: First, you don't know until you ask, and second, there are win-wins in business blogging.

TIP

Asking someone to sponsor you can be an intimidating thing to do. Get over it. Although you might run into a lot of rejections, you will *never* get a "yes" if you don't ask. At the end of the day, if the worst thing a person can tell you is "no," you really haven't lost anything.

Nowadays, I tend to seek sponsorships to cover the costs of going to conferences. If I want to attend a conference where I'm not speaking, I offer to blog the sessions for a company, giving them the always nice "My attendance and these posts are sponsored by..." line at the end of my posts. The direct win for the sponsor is more along the lines of being associated with a prominent blogger and "getting the scoop" at a conference.

There is a concern about sponsorships, however, which is that you as the blogger could be tainted by the sponsorship. The fear is that you won't say something bad about the sponsor or their product because they have sponsored you. This is a legitimate concern and something that all of us who have accepted sponsorship money or support have faced. The best way to handle this is to make it very clear who is backing you, so if there is any accusation of bias, at least it's out in the open. In terms of conflicts of interest, the biggest problems between bloggers and their readers occur when it looks like the blogger has something to hide.

Additionally, there's a trust element between you and your readers that takes time to build. I've built up a reputation through many years of blogging that even if I'm given a free product or access to a product to try (like testing computers, laptops, phones, or printers), I'm going to give the straight story. I might love or hate the product. I might even pan it (politely), but privately give the company detailed feedback on the product so they can improve it. You can be honest without being hurtful. Sponsors appreciate this because they don't want tainted bloggers writing about their products. Bloggers who are not trusted by their readers are useless to a sponsor because if people think a review is biased, it's a worthless review, no matter how glowing the praise. You can't *always love* the products you try. I don't love all the software or hardware I own. Ultimately, it's about balance. Few things are all good or all bad. I love my Mac, but sometimes it drives me nuts. I have received lots of free useful apps, but that doesn't mean I don't have constructive criticism about them.

The key to getting sponsorships is to be real, honest, valuable, and helpful to the sponsors. Along the way, you're going to have to prove to others that you can be unbiased, and if you receive sponsorship for something, you disclose it. Beyond that there is only one other thing to remember: You don't know until you ask.

Writing Posts on Other Blogs
You might already have guessed that this is my preferred method for making money from my

WHAT IF YOU REALLY DON'T LIKE IT? HANDLING PR PITCHES AND REVIEWS

Although bloggers often receive things to test, contrary to popular belief bloggers aren't showered with freebies galore (sorry). When you do receive something and are asked to review it, what do you do if you don't like it? What if you are getting email after email from a PR person asking you to review something that you aren't interested in?

Honesty and open communication are the best policies. If a PR company is dying for a stellar review and you just can't give it, be honest about it. If I've received something to test, and I know that I'm not going to give the most glowing review, I give my PR contact a little heads up and also additional feedback about my experience. Nine times out of ten, the PR people I've worked with, and developers themselves, have appreciated my honest (and polite) feedback. Building a good rapport with companies is key to both their and your success. You can be both a critic and supporter of a company at the same time and still be an asset to the company.

However, being bullied to write a great review or fearing to be cut off from early access is something that many bloggers will make public. PR companies are not under unprecedented scrutiny, and potential clients don't want to see that a PR firm has been blackballed by bloggers for being unprofessional. Often overzealous PR people will try to get you to write *anything* about their client's product. If I'm not interested, I tell the person straight away. If I am interested, but it's a PC application (I have a Mac), I say that I have a Mac, and if they offer a Mac version in the future I'd be happy to look at it.

PR people have a tough job and are under tremendous pressure to perform for their clients. Although this is no excuse for unprofessional behavior, a little communication goes a long way to keeping everyone happy.

FINDING BLOGGING GIGS

Although the notion of being a professional blogger isn't making headlines anymore, that doesn't mean that you can't still become one. Keep an eye on the Problogger Job Board and Bloggers for Hire for potential gigs.

When you apply to blog for others, they are going to ask to see examples of your work. Don't worry if you haven't blogged on a particular topic before; the important thing is to have an established blog with a good track record of posts and using all the current social media tools. It's most important to show that you "get" the medium, not as much that you're an expert in a particular topic.

The key to getting a job writing for other people is showing that you not only can write well, but that you understand how blogging/social media works and know how to research information on topics quickly. Really good professional bloggers don't have to be subject matter experts on everything, they just need to be able to find what the hot topics are, analyze what others are saying, and write some good commentary about it. Being able to quickly understand a topic enough to comment on it is one of the things that separates great probloggers from just okay ones—that and being able to type at preternatural speeds.

blogs. Before I had my first sponsorship, I was writing posts for other blogs. I was one of the first "professional bloggers" hired to contribute nothing but blog posts. My job was simple: Here is a blog on Topic A; write a post a day on it and we'll pay you x dollars. At the peak of my pro blogging I was *trying* to maintain close to twenty blogs. That meant reading hundreds, thousands maybe, of other people's blog posts to get source information, and then write something interesting given the news of the day. If there was no news of the day, I had to find a new angle on the topic that I thought might be interesting. This was hard work.

To give you an idea of what sorts of direct hire opportunities are out there, during my career as a professional blogger, I've been part of the third-largest blog network (b5media), have been a partner in one of the first professional blogging agencies (Bloggers for Hire), and…completely burned out on blogging.

Sure, it was a lot of fun and I wouldn't be where I am now if I hadn't gone pro, but I also remember trying to get a day's quota in the meager 30 minutes I had left in the day (that set my 12 posts in 20 minutes record). Would I do it all over again? Yes, without hesitation. I wouldn't be writing this book (the first or second time) without having started off as a professional blogger. My work as a writer, teacher, consultant, and marketer are *all* thanks to starting off blogging (on a whim, remember). Although I don't blog professionally any more (but I always do wind up being "the blogger" at whatever place I'm working), I wouldn't change a thing.

If you want to make the jump to professional blogging full time (most probloggers are part-time folks writing for a little extra spending money), you have to know how much you can write during a given day. Not just *write* but write good posts of about 200 words each, with links to sources and good tags for SEO. Believe me, the people who I know that do it full time work hard (and type fast).

If you want to make the jump to professional blogging full time (most probloggers are part-time folks writing for a little extra spending money), you have to know how much you can write during a given day.

The first step to going pro is to write and maintain a blog for several months and show that you have solid knowledge *and* passion for your topic. It doesn't matter if your blog is on computers or coin collecting, you have to write good, smart stuff to go pro.

Think you're up for the challenge? Start writing.

Selling Things Online

This is the most obvious way for you to make money from your blog—if you already have a business or hobby where you sell things. You can sell ebooks, music, jewelry, cards, clothing—whatever it is that you want or can sell. The most interesting part of these blogs is that they span almost all the kinds of blogs in this book. They are personal, business, and portfolio blogs all at once. Selling things that you have made or created yourself is so tied to you that you have to be passionate about them. You must present them in the best light possible, and you have a big challenge.

If you're selling something physical or at least semitangible (like ebooks or downloads or music), you're going to need an eCommerce/shopping cart system to make this happen. If you've gone the DIY route already, you could install an eCommerce engine via Fantastico or install one of the several WordPress plugins for eCommerce (or whatever blog engine you chose—if you chose to ignore my advice completely and picked something other than WordPress), but frankly there are times when it's best to leave things to the pros. This is one of those times.

Whether you use eBay (www.ebay.com), Etsy (www.etsy.com) for arts and crafts (see Figure 11.1), PayPal (www.paypal.com), or Shopify (www.shopify.com) to sell, let them do the heavy lifting. They have made setting up an online store drop-dead simple. I've gone both routes and would much rather spend my time doing almost anything other than trying to configure and get a shopping cart working on my own. Etsy and eBay have all the hard stuff worked out. They accept payments, they can handle downloads, they handle receipts, and they take a cut. I think the cut is worth it (usually just a small percentage of the purchase price) given how unfun it is to set up a cart, get transactions working (and secured), and handle all the other easily forgotten details.

Earning money directly from your blog is very satisfying. You've worked hard, you've created something that other people value, and you've earned something for it. It gives me a thrill to see the check or deposit as payment for something I've written. On the other hand, it is nice to earn money just by having my site or blog *be there* and not have to do anything day to day with it. That's the world of *indirect* earning.

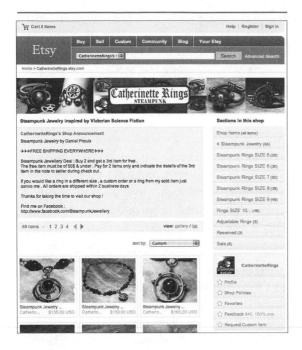

FIGURE 11.1
The Etsy storefront for Canadian jewelry maker Catherinette Rings.

Making Money Indirectly

As mentioned earlier in the chapter, "indirect" means that after a particular system is set up, it runs itself. It doesn't mean that there isn't work to be done to optimize or tweak; just that left to its own devices, the money comes in from your blog. If you frequent the Internet, which was 40 years old in 2009, you've seen one of the most dominant forms of passive income generation: Google AdSense. There is, however, more to life than AdSense or simple banner ads. You can make money by suggesting products and services to people (affiliate

programs), or you can sell space on your blog directly, or you can use many other schemes for leveraging the traffic and audience of your blog for monetary gain.

When sites like GeoCities, Blogger, and other free services started to crop up (ones that offered a "free homepage/website"), they were supported by the ads surrounding your content. People, by and large, accepted this because they were getting a free website and the ads surrounding their content were paying for this privilege. After people started having their own sites—sites they built and controlled themselves—they wanted to earn their own money from their content. Thus, the ad network was born.

> **CAUTION**
>
> There is a really big "but…" in this discussion of ads and ad networks. If you use WordPress.com, you cannot put ads on your site. That is a violation of the Terms Of Service (TOS), and it will get your blog deleted with little or no warning. The folks at Automattic (the company that runs WordPress.com) are very firm on this. They do not want WP.com to become like other services infested with spam blogs. So, no ads. You've been warned.

Let's get back to AdSense. Google didn't invent the ad network, nor did they really invent a new idea with text-based contextual ads; they just found a way to do it really well. Because Google AdSense is one of the easiest ways to make money from your blog, let's cover it first. I am, however, convinced that making money with AdSense is somewhat of a dark art. Some people manage to make *lots and lots* of money with AdSense and others, pretty much nothing. With that caveat in place, let's continue.

Google AdSense

If you pick nearly any random scattering of blogs, you will see ads on them, and chances are those ads are Google AdSense. The reason for this is simple: Putting AdSense ads on your site or blog is easy. The amount of configuring you have to do for a basic set of ads to show up is minimal. The payouts on AdSense can be great or they can be nonexistent. The key with AdSense is putting the ads in the right place *and* writing good content that triggers good ads. AdSense ads are *contextual* ads. If you have ever used Google to search the Web (and who hasn't?), you've seen this in action. For example, a search on google.ca for "Vancouver tours" yields the results shown in Figure 11.2 (at the time I wrote this).

Companies pay (bid, actually) to have their ads appear on pages like this one. The companies at the top, just above the search results, paid the most to have their ad there. For a time, it was a little hard to see on Google where the "sponsored links" stopped and the results started because the ads didn't look much different from the regular search results. They were relevant to what you were looking for, right? Sure, but people *paid* to have them there, on top, for you to see and hopefully click on *before* you saw the actual search results. That's the power of textual ads, which is the same as you might see in Gmail and the same as you *want* to appear on your blog. If you're writing about fly fishing in Idaho, having ads for crocheted tea cozy patterns isn't going to match your audience.

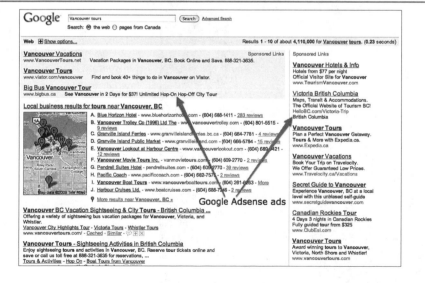

In addition to some template tricks that I discuss later, the following are some tips for how to write for contextual ads:

▸ **Use descriptive titles like "Best MP3 player for joggers and runners."** Titles with strong keywords not only help Google index your post better, but help to match the content to appropriate ads as well.

▸ **Break out the thesaurus.** There is more than one way to skin a cat and there is more than one way to describe a product, idea, or service. Within the framework of your natural writing style, work in as many variations of the idea as you can.

▸ **Use descriptive tags and categories.** Using categories like "News" or "Products" aren't as good as "Music News" or "Audio recording products." Don't make readers, search engines, or AdSense guess what the topic is about.

Getting started with AdSense is just a form field away.

1. Go to www.google.com/adsense and log in with your Google ID (see Figure 11.3).

2. If your account *doesn't* have an AdSense account associated with it, you'll see a page like the one shown in Figure 11.4.

3. Fill out the required information and click the Submit Information button at the bottom of the page.

After your account is approved (essentially, everyone is), you'll be in a position to start adding code to your blog and tweaking the ads. I'll save that for more of a nuts-and-bolts part of the chapter (just a few more pages, I promise). The important thing to keep in mind is that AdSense isn't the be all and end all of ad networks/ad programs. Sure, Google is proud of the system they built (and rightfully so, in my opinion), but it is neither perfect nor the best solution for everyone.

How much can you earn from AdSense? Essentially, it can range from nothing to thousands of dollars a month. You earn money from AdSense when someone clicks an ad on your site. Generally that single click pays you a few cents. No, that's not very much, but AdSense is a game of scale and numbers. To make money with AdSense, you need enough people to click the ads. To do this, you also have to *attract* a lot of people to your site in the first place. Generally, people put AdSense on their blogs when they reach a certain level of traffic per day (between 400 to 1,000 page views a day), a level that represents a sort of critical mass of potential people to click the ads.

FIGURE 11.3

Logging into AdSense.

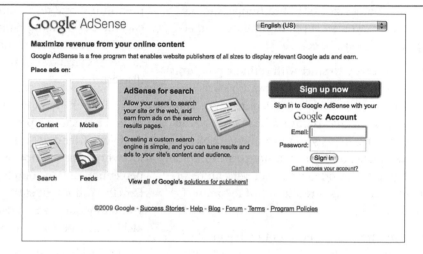

FIGURE 11.3

Logging into AdSense.

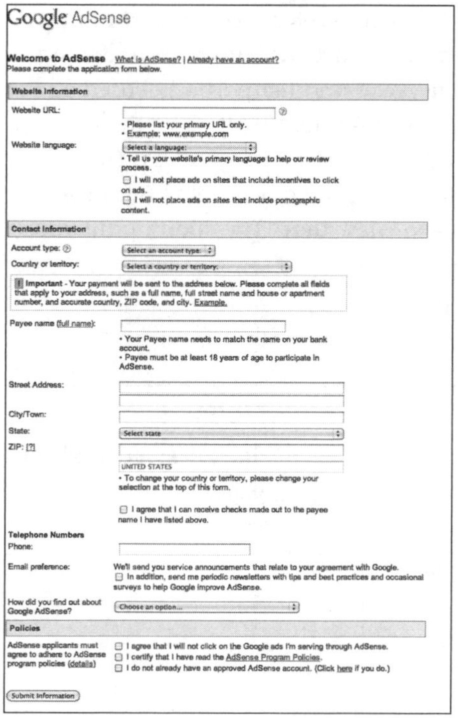

FIGURE 11.4

Application for AdSense.

What else is there? Okay, how about if you got a 5% kickback from a store every time you sent someone there and they bought something? Sounds pretty good, huh? Welcome to the world of affiliate programs.

Affiliate Programs

You like to recommend products to your friends, right? Generally when you tell a friend to go to a certain store or buy a brand of detergent, you don't get anything out of it (maybe the thanks of your friend). So, what if your recommendations earned you 5% of what your friends spent? Yeah, that's cool, eh? That is how affiliate programs work.

You sign up for a program, often a service you use already, and they give you a special link or coupon code that you give to friends. It doesn't stop there—you can sign up for affiliate programs for all sorts of products and services. In fact, affiliate marketing is big business. There are millions affiliate marketers in North America bringing in billions of dollars a year.

How do you get started? That happens to be pretty easy—you start out at affiliate marketing how-to blogs, of course!

The easiest way to start with affiliate programs is to go with the folks you know. Let's use Amazon as an example (see Figure 11.5). The Amazon Associates program has been around for years, and it lets you recommend books, movies, music, and other things (depending on where you live) and get a small percentage of any sales made as a result of traffic coming from your site.

Amazon's program might not be the most lucrative one of its kind, but people certainly trust buying from Amazon, and trust is important when you're using affiliate programs on your blog. Part of the hesitation people have with buying things is whether it's a good deal. When a friend recommends something to you, you feel more confident in your purchase (unless it's coming from crazy Uncle Louie). Now, if you have an affiliate link or offer on your blog, this is a statement that you recommend this product to your friends. Whether it is buying a domain name or web hosting or

premium WordPress themes, your readers are clicking and making a purchasing decision based on *your* recommendation. This brings me to the next important part of affiliate links: disclosure.

What if your friend told you to buy a computer from a particular store and you later learned that your friend got a kickback from the store for every referral? How would that color your perception of your purchase and your friend? Exactly. You might start wondering whether you really got the best deal and what other kickbacks your friend is getting.

Using "kickback" instead of "commission" or "percentage of the sale" colors how you perceived the questions, but the idea is still the same. When you receive a commission from the sale of a product, you are recommending one product over another partially based on money. Sure, you might really love the product and would recommend it regardless. The commission is just a bonus, right? But how do your readers know that? They don't until you tell them.

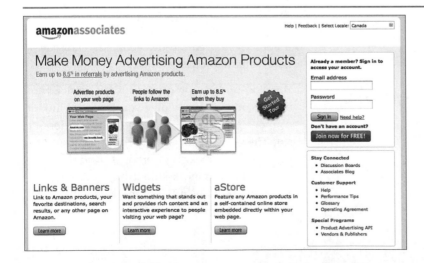

FIGURE 11.5
Amazon Associates home page.

Using "kickback" instead of "commission" or "percentage of the sale" colors how you perceived the questions, but the idea is still the same. When you receive a commission from the sale of a product, you are recommending one product over another partially based on money.

Although Amazon Affiliate links and Google AdSense are clearly ads, other affiliate links might not be so obvious. It's good practice to disclose an affiliate link. Just saying that tells the reader, "I like this product, but you should also know that I'm getting a commission when you buy it."

One of the hallmarks of blogging has been its culture of transparency and openness, which means that it is expected that you will disclose affiliate links and other similar things (like when I receive a free product for review that I get to keep). Not disclosing this information can get you in hot water. It's happened to even prominent bloggers (who should know better), so don't feel alone, but it's best to avoid the whole issue and let people know.

How do you choose what to sign on with? Start with the things you already use. For example, I like to use Namecheap (namecheap.com) to register my domains, and they recently came out with an affiliate program. Because I like them a lot and have recommended them in the past, I'll probably join the program. Same goes with hosts I use (and like), and the themes from StudioPress and DIYthemes. There are affiliate programs for almost everything. I think there are even affiliate programs for referring affiliate programs!

When you decide to join a program, do a little Google research to see whether complaints or other issues come up. If you know people who are already in the program, ask them about it. After you sign up, you get special codes and links to use and information on how to track your sales. These vary from program to program. It's also important to read the fine print of the program, such as how long after clicking a link (referral) does a purchase count toward your commission. For example, someone might click a link from your blog so they can get a look at a hard drive on Amazon, but not buy it until a couple days later. Will you still get credit for the sale? In Amazon's case, most likely yes, because it stores a cookie on the person's machine. Other affiliate programs might not work that way, so it's important to check. Sometimes the devil is in the details.

All caution aside, I have several friends who earn money that ranges from paying for "a nice dinner out" to "quit my job and do this full time" in affiliate marketing. The important thing is to do some research, ask around, and try the program for a little while.

Other Ad Networks

More than just Google and Amazon exist out there in the online ad world. There are many other ad networks that you can join. Sometimes they are specific to a niche or product and sometimes they are more general, just like the banners you see all over the Internet.

Like AdSense or affiliate programs, it's important to look into these programs carefully and see what kinds of ads they run. Are there restrictions on how many ads you can have per page? Are there restrictions on *your* content? Can you put restrictions on *their* ads? (Having an adult-dating site ad appearing on a children's clothing blog isn't really a good thing.) All these are questions to investigate.

When you get to the point of signing up, check the sites that also carry the ads. You don't want to fall into "the wrong crowd" on the Internet (spammers and other malcontents). I'm always hesitant to give blanket "Oh, these folks are great…" endorsements because sometimes ad networks have done things like generate codes for you to embed in your site that Google doesn't like (for search indexing). Another thing to keep in mind is that Google in particular doesn't allow competing ad networks on your site. If the ads you're inserting in addition to Google's are also contextual, where the ads change to relate to the content on the page, Google will kick you out of AdSense. Believe me, you don't want to be on Google's bad side.

Final Word on Ads

If you've looked at any of my blogs while you've been reading this book, you will notice that I don't have ads on my sites. I debated whether to put Google AdSense back on my blogs (they used to be there), but I generally don't bother. Don't take this to mean that I'm anti-ads or anti-affiliate programs. I've tried them and have chosen to earn money through my writing or sponsorships, not through ads. I think this is one of the hallmarks for what blogging is—the freedom and ability to choose how you want to run your blog. Of course, you are able to buy this book through Amazon on my blogs; I think that's a pretty understandable thing, though.

Pulling It Together on Your Blog

Have you picked your ad program of choice yet? AdSense? Amazon Associates or another affiliate program? Regardless of which one you choose, there is one unifying factor among all of them—they require you to paste various HTML codes into your blog to make them work. You also need to make sure that the ads are placed so that people will see *and* click them (an unclicked ad is just a pretty picture, after all). At the same time, they must not be obtrusive and interfere with your readers' ability to digest your content.

After you have ads on your blog, you need to track how well the ads are doing, which means doing a little more web stats work than your average blogger. Not to worry—like all the things in this book, none of this is rocket science. If you can copy and paste, you can do it all with ease and aplomb.

Ad Codes 101

Let's talk ad codes for a second (maybe more than a second). The first thing to know is which ad codes can (or should) go into your posts and which are best kept in the header, footer, and sidebars. (If you're really cool, you might be able to sneak them in between posts, but that's some pretty tricky handcoding.) The second thing to know is that ad code tends to be fragile. Yes, it can break.

Fragile code isn't that different from that antique vase your Aunt Minnie gave you. Jostle it around and the results might be unpleasant. Functionally, this means that when you're pasting code—into your posts especially—you need to do it in HTML mode, *not* the visual editor. Visual editors make life easy by keeping messy HTML code away from you, but this also means that if you paste HTML code *into* a visual editor it will essentially neuter the code and make it just funny looking text.

Because you might not like working in HTML mode, some kind souls have made plug-ins where you can paste the code into a separate window and let it inject the code into your post without breaking the code or messing up the rest of the editor. For the sake of teaching you, let's pretend you're going to do this the old-fashioned way and just paste things into posts.

In the realm of ad code you can paste, Google AdSense is not code that works very well within posts. To get AdSense code *within* your posts, you have to edit your blog's template to have code in by default, not as you write the post. Affiliate links and Amazon code is generally okay to paste into posts as long as you remember to stay in HTML mode after you paste the code in until you save your post.

NOTE

I might be considered overly cautious for this approach of staying in HTML mode after I've pasted code into my post (until I publish it), but it's better to be safe than sorry.

HTML mode is important for any ad code that has the magic word "JavaScript" in it. I'll caution now that sometimes JavaScript is stripped out when you publish a post. This is a safety and security precaution and doesn't mean that you did anything wrong. If you can

see a preview of the ad *before* you copy and paste the code, you can usually tell right away if you're going to need to switch into HTML mode to paste it in.

The biggest clue is if there are images or any kind of dynamic interaction going on. These are codes that have some cool things, and cool things often don't like being pasted in visual mode. Affiliate links are often the easiest to handle because the link is just a normal link with extra codes in it. Even Amazon has basic, simple, boring HTML link URLs that you don't have to switch into HTML mode to use.

Thus far I've been talking about pasting ads into your *posts*, but what if you want to have them in the header, footer, or sides of your blog? This is a much easier proposition, believe me. Let's start with sidebars. In WordPress and most other blog templates, you can create "text widgets," which are simply containers for HTML code to go into the sidebars of your blog. Yep, they are built to take HTML code and actually use it instead of breaking it. Figure 11.6 shows what pasting some HTML code into a sidebar widget looks like.

It probably looks pretty geeky and difficult, but it really isn't. The process follows these steps:

1. Copy the code from Google, Amazon, or whomever your ad provider is.

2. Go to the administration portion of your blog where you are able to add widgets to your theme (for WordPress, it's the Appearance button and the Widgets link).

3. Create a text widget (in WordPress, this mean dragging a text widget to one of the sidebar areas) and paste the code into it.

4. Save the widget.

5. Enjoy, because you're done.

FIGURE 11.6
Pasting code into a WordPress widget.

Paste code here

In fact, if you've been tricking out your blog, you already have been playing around with pasting things into sidebar widgets. It doesn't matter if it's a Flickr widget or an Amazon ad for the Deal of the Day, because they all work the same way. This is another nice thing about blogs—nothing is really *that* hard. Mostly it's copying, pasting, pointing, and clicking. You can do a lot with just a few clicks and some practice.

Putting ads into the header and footer is a little trickier. This usually involves editing your theme's template (the header and footer files, in fact) and understanding a little more about how your blog works. Again, it's not hard, but something that you should do a little more investigating before trying out. The trickiest part of editing a template file is making sure you don't accidentally delete something important. There are in-depth tutorials on how to do this for all major blog platforms; a little Googling is all it takes to find them. I said "usually" because more and more theme developers are providing header and footer widgets where you can include text widgets for ads.

This makes creating dynamic-looking sites very simple and probably reduces the number of emails the developers get from people who have broken their themes.

Hopefully, when you're done inserting ads into your blog, it doesn't look like a mess, but if it does, let's hit that as the next step—optimizing your template for ad performance and aesthetics.

Optimizing Your Blog's Template

You've seen sites and blogs that look so cluttered and chock full of ads that it looks like...well, you know. Let's try to avoid that happening to you, okay? The best way to do this is to be judicious with your ad placements. You don't need to fill every space in your sidebar, in your header, in your footer, within posts, and between posts with ads.

I'm of the "less is more" school of thought when it comes to ads. I might put an AdSense block at the top of the sidebar, and then an Amazon banner in the sidebar (one of the tall ones). If I'm writing about a particular item or book, I will include an affiliate link within the post. My style is not to beat people over the head with ads, but to offer ads in a way that seems natural and part of the design.

Design is only part of the optimization strategy here. The other part is bringing visitors to your blog who are *looking* for what you have ads for. Yep, you guessed it; this falls under the wonderful world of Search Engine Optimization (SEO) again. If you've been following along with my SEO recommendations thus far, you're well ahead of the game. For AdSense in particular, you can add these magic codes around your content (again, this is a template editing thing):

```
<!-- google_ad_section_start -->
<!-- google_ad_section_end -->
```

And then add this variation around the sidebar:

```
<!-- google_ad_section_start(weight=ignore)
➡ -->
<!-- google_ad_section_end -->
```

These codes focus the Google AdSense codes so when the magic of Google is picking which ad to display, it considers content within the first set and *excludes* content within the second set. This helps to make your AdSense ads more relevant to the content you've written on that page. This section, and the one following on tracking performance, dovetail into one another.

As you get a solid baseline of data (I suggest a month at least), you can see how well the ads are performing. If something isn't working, you can adjust your ads. Maybe the colors blend too much into the page. Maybe they aren't big

enough. Maybe they aren't relevant enough. The more you look into the data, the more you can decide whether a particular kind of ad or affiliate program is working for you.

Tracking Your Performance

Earlier in the book I touched on web stats or analytics for bloggers. One of the fullest featured ones for seeing how Google AdSense is working on your blog is, yep, Google Analytics, which Chapter 2, "Installing and Setting Up Your First Blog," examines in depth. Coupled together, you get great insight into how well the ads on your blog are targeted and whether people are clicking them. Now, for other programs, you'll need to rely on the data you get from Amazon or another ad provider. Look for the following:

▶ Number of impressions (the number of times an ad was displayed on your site overall)

▶ Number of clicks

▶ Number of conversions

From these data, you can discern a lot. For Google AdSense, which are pay-per-click (PPC) ads, you only have to worry about the first two metrics. Look at the ratio of clicks to impressions; this is your click-through rate (CTR). It won't be terribly high—maybe a few percent points. That's fine; it's normal. You get paid just for someone clicking an AdSense ad.

For ads like Amazon, just clicking isn't enough; they have to click *and* buy for you to get paid. These are pay-per-conversion ads. Looking is step one, clicking is step two, and buying is step three. If you aren't offering something that people will be interested in if they do click, you might think about either offering something else or picking a different affiliate program. Something that looks good on the ad but doesn't seem quite right when people get to the site isn't going to earn you any money.

If you're selling your posts or syndicating, your metrics are a little different. If you are paid a flat fee regardless of how the post does traffic-wise, that's easy, but if you have a fee plus performance bonus, you need the metrics on readership, search engine traffic, and referrers to know if you're hitting the mark.

If you've gone the route of sponsorships, you might be asked by your sponsor for your monthly traffic, the number of impressions that ad has had, and the number of clicks. These data aren't hard to gather and give, if you plan for them. Before you get into offering banner ads yourself, look into ad management plug-ins for your blog engine. These save you time, energy, and hassle by not only managing your inventory, but also providing you with the metrics you need to gauge ad performance.

Obviously, if you're selling goods yourself, you'll have all the data you need. You'll know the traffic on your site, and you'll know exactly how much you've sold. You also are keeping everything in-house so there isn't as much pressure to report the data to someone else!

Figure 11.7 shows you what keywords people use to reach one of my blogs. In addition to the traffic data, knowing these keywords helps you determine whether your posts are tuned correctly for search engines. If you are selling things directly, this is critical to getting customers. If you have general ads on your site, these data can help you better tune your offerings to your visitors.

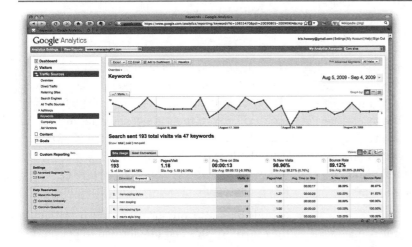

FIGURE 11.7
Keywords on Manscaping411.com.

Summary

Making money through your blog is both easy and hard. It's easy in that there are lots of different ways to do it, and it's hard in that you have to choose which one is right for you and then actually make money utilizing it. You can make money directly by selling your own ad space (sponsorships), writing for other people or syndicating your content, or selling goods or services that you offer (and explain on the blog). You can also make money *indirectly* through various ad networks and programs. Altogether it is possible, but difficult, to earn a nice amount of money from your work. The key for you as a blogger is to offer the right kinds of ads, have the right kinds of metrics, and keep the layout optimized so your readers can enjoy the content *and* have your ads still perform well.

Index

FREE
Online Edition

Your purchase of *Create Your Own Blog: 6 Easy Projects to Start Blogging Like a Pro* includes access to a free online edition for 45 days through the **Safari Books Online** subscription service. Nearly every Sams book is available online through **Safari Books Online**, along with thousands of books and videos from publishers such as Addison-Wesley Professional, Cisco Press, Exam Cram, IBM Press, O'Reilly Media, Prentice Hall, Que, and VMware Press.

Safari Books Online is a digital library providing searchable, on-demand access to thousands of technology, digital media, and professional development books and videos from leading publishers. With one monthly or yearly subscription price, you get unlimited access to learning tools and information on topics including mobile app and software development, tips and tricks on using your favorite gadgets, networking, project management, graphic design, and much more.

Activate your FREE Online Edition at
informit.com/safarifree

STEP 1: Enter the coupon code: NVQLOGA.

STEP 2: New Safari users, complete the brief registration form. Safari subscribers, just log in.

If you have difficulty registering on Safari or accessing the online edition, please e-mail customer-service@safaribooksonline.com